GROSS NATIONAL HAPPINESS

GROSS
NATIONAL
HAPPINESS

Why Happiness Matters for America
—and How We Can Get More of It

ARTHUR C. BROOKS

BASIC
BOOKS

A Member of the Perseus Books Group
New York

Set in 12 point Adobe Caslon

Library of Congress Cataloging-in-Publication Data

Brooks, Arthur C., 1964–
    Gross national happiness : why happiness matters for America — and
how we can get more of it / Arthur C. Brooks.
        p.   cm.
    Includes bibliographical references and index.
    ISBN 978-0-465-00278-8
    1. Happiness—Social aspects—United States. I. Title.
BF575.H27B76 2008
302'.14—dc22   2007052221

10 9 8 7 6 5 4 3 2 1

For Quimet, Carlos, and Marina

Happy the man, and happy he alone,
He who can call today his own:
He who, secure within, can say,
Tomorrow do thy worst, for I have lived today.
Be fair or foul or rain or shine
The joys I have possessed, in spite of fate, are mine.
Not Heaven itself upon the past has power,
But what has been, has been, and I have had my hour.

—JOHN DRYDEN, "HAPPY THE MAN" (1685)

Contents

INTRODUCTION

America's Pursuit of Happiness

*We hold these truths to be self-evident, that
all men are created equal, that they are
endowed by their Creator with certain
unalienable Rights, that among these are
Life, Liberty and the pursuit of Happiness.*
                    —U.S. DECLARATION OF INDEPENDENCE,
                                          JULY 4, 1776

You want to be happy. I am going to assume this right off the
bat, and I am in pretty smart company when I make this sort of
assumption. Socrates once asked his students, "Do not all men
desire happiness? And yet, perhaps, this is one of those ridiculous
questions which I am afraid to ask, and which ought not to be
asked by a sensible man: for what human being is there who does
not desire happiness?" One student answered him: "There is no
one who does not."[1]

If Socrates was right—if everyone wants happiness—then isn't it reasonable to assume that a decent nation will, at minimum, create the conditions in which its citizens can best pursue happiness?

This idea is as old as America itself. In the Declaration of Independence, the founders did not treat happiness as some fuzzy concept—they obviously believed people knew it, wanted it, and had the right to pursue it. Happiness was—along with life and liberty—the connection between the Creator and our nation's destiny. The ability of citizens to pursue and achieve their happiness was a measure of the effectiveness and morality of the state.

Yet our leaders and policymakers today seem to have forgotten this. To hear the way politicians talk about gross domestic product, health care reform, and social security, you would think that this nation's founding fathers held as "self-evident that we are endowed by our Creator to purchase new high-quality consumer durables each and every year," or "to enjoy healthy economic growth with low inflation and full employment." The founders didn't talk about such things not because they are unimportant, but because they believed that happiness went *deeper*.

You have probably heard the "pursuit of happiness" line from the Declaration a thousand times. By sheer force of repetition, the idea that a nation should commit itself to the happiness of its citizens no longer seems profound to us, which is why so many of today's leaders ignore it. But it was a truly radical idea at the time. No other government in the world had proclaimed that all of its people—not just people of noble birth or special privilege—had an equal right to chase after happiness as they defined it. In fact, it took 194 years for another country to enshrine happiness as a political ideal—and that happened in the tiny kingdom of Bhutan.[2]

Bhutan, surrounded by the Himalayan Mountains, is roughly the size of Switzerland and has a population of slightly under 1 million people. In the early 1970s, poor nations like Bhutan around the world were deluged with ideas on how they might develop into prosperous countries. Virtually all the strategies—from postcolonial nationalism to market capitalism to doctrinaire Marxism—were focused on economic success. But Bhutan's newly acceded sixteen-year-old king, Jigme Singye Wangchuck, believed a purely economic strategy dehumanized the development process by stripping it of moral values. He devised a development approach that aimed to maximize what he called "gross national happiness." The success of the country, according to this philosophy, would be judged not by how rich it was, but according to how people felt about their lives. Bhutanese gross national happiness would be maximized by minimizing access and exposure to foreign culture, so that the Bhutanese could maintain their traditional Buddhist values.[3]

You will notice immediately that there is a major difference between the American idea, that we have a right to *pursue* happiness, and the Bhutanese monarch's goal, to *deliver* happiness to his people. This difference is reflected in the fact that Bhutan guarantees neither economic nor political rights to its citizens, and it has largely been governed as a closed, authoritarian regime. Few Americans would propose actually following Bhutan's model for achieving happiness.[4]

Nonetheless, we too should take seriously the *idea* of measuring our gross national happiness, because it brings us back to our own founding ideals. It makes us ask: Are we improving as a nation in protecting and exercising our right to pursue happiness? What can we—what *should* we—do differently? If we're serious about pursuing happiness, what should we as citizens demand of our leaders, present and future?

———

Before we can even begin to tackle these questions, we have to ask a much more obvious one: What is happiness?

This is the kind of question that sounds simple until you think about it—but the harder you think, the less clear the subject becomes. Is happiness a momentary feeling of elation, a generally positive assessment of one's life, a sense of contentment, a morally upright existence, an absence of pain, or some combination of these things? Describing pornography in 1964, Supreme Court Justice Potter Stewart simply said, "I know it when I see it." He could just as easily have been referring to happiness. Indeed, it is easy to tell when someone is happy; it's not so easy to explain exactly why or in what sense he or she is happy, or to know how to reproduce that happiness in others.

Not surprisingly, psychologists and philosophers have long searched for more quantifiable ways of describing and measuring happiness. They have done us the favor of defining three distinct forms of happiness that can be summed up by succinct phrases: "fleeting feelings of happiness," "happiness on balance," and "moral quality of life."[5]

Fleeting feelings of happiness are what we think of as joy, or euphoria. In our best moments, they are those short-lived flashes of bliss that C. S. Lewis believed were earthly glimpses of Heaven— what he called "joy." They are the little rushes you get when you see people you love after a long absence, the strange pleasure you experience when you hear a song that was popular during a happy time of your life, or when you smell food that reminds you of your mother's cooking. But some people experience euphoria at the end of a crack pipe or the bottom of a bottle of gin. These fleeting feelings are not reliable or enduring, and thus are not what most researchers mean when they talk about happiness.

Happiness on balance involves an assessment of the good and bad in our lives, the emotional balance sheet we keep that allows us to tell honestly whether we are living, all things considered, a happy life. Determining that you are happy at this level does not deny the presence of unpleasantness in life—you can be "happy" in spite of bad things around you—but it does mean that, on balance, your life has more joy than sorrow in it. This is the level most often studied by social scientists, and it is the level measured in the survey data I will use in this book. Some authors call it "psychological happiness."[6]

Moral quality of life has little to do with a sense of happiness—it is the well-lived life, in which a person realizes his or her true potential. This is an ancient, moral concept of happiness that Aristotle termed *eudaimonia*. Happiness is, in Aristotle's words, "an activity of the soul expressing virtue." As contradictory as it seems, this philosophical definition can be absolutely compatible with psychological *un*happiness. You could be drowning in depression, but if you are living virtuously, and are true to yourself, you are axiomatically happy. In ancient times, this was the most commonly understood definition of happiness, which makes it all the stranger that today it sounds the least like true happiness of the three types noted here.[7]

What about unhappiness? Your intuition might skip to the answer that unhappiness is simply the opposite of happiness, and for many years, mental health professionals worked more or less on that model. The word "unhappy" does denote the absence of happiness, at least in the dictionary. But it turns out that happiness and unhappiness, while not unconnected, are not exactly opposites either. Images of the brain show that the left cerebral cortex is more active than the right when we are experiencing happiness, whereas the right side becomes active when we are unhappy. When you experience stage fright, or someone insults you, or you eat something unpleasant, the right side of your brain goes into overdrive, while the left side remains quiet. When you are complimented, or taste something you like, the left side becomes active. When the left side is damaged, as by a stroke, patients often become unable to experience happiness; similarly, people can become eerily cheerful when they experience damage to the other side.[8]

Strange as it may seem, being happier than average does not mean that you can't also be *un*happier than average. One test used to assess both happiness and unhappiness, the Positive Affectivity and Negative Affectivity Scale (PANAS)–Momentary Feedback Test, makes this point clear. This is a self-rated test of moods— good and bad. I took the test myself and found that, for happy feelings, I am at the very top for people of my age, sex, occupation, and education group. But for unhappy feelings, I get a high score as well. Which makes me, perhaps, the most ebullient grouch you've ever met.[9]

So we know what happiness *is*—but can we measure it? In PANAS and in most of the academic studies dealing with happiness, researchers rely on "self-reports," in which respondents are asked to answer survey questions like the following: "All things considered, how happy would you say you are?" These surveys are often multiple choice; the choices include such answers as "very happy," "somewhat happy," and "not so happy." Or the respondent must circle a number on a 1–7 scale, where 1 might mean, say, "extremely unhappy" and 7 means "extremely happy."

You might ask yourself whether this kind of survey measurement of happiness really measures much at all. My first thought, when I started looking at the research on happiness, was that putting a number on happiness would be meaningless—it seemed hopelessly subjective. The number I use to designate how I feel about my life might exist on a scale totally different from the scale that serves as *your* measuring tool. If we were both asked to rate our happiness on a scale of 1–7, who is to say that *your* 5 and *my* 5 would have any comparability whatsoever? Maybe 5 means a good mood to you, while I have higher expectations for happiness and consider anything below a 6 to be lousy. Or maybe I am really in touch with my feelings and give myself a score that is lower than the one you checked off, but it is because I *think* about happiness more than you do. Perhaps you are repressing some dark past, and walk around giving yourself a 7 even though, deep down, you are an unhappy, injured soul. Or let's say that you are a normal, honest, upbeat American and answer a survey straightforwardly, while I am (hypothetically) a cynical college professor who teaches young people that the world is a depressing, exploitative hell. Won't we naturally answer happiness surveys differently? Does our true happiness have any relation at all to a numerical measure?[10]

When we move across time and geographical borders, our ability to compare measures of happiness becomes even more fraught with uncertainty. Some scholars have pointed out, for example, that there are not equivalent words for "happiness" in every language, and that the concept of happiness has changed dramatically over time.[11]

Even the "experts" on happiness have had such doubts, and they have diligently faced them. Psychologists, statisticians, and neuroscientists have dedicated a great deal of research to the question of whether or not self-reports are useful for measuring happiness. The surprising consensus is that these surveys, while far from perfect, are actually quite accurate and comparable between individuals. We *can* estimate our happiness on a survey, the researchers conclude, and we all more or less estimate our happiness in the same way.

The best way to demonstrate the reliability of self-reports is to compare them to other measures of happiness and see if they match up. What if, for example, you could compare the happiness scores an individual gives himself with the happiness scores that other people give him? Two researchers in 1991 did just that, interviewing groups of well-acquainted peers. They found that if someone said he was very happy (or very unhappy, for that matter), his friends generally said the same thing about him. In other words, it's not common to find a person who appears sad to his friends, but who thinks he's actually happy, or vice versa.[12]

There are other ways to measure happiness. We can gather evidence by hooking electrodes up to people's heads and observing brain activity, for example, or by asking people to write down lists of words and then assessing the content for positive and negative emotions. These objective types of tests correlate strongly with self-reports of happiness. For example, researchers in one study asked people to list as many words as came to mind in 60 seconds after hearing "stimulus" words such as *disappointed, generous, peace,* and *pain.* People who say they are happy generally have the easiest time coming up with associations with the "happy" words; unhappy people are more inspired when presented with the "sad" words.[13]

People differ in a multitude of ways—but it appears we all experience happiness and unhappiness in much the same way. Researchers have demonstrated this by showing that happiness produces the same physiological responses in people, such as in the way they smile. It turns out humans are capable of producing nineteen distinct smiles, but only one of them—the "Duchenne smile," named for the nineteenth-century French physiologist Guillaume-Benjamin Duchenne—occurs when people are truly happy. (This smile is the only one that involves the *orbicularis oculi* muscles in the upper half of the cheeks.) Researchers have found that the Duchenne smile is not culturally specific. Anthropologists have found that natives of Papua New Guinea, who were so isolated they had never seen people from another tribe, let alone another country, produced a Duchenne smile when they were happy exactly like modern American urbanites do.[14]

So people can, in general, accurately estimate their own degree of happiness and report on it in surveys. In general, subjective experience of happiness seems to mesh with more objective forms of evidence. Still, one person's score of 5 on a happiness scale may mean something quite different from another person's score of 5. Does this mean the data are meaningless? Fortunately, the answer is no. To solve this problem, we survey large numbers of people: When we ask 1,000 people how happy they are, we can assume that happy people *on average* will answer the same way, and so will unhappy people. Survey data are valuable because they smooth out the variation in the way people answer questions, and, assuming the survey is done right, we can start to see patterns in the population at large. So although it would be foolish to compare your individual survey responses to mine, hundreds of people together start to get us someplace.

The bottom line is that we may not know much, but we do know when we're happy. It is a universally human cognition. Even more amazing, researchers can measure it fairly well by surveying people about their own happiness. And that means it is also possible to find out what parts of our lives are associated with happiness, and which are not.

Happiness is measurable. But to make this fact meaningful (as opposed to just interesting), we have to be able to *affect* happiness as well. If we can't, then a book on our national happiness is of little use to us. Such a treatise would be like a book on the rock formations on Mars: intellectually stimulating, but lacking any power to influence personal behavior or public policy. If we can, however, alter our happiness, then it would be foolish not to study it. And if we can change the happiness of our fellow citizens through proper values and correct policies, we would be ethically remiss to ignore the subject.

So can we change our happiness quotient? And if so, how much can we change it? Sometimes you might think that you can't; you might have the feeling that you are "wired" to a certain level of happiness. You may have noticed—or maybe your family has complained—that, even after really great things happen to you, you tend to return to your typical foul moods. We often comment on the fact that many of the people who theoretically have the best lives—filthy rich heiresses, famous movie stars, professional athletes—are miserable. Or perhaps you're one of those lucky, cheerful people who always seem to feel upbeat, even when setbacks occur in your life. You see the blessings in disguise, the silver linings. Or, you might have noticed that you tend toward a baseline set of moods that resembles those of your parents. Grouchy parents tend to have grouchy kids, and vice versa.

These patterns have not gone unnoticed by researchers, who have shown quite conclusively that there is a strong genetic component to happiness. Your state of mind is due in significant part to the wiring you get from your parents. Psychologists at the University of Minnesota conducted a study of 2,310 twins born between 1936 and 1955, asking them to report their self-judged happiness. The purpose was to compare their happiness levels and see if they were influenced more by their different surroundings or by their common genes. The researchers found that no demographic circumstance—not income, education, race, gender, or social status—could account for more than 3 percent of a person's reported happiness. Twins, even if separated at birth and brought up in very different life circumstances, tended to be similarly happy (or unhappy). In fact, the researchers concluded that at least half of one's "baseline happiness" (the happiness reported in the absence of unusually good or bad life events) is hereditary.[15]

So at least 50 percent of one's happiness level is a given, the product of nature. If less than half is subject to outside influence, or nurture, can an investigation of the values associated with happy people really be that useful? Is there any point to gathering this information? The answer, I believe, is "yes." If we truly can affect just half our happiness, this raises the stakes enormously for getting things right in our lives. Imagine that today you learned that you had only half as many years of life left as you had hoped. This is not an unrealistic scenario. I have a friend who is in his early forties, like me. Recently, he received reliable information from his doctor that a medical condition makes it highly likely that he will die before he is sixty. This came as a complete shock to him. His immediate reaction was to think about all the fun things he wanted to do with the fifteen years or so he most likely has left. Having half your happiness to work with is pretty similar: It's only sensible to try hard to live in a way that uses this half well.

Furthermore, just because a trait is inherited doesn't mean it's immutable. There are many things we are born with that we can change. Most substance-abuse experts believe (and the twins studies confirm) that alcoholism stems in part from inherited tendencies to addiction. Does this mean that if your father was an alcoholic, you will be as well? Of course not. If you don't drink, you won't get hooked, period. It is *entirely* under your control whether your genetic proclivity to abuse booze has any effect on your life at all. Martin Seligman, the eminent psychologist who has done more than any other scholar to popularize the study of positive moods, believes that happiness (like alcoholism) is one of the traits over which we have significant behavioral control.[16]

Understanding happiness is more than just worthwhile. It is silly *not* to take the time to do it.

————

This is a book about America's happiness—which is to say, the number of Americans who are happy, versus those who are not. Doing sums across our population, can we say that the United States is a happy country?

The answer to this question is not as neat as "yes" or "no," because we obviously have citizens who fall all along the happiness spectrum. In general, about a third of American adults say they are very happy; between 10 and 15 percent say they are not too happy; and the rest are somewhere in between.

America's happiness is not evenly distributed—some folks are doing more than their part for our gross national happiness. Research has been devoted to asking whether certain demographic groups are happier than others, and the results are interesting: Older people are slightly likelier than younger folks to be very happy, but also slightly likelier to be unhappy. Whites and blacks have a similar probability of saying they are very happy, but blacks are 50 percent likelier to say they are unhappy. Women are slightly happier than men, on average. But in general, these demographic differences are far less important to reported happiness than differences in attitudes, behaviors, and lifestyles.

How do Americans compare in happiness with the rest of the world? This question has spawned many surveys, a number of different answers, and a lot of press. One British study from 2006 compared responses from 128 countries and concluded that the Danes were the happiest people on Earth. Of course, this grabbed the attention of the media in Europe and the United States. The Europeans interpreted the results as support for social democratic systems and an indictment of America's capitalistic society.[17]

Before you make plans to move to Denmark, however, you should note that it is far from settled that Denmark whips America in happiness. According to other data sources, Americans are happier. In 2002, a major international survey gauged happiness among 45,000 people in thirty-five countries and found that Americans outranked the Danes, and also the citizens of all the other developed nations (except, for some reason, the people of Cyprus). Indeed, the data tell us that while 56 percent of Americans surveyed that year said they were either very happy or completely happy, only 44 percent of Danes gave one of these answers. This is not to say that the Danes are unhappy—compared with many other Europeans they look downright ecstatic. Indeed, only 10 percent of the Bulgarians in the 2002 survey said they were very or completely happy.[18]

The fact that Americans are generally quite happy actually has a downside. Researchers have found that as a result of being generally accustomed to happiness, negative events bring us down more than they do people in other countries, and positive events have less of an uplifting effect on us. A 2007 study measured the number of positive events it takes to offset a negative event in our lives. For Americans, this number is about two. For Koreans and Japanese—whose baseline happiness levels are quite a bit lower than Americans'—the number is closer to one. In other words, greater average happiness brings greater expectations.[19]

You might suspect that America is getting happier over time. After all, we are getting richer, and this should make us better able and equipped to pursue our dreams. On the other hand, people talk about the good old days, when (we hear) you could let your kids play outside without worrying that somebody would abduct them or try to sell them heroin. In point of fact, average happiness levels in America have stayed largely constant for many years. In 1972, 30 percent of the population said they were very happy with their lives. In 1982, 31 percent said so; in 1993, 32 percent; and in 2006, 31 percent. The percent saying they were not too happy was similarly constant, generally hovering around 13 percent (see the following graph).[20]

It might be that looking at "average happiness" over time gives an inaccurate picture, however. Maybe some people have gotten happier while others have gotten unhappier. After all, we keep hearing that the rich are getting richer while the poor are getting poorer: Might it not be the same with happiness? Perhaps the happy are getting happier while the unhappy are getting even more miserable. If we are getting both happier *and* sadder as a nation, it hardly means that happiness is unchanged—it means we have an alarming story of winners and losers on our hands. But it turns out not to be the case. On the contrary, from 1972 to 2004, the range in reported happiness across the American population actually shrank.[21]

Some researchers have suggested that the best way to measure changes in happiness, in the United States or anyplace else, is to look at how many "happy life years" we are enjoying. In other words, we need to take into account not just how happy we say we are, but also how long we are around to enjoy our happiness (or endure our misery). Using this measure, one of Europe's most distinguished happiness researchers, Ruut Veenhoven, found that the average number of happy years of life per American has increased over the past three decades by more than six. The average

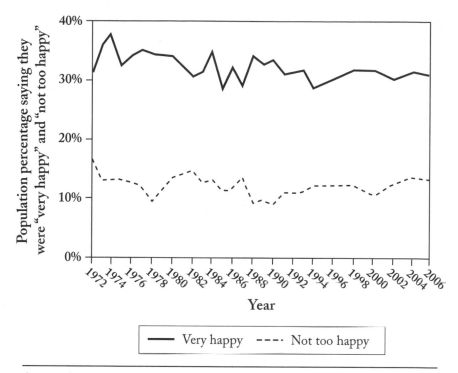

Average happiness levels in America, 1972–2006

SOURCE: James A. Davis, Tom W. Smith, and Peter V. Marsden, principal investigators, *General Social Surveys*, 1972–2006 [machine-readable data file] (Chicago: National Opinion Research Center [producer]; Storrs, Conn.: The Roper Center for Public Opinion Research, University of Connecticut [distributor], 2006).

number of happy life years in the United States is currently 62, versus 51 across the European Union, 47 in Japan, and less than 20 in many parts of the developing world.[22]

You might have seen facts like these about happiness before. Happiness is in the general American *zeitgeist* these days. Over the past several years, a number of popular and serious books on happiness research have appeared. Entertaining and informative bestsellers by prominent psychologists have provided an opportunity for laypeople to look at the psychological research on happiness, to understand some of its counterintuitive nuances, to get happier by avoiding common decisionmaking errors, and even to understand some of the brain science behind our happiness and unhappiness. For those with slightly more esoteric tastes, there's even a whole academic journal dedicated to studying happiness: *The Journal of Happiness Studies,* which comes out every quarter, chock full of technical articles about the psychology and physiology behind our bliss.

Those who consume the growing literature can learn a great deal about human happiness as a concept, an emotion, a demographic characteristic, and a physiological phenomenon. One thing that stands out about this body of work, however, is that it tends to treat happiness as a subject divorced from its political and cultural context. The authors, intelligent and prudent men and women all, do not shed much light, for example, on whether either side in our hot political and social controversies has an edge over the other in terms of adding to our happiness. In other words, there is very little advice out there on how America can get happier as a nation by tending to our values, improving our policies, and changing our politics. But given the tremendous amount of evidence on what makes us happy and what curtails our happiness on an individual level, surely there are some lessons to instruct us on how we, as a nation, might meet the challenge to pursue happiness posed to us in our Declaration of Independence.

I look for these lessons in this book. I do so because I believe that the pursuit of happiness is a deeply *moral* obligation, on both the personal and the national level. You will learn in this book that *your* happiness affects *me.* Happy people treat others better than unhappy people do. They are more charitable than unhappy people, have better marriages, are better parents, act with greater integrity, and are better citizens. Happy people not only work harder than unhappy people, but volunteer more, too—meaning that they increase our nation's prosperity and strengthen our communities. In short, happy citizens are *better* citizens. Better citizens are vital to making our nation healthy and strong. And a strong, prosperous America can and should be a happy leader for the world.

In short, we have the right to pursue happiness. But we also have an ethical responsibility to exercise that right, and to guide our values, policies, and politics as a nation in a way that makes it possible for our fellow citizens and those around the world to pursue happiness as well.

This book is based completely on data—large surveys conducted by the best and most impartial data-collection organizations in the world—as well as on a synthesis of the work of the finest researchers currently working on the subject of happiness. I try to uncover the truth about our gross national happiness and how we can improve it.

Looking for the truth in the data on happiness is actually a slightly unnerving thing to do. Like anybody else, I have lots of preconceived notions and beliefs about what brings happiness and what doesn't. I want to think that the way *I* vote, worship, earn money, and live leads my community and my country to be happier, not unhappier. I certainly don't want to find out that I've been hurting my neighbors with my attitudes and behaviors, or that my ideology is part of a force that makes America less happy. Nobody wants to learn these things.

In fact, we're quite adept at making sure we do *not* learn such things. All through our lives, we convince ourselves that we are right by avoiding questions where the expected answer is not what we want to hear. This is why so many people shun doctors. We also protect people we care about from hurtful truths—which is why, if someone writes a bad review of this book, my publisher probably won't send it to me (delicate artist that I am). We stack the deck to gather the evidence we want, and ignore or reject the data we dislike.

Writing this book meant opening myself up to the possibility—and indeed, the reality—that much of what I always thought about how to be happier or how to make America a happier place was wrong. I found some of the truths about happiness to be extremely surprising, and even uncomfortable. But I am convinced that what I found is right, whether I like all of it or not. This is not a book of philosophy or conjecture. I leave theories about happiness largely to others. Instead, I go where the data take me when I write about happiness in America and how we can get more of it. On that basis, you will hear a story—sometimes a controversial one—about who is happy, who isn't, why it matters, and how we as a nation can do better. This story has changed my mind about many things. It just might change yours, too.[23]

PART I

THE CULTURE OF HAPPINESS

CHAPTER 1

THE POLITICS OF HAPPINESS

Happiness is a political subject. It is a political subject because Americans tend to vote for politicians who have made their lives happier in the past, or who they think will make their lives happier in the future. So we start by asking: What brand of politics—Left or Right—brings the most happiness to America?

At the outset of his doomed presidential campaign forty years ago, Hubert Humphrey asserted that the Democrats represented nothing less than the "politics of happiness." By this, he meant that his party's program of income redistribution, expanded government services, liberal social policies, and protections from the evils of the free market offered America a roadmap to utopia. In 1972, Democrat George McGovern laid similar claim to the politics of happiness shortly before his epic crash-and-burn defeat at the hands of the unhappy and unlovable Richard Nixon.[1]

The politics of happiness no longer seemed to be associated with the Democrats a few years later. When President Jimmy Carter delivered his famously dour "malaise speech" in 1979, he told us that we were suffering from a "crisis of confidence." Carter's unhappiness helped ensure the success of his opponent in 1980, the sunny Republican Ronald Reagan, who assured voters that it was "morning again in America." And indeed, Reagan's presidency is remembered today as a happy time for conservatives—and a miserable one for liberals.

Over the past two decades, happiness has continued to appear to swing from one political side to the other. In 1992, Bill Clinton swept into the White House after running a campaign that adopted the optimistic slogan "Don't Stop Thinking About Tomorrow," from the famous song by the 1970s rock band Fleetwood Mac—a feel-good anthem intended to stimulate happy memories for millions of baby-boom voters. The cultural and political conflicts of the Clinton years solidified a stereotype that liberals were tolerant and cheerful, while conservatives were a bunch of repressed, unhappy stiffs.

Nothing captured this stereotype better than the "Monica Lewinsky scandal," in which Clinton pursued an adulterous affair with a twenty-two-year-old White House intern, lied under oath about the relationship, then had a conservative special prosecutor hound him for it as a Republican Congress tried to impeach him. The Left dismissed the scandal as being "only about sex," while right-wing commentators and politicians went into overdrive in nightly television debates, all but predicting the end of Western civilization—because the president of the United States had turned out to be an adulterer and a liar (and a bit of a pervert to boot). Conservatives emerged from the affair looking censorious, puritanical, and humorless, while liberals came off seeming open-minded and bemused.

But all of a sudden, something happened to all those supposedly happy and tolerant liberals. Or rather, some*one:* George W.

Bush was elected president in the hotly contested 2000 race, losing the popular vote to Democrat Al Gore and only winning the electoral vote after a legal showdown over vote-recount procedures adjudicated by an ideologically riven U.S. Supreme Court.

Almost overnight, political unhappiness took off its wingtips and put on Birkenstocks. Liberal activists compared Bush to Hitler and claimed American democracy was becoming a sham. In a climate of disgust and despair at the Bush administration's conservative policies, many lifelong Democrats became miserable conspiracy theorists, arguing that when Democrats lost elections it was because they were rigged as part of some vast right-wing conspiracy—and when Democrats won, it was only because the Right had rigged the elections incompetently.

Liberal rage was suddenly all the rage. The Academy Award–winning (and perennially outraged) filmmaker Michael Moore became a liberal icon, publicly ranting in 2004 that "The right wing, that is not where America's at. . . . It's just a small minority of people who hate. They hate. They exist in the politics of hate. . . . They are hate-triots, and they believe in the politics of hate-triotism. Hate-triotism is where they stand." The culture wars of the Clinton years had come to seem positively jovial by comparison.[2]

So which side can lay claim to being the happy side of the American political debate? A casual review of the past few decades of American political history provides a mixed answer. Sometimes the Right looks happier, and sometimes the Left.

For a more definitive answer, we might try turning to the academic world. Most scholars and intellectuals would tell you in no uncertain terms that, notwithstanding all the rage and despair of the political left during the presidency of George W. Bush, liberals are, and always have been, happier than conservatives. But this is hardly surprising; after all, intellectuals are disproportionately politically liberal. And it is human nature to believe your own tribe has the best minds, the best looks, the best jokes—and the happiest people.

The liberal academic world has developed a set of theories to support the idea that liberals are happy and conservatives are not. These theories revolve around the "natural personalities" of conservatives and liberals: Conservatives are emotionally rigid, the story goes; they require a lot of structure in their lives and cannot tolerate anything but black and white—and consequently the real world leaves them insecure and angry. Liberals, in contrast, are emotionally flexible, are able to understand nuance, and have less trouble adjusting to a changing storyline; they are thus happier and more comfortable in the modern world.

Berkeley linguistics professor and Democratic political adviser George Lakoff developed this idea in his 2004 bestseller *Don't Think of an Elephant: Know Your Values and Frame the Debate.* Conservatives, he explained, have a "strict father" model of life, whereas liberals subscribe to a "nurturing parent" model. According to Lakoff, for conservatives "the world is a dangerous place. It's a difficult place. And kids are born bad and have to be made good." For liberals, "children are born good and should be kept that way." Lakoff's ideas are not wholly new—they emerge out of a rich intellectual tradition that includes Theodor Adorno's 1950 classic *The Authoritarian Personality,* in which he argued that conservative ideology was a prefascist personality type, and psychologist Robert Altemeyer's *Enemies of Freedom: Understanding Right-Wing Authoritarianism.*[3]

Some academics have sought statistical support for their claims that conservatives are emotionally rigid and unhappy. Indeed, in one study researchers traced the ideology and worldview of people in their early twenties back to the personalities they had exhibited as toddlers. They calculated measures of the "conservatism" and "liberalism" of the study participants on values such as religion, patriotism, law and order, moral standards, and support for capitalism. Then, they compared these measures with assessments of the same people made by researchers at their nursery school decades before. The results were stark. The liberal young men had these principal traits as toddlers: resourcefulness in initiating activities, independence and autonomy, and pride in accomplishments. Liberal young women had similarly happy characteristics. In contrast, as toddlers the conservative young men had been easily offended, immobilized under stress, brooding and worried, and suspicious of others. Conservative young women had cried the most easily.[4]

The lead investigator of the study, explaining the correlation between youthful unhappiness and conservatism in an interview following publication of the study, contended that insecure children seek "reassurance provided by tradition and authority, and find it in conservative politics. The more confident kids are eager to explore alternatives to the way things are, and find liberal politics more congenial."[5]

There are a great many reasons to challenge the study's conclusions. All of the study participants, for instance, lived in the San Francisco Bay Area—arguably America's most left-wing region. Living in San Francisco by itself would make a conservative of *any* age emotionally rigid and prone to weeping. More importantly, it seems unfair to base judgments about a person's adult worldview on an assessment done when he was in his early twenties. Still, this limited study bolstered elite stereotypes about unhappy conservatives and happy liberals.

For many academics, there is really no need to explain the link between political affiliation and happiness because it is so obvious.

One psychologist conducting research on happiness even told the *New York Times* that he didn't "see how anybody could study happiness and not find himself leaning left politically." This logic is common on the left: Anyone who cares about happiness on a national level must, by definition, be a liberal. The argument is an economic one: Income should be redistributed to allow the greatest happiness for the greatest number. Liberals are far more committed to forms of economic redistribution than conservatives are—and so happiness proponents should, by all rights, be liberals.[6]

There is a logical sleight-of-hand in this argument, and it also turns out to be incorrect—but we haven't gotten to that part of the story just yet.

———

For most of my life, I didn't question the elite wisdom about happy liberals and unhappy conservatives. I had never been particularly encouraged to question this view, either, while growing up in liberal Seattle or in the even more liberal academic world I came to inhabit professionally. After all, I rarely *met* conservatives—much less talked with them about their happiness. In my world, we all just knew liberals were happiest. But the foam-flecked liberal rage that followed the election of George W. Bush took me aback. All the fancy theories I had learned about grim, authoritarian personality types and the emotional rigidity of conservatives seemed to ring more and more hollow with each venomous anti-Bush yard sign that popped up in my university neighborhood and every paranoid liberal claim I heard about America becoming a police state. Maybe it was just temporary insanity. But maybe, just maybe, liberal happiness wasn't everything it was cracked up to be.

On a lark, I decided to glance at the survey data—something the theorists didn't ever seem to do, for some reason—and see who was *really* happier. And, lo and behold, it quickly emerged that I had been wrong all this time. In fact, it is political conservatives who take the happiness prize, hands down. And not just since 2000, when their man took the presidency. They've *always* been happier than liberals—even during Clinton's sex scandals, when grim conservative spokespeople looked like they had just stepped out of Grant Wood's famous painting *American Gothic*. The happiness gap between conservatives and liberals is, in fact, astonishingly large and enduring, and it doesn't have anything to do with who is winning elections.

In 2004, people who said they were conservative or very conservative were nearly twice as likely to say they were very happy as people who called themselves liberal or very liberal (44 percent versus 25 percent). Conservatives were only half as likely to say they were not too happy (9 versus 18 percent). Political conservatives were also far less likely than liberals to express maladjustment to their adult lives. For example, adults on the political right were only half as likely as those on the left to say, "at times, I think I am no good at all." They were also less likely to say they were dissatisfied with themselves or that they were inclined to feel like a failure or to be pessimistic about their futures. Further, in a 2007 survey, 58 percent of Republicans rated their mental health as "excellent," versus 43 percent of political independents and just 38 percent of Democrats.[7]

This gap has persisted for at least thirty-five years. Liberals were no happier, and conservatives no unhappier, during the Republican meltdown after Watergate, Jimmy Carter's "malaise," the conservative reign of Ronald Reagan, or the "culture wars" of Bill Clinton's presidency. Indeed, the difference was slightly greater under Bill Clinton in 1993 than it was under George W. Bush in 2002. Democrats may very well win the presidency in 2008, and conservatives will certainly be displeased about that—but the data promise that they will still be happier people than liberals (see the following graph).[8]

———

Now, it is of course possible that the enormous happiness disparities between right and left could be explained by something other than politics per se. You might immediately suspect that conservatives earn more money than liberals (although studies have not uniformly concluded this—some find that liberals actually earn more). In truth, income does not matter in the left-right happiness gap. But there are two demographic differences between liberals and conservatives that do matter: religion and marriage.

As everybody knows, political conservatives tend to be more religious than liberals in America today. In fact, in 2004, conservatives were more than twice as likely as liberals to attend a house of worship weekly, whereas liberals were twice as likely as conservatives to attend seldom or never. There are indeed religious liberals in America, but they are outnumbered by religious conservatives by about four to one. Furthermore, the American left is gradually secularizing. While 27 percent of American liberals attended church weekly in 1974, only 16 percent did so by 2004. In contrast, the percentage of church-attending conservatives rose over the same period from 38 percent to 46 percent.[9]

Politics aside, practicing a religion makes people very happy, on average—this is the topic of the next chapter. But when we *combine* religion and politics, happiness differences explode. Equal percentages of secular liberals say they are very happy as not too

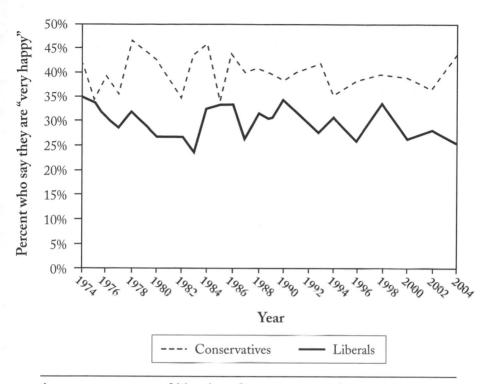

Average percentages of liberals and conservatives who say they are "very happy," 1974–2004

Source: James A. Davis, Tom W. Smith, and Peter V. Marsden, principal investigators, *General Social Surveys*, 1974–2004 [machine-readable data file] (Chicago: National Opinion Research Center [producer]; Storrs, Conn.: The Roper Center for Public Opinion Research, University of Connecticut [distributor], 2004).

happy (22 percent). Compare this with religious conservatives, who are ten times likelier to say they are very happy than not too happy (50 percent versus 5 percent). Interestingly, religious liberals are about as happy as secular conservatives: About a third of each group say they are very happy.[10]

Conservatives and liberals also organize their families differently, and this fact also plays a significant role in the happiness gap between right and left. Conservatives, for instance, are much likelier than liberals to be married. Indeed, two-thirds of conservatives are married versus only a third of liberals. To some extent, this divergence is explained by the fact that liberals are on average younger than conservatives. But it goes beyond the age differences, because conservatives are more likely to be married within every age category.

A bit later we will find that married people from all political groups are nearly twice as likely as singles to say they are very happy. As in the case of religion, politics exacerbates these differences: Married conservatives are more than three times likelier than single liberals to say they are very happy. And this is probably underestimating the difference, given the fact that there is no evidence that nonmarried, cohabiting couples—who are disproportionately liberal—are dramatically unhappier than married couples. If we counted only the truly single liberals, in other words, we would likely find that they were even unhappier than liberals who describe themselves as single but are living with a partner as though married.[11]

Religion and marriage account for some of the political happiness gap, but not all of it. Even when we correct for all the demographic differences between right and left, a large gap persists. Imagine two people who are identical in religion, marriage, income, age, education, and race. The only difference is that one is a liberal, and the other is a conservative. The conservative will still be 10 percentage points more likely than the liberal to say he or she is very happy.[12]

There is an authentic worldview disparity between liberals and conservatives that explains this persistent happiness gap, a disparity that centers on the role of the individual in society. Conservatives generally look at society and see a collection of individuals. They naturally believe, therefore, that individual action—personal action—is the right focus for our attention. Liberals are much stronger at the level of the collective. For many on the left, individual action is a silly, futile focus if we want to make any meaningful social change; the community or all society requires change in order for real progress to be made. Legendary social activist Jane Addams defined the progressive agenda for a century when she said, "We must demand that the individual shall be willing to lose the sense of personal achievement, and shall be content to realize his activity only in the connection with the activity of the many."[13]

Individualism affects all sorts of behavior. Consider how conservatives serve others in need: They tend to give substantially more of their private resources to charity than liberals do. This fact reflects the divergence between liberals and conservatives in thinking about the role of the individual versus the collective: People who support government solutions to social problems tend to donate substantially less to charity than those who do not support government efforts. In 1996, people who believed the government should take greater measures to reduce income inequality gave, on average, only one-fourth as much money to charity each year as those who believed the government should *not* equalize incomes more. This result persists even after correcting for other demographics such as income, age, and education. It also holds for all sorts of giving that does not involve money, such as volunteering for a good cause and donating blood.[14]

I think most people would agree that both the individual *and* the collective are important for social progress. Societies, after all, are made up of individuals, so collective action requires changes in individual behavior. But real change means change in the behavior of sufficient numbers of individuals to make a difference. Even without taking a position here on whether it is worse to marginalize the individual (as liberals often do) or the collective (as conservatives often do), we can see how this worldview difference affects happiness levels. Simply put, it is easier to feel successful when you are relying on your own actions to affect things that are important to you than it is when you feel you must depend on the actions of everyone else.[15]

The conservative reliance on oneself—as opposed to others, or the government—makes happiness, as columnist George Will puts it, a *project* rather than an *entitlement*. In the colorful words of former U.S. House Speaker Newt Gingrich, the Declaration of Independence asserts that we deserve "not happiness stamps; not a department of happiness; not therapy for happiness. Pursuit."[16]

Reliance on any sort of entitlement—whether for services or for happiness itself—cedes control over important parts of one's life. And as mental health professionals have known for many years, a perceived lack of personal control brings misery: It is terrible to feel like you are at the mercy of circumstances or other people. An example that makes this point vividly is commuting to work, which is one of the least pleasurable activities people regularly undertake. In one study, researchers asked people to rate the happiness they received from daily activities such as socializing, eating, and working. Commuting was rated dead last, delivering the most unhappiness of any daily activity. Why is this? Commuting certainly wastes time and resources. Even worse, though, is the effect it has on our perceived control: We are cooped up in a car at the mercy of traffic patterns day after day after day. Depriving us daily of the ability to control our circumstances, commuting is like a mild form of torture.[17]

The relationship between control and happiness helps explain not just why conservatives are happier than liberals, but how political liberals *perpetuate* their own unhappiness. The American left has occupied itself for decades with the plight of victims—victims of discrimination, of class, of circumstance, and of exploitation—

who lack control over their fate. In many cases, such as during the American civil rights movement of the 1950s and 1960s, this focus was not only justifiable, but noble and important for America, and instrumental in giving victims more control over their lives. But inasmuch as the American left is now a coalition of groups that *define* themselves as victims of social and economic forces, and inasmuch as liberals encourage these feelings of victimization in order to mobilize votes, liberal leaders inevitably make themselves and their constituents unhappy.[18]

The political right should take careful note of these patterns as well. There is a growing tendency for conservative groups to seek power and advantage in the politics of victimhood. On college campuses around the country, conservative student groups have turned to the tactics of the Left to gain power—citing examples of the discrimination they suffer at the hands of liberal professors and administrators. Whether the abuses they face are real or not, campus conservatives imperil their happiness edge with this approach.

The political right is happier than the left, but what about the political extremes versus the middle? It always seemed to me that political extremism and happiness were incompatible. Surely only misery could motivate someone to put a "Who Would Jesus Bomb?" bumper sticker on his car, or claim that AIDS was God's way of punishing America for tolerating homosexuals.

Alas, once again the data proved me wrong. Americans who describe themselves as holding extreme political views—somewhere between 10 and 20 percent of the population—are among the happiest people in America. All of those angry protesters who denounce Dick Cheney as a murderer; all of the professional political pundits who use the rhetoric of rage and misery to get on cable television—it turns out they're not miserable at all. On the contrary, they're enjoying themselves rather a lot.

In 2004, 35 percent of people who said they were extremely liberal were very happy (versus 22 percent of people who were just liberal). At the same time, a whopping 48 percent of people who were extremely conservative gave this response (compared with 43 percent of nonextreme conservatives). Indeed, the gusto with which Bill Clinton's attackers in 1998 went after him was really a clue that they were having a grand old time. George W. Bush's harshest critics—those who have felt the predations of the Bush administration to the very depths of their soul—are quite likely to be a great deal happier than more moderate liberals.[19]

Why are ideologues so happy? The most plausible reason is religion—not *real* religion, but rather, a secular substitute in which they believe with perfect certainty in the correctness of their political dogmas. People want to hold the truth; questioning is uncomfortable. It is easy to live by the creed that our nation's ills are because of George W. Bush; it is much harder to acknowledge that no administration is perfect—or perfectly awful. True political believers are martyrs after a fashion, willing to shout slogans in public for causes they are sure are good, or against causes they are convinced are evil. They are happy because—unlike you, probably—they are *positive* they are right. No data could change their minds.

But, importantly, the happiness of political extremists is an unhappy fact for America. They may themselves be happy, but they make others unhappy—that is, they actually lower our gross national happiness.

In many cases, extremists actually *intend* to upset people—it is part of their strategy. If you happened to be walking in my neighborhood before the 2004 presidential election, you would have seen hundreds of anti-Bush yard signs with the slogan, "Human Need, Not Corporate Greed." If you were a liberal, this would be intended to alarm you and stir up your negative feelings toward conservatives and the Bush administration. The few rare hard-boiled conservatives in my town responded to this provocation in kind, displaying signs that said, "America Protected, Not Terrorism Accepted." This was obviously supposed to rile up the conservative base, even at the cost of their happiness. In the extremist's mind, it's *good* if you get angry. This is what hard-core Bush-haters meant with their slogan, "If you're not outraged, you're not paying attention."

Extremists are happy to stir up their own ranks, but they are even happier when they cause misery for their political opponents. For people on the far left and right, people who do not share their views are not just mistaken, but *bad* people, who are also stupid and selfish. They deserve to be unhappy. If you were a Bush supporter in 2004, the yard-sign slogan "Human Need, Not Corporate Greed" was intended as a profoundly insulting moral statement about *you:* Since you supported the president, you obviously favored *greed* over the needs of your fellow man. Meanwhile, "America Protected, Not Terrorism Accepted" criticized liberals for selling America out to terrorists by refusing to support the president in 2004.

Extremists thrive on dehumanizing their opponents. This fact is evident not just in yard signs, but in data as well. To study degrees of dislike and intolerance for others among large segments of the population, political scientists use "feeling thermometers," a public opinion survey tool in which respondents are asked to express their personal feelings about people and issues on a 0–100 scale. A freezing score of zero is basically absolute hatred (think Hitler), while 100 means adoration (Santa Claus). Respondents are told that a score of 50 means "neutral." Unsurprisingly, this kind of data always shows that conservatives like other conservatives much more than liberals do, and vice versa. In 2004, conservatives gave themselves a toasty average score of 81 but gave liberals a cool 39. Liberals gave themselves 75 but rated conservatives 38.[20]

Political extremists make these temperature differences look paltry. People who say they are extremely liberal or conservative generally give their political foes scores of 20 or below. Below 20 is an unusually chilly score, which you might reserve for highly unpopular figures, not fellow average citizens. In 2002, for example, Americans gave Fidel Castro and Yasser Arafat average scores of 22. In 2006, the countries of Cuba and Iran—avowed enemies of the United States—each received average scores of 27. Yet two-thirds of those who called themselves extremely liberal in 2004 gave conservatives a thermometer score of 20 or below, and half of extremely conservative people gave liberals this kind of score. About one in five of those on the far left gave conservatives the lowest possible score: zero. In 2002, even Saddam Hussein received an average score of 8 from Americans across the political spectrum.[21]

These thermometer scores are ratings of people, not ideas: An ice-cold score is equivalent to saying, "I dislike a certain class of people simply because of the views they hold." This is the essence of intolerance, and it describes two-thirds of America's Far Left today and nearly half of America's Far Right. Extreme liberals, regardless of what they might claim in polite company, happily detest conservative people almost as much as they do the president himself. When liberal political power inevitably returns to the White House, we should remember these findings, particularly when we hear the predictable progressive homilies on the importance of tolerance for a good society.

But it gets worse. The unhappiness created by happy people with extreme political views extends far beyond those stuck behind them in traffic and exposed to their bumper stickers. There is evidence that people with extreme views affect everybody adversely, because they are less compassionate than average, less honest, and less concerned for others.

People with extreme politics tend to have a high opinion of their love for others—but their personal actions tell a different story. Consider the Far Left. In 2002 and 2004, those who said they were extremely liberal were 20 percentage points more likely than moderates to say they felt concern for less fortunate people. But this didn't translate well to a deep concern for any individual: This group was also 20 points less likely than moderates to say they'd "endure all things for the one I love." You've probably heard the old joke that a socialist is a man who loves humanity—but only in groups of 1 million and above. These data show there's more than a grain of truth there.[22]

Extreme conservatives are also more caring in theory than in practice. People who say they are extremely conservative are slightly more likely than people with nonextreme views to say they "feel protective of people who are taken advantage of." Unless, it seems, they are the ones taking advantage: It turns out they are substantially less likely than others to act honestly in small ways, such as returning change mistakenly given them by a cashier.[23]

What creates ideological extremism? This question has occupied millions of pages of speculation in the past decade, especially as we struggle to understand the lethal extremism of Islamic militants bent on our destruction, or even the homegrown craziness of Oklahoma City bomber Timothy McVeigh. Of course, most people who say they are extremely liberal or conservative are totally benign by comparison, but it is still worth noting that our political system creates the incentives for these views. Political campaigns cater to highly mobilized activists to win primaries, which is why national candidates always sound more extreme when seeking their party's nomination than they do in a general election. The partisan political machine today, in toadying to happy (but unhappiness-producing) activists, gears itself toward the destruction of opponents and sanctions the argument that the other side is not just misguided, but evil.

The bottom line is that political extremists—a relatively small minority—have happily hijacked our politics. And our political system has encouraged them to do so. The solution is for the level-headed masses—from liberal to conservative—to take back our political discourse. Our mainstream presidential candidates are not radicals or reactionaries, and they should have the courage and integrity not to cater to the fringes in trying to win elections. The rest of us, for our own happiness, need to send market signals that devalue the radicals—by shutting off their shrill voices when they are presented to us by the media as cheap entertainment, by participating in politics ourselves, and by refusing to vote for the most extreme political candidates.

————

I know that my conclusions about the liberal-conservative happiness gap will be controversial, so I want to underscore what I am *not* saying.

First, the data do not reveal that all conservatives are happy, that all liberals are unhappy, or that all conservatives are happier than all liberals. Such claims would be manifestly incorrect—there are many counterexamples to all of them. Rather, the data simply reveal that, if you meet a random liberal on the street, she will be more likely to say that she feels she is no good at all than that she is very happy. A random conservative, in contrast, is three times as likely to be very happy than to feel he is no good at all. Still, given an adult American population in which about 30 percent call themselves liberals, there are about 17 million very happy liberals in America. Maybe you are one of them—in which case, I congratulate you and hope this book does not dampen your high spirits.[24]

Second, the happiness differences reported here do not say that conservatives are in any way *better* than liberals, *righter* than liberals, or even that they *deserve* to be happier. In fact, a major criticism of conservatives by liberals is that they have no right to be so happy—that they really *should* feel worse because they are misguided, or even malevolent. Many liberals might take comfort in John Stuart Mill's claim that "it is better to be a human being dissatisfied than a pig satisfied." Recently, during an interview on a radio call-in show, a liberal caller who was vexed with my findings summed up the left-right happiness gap with the old axiom that "ignorance is bliss." I make no claim that the right wing merits its relative happiness. You can be the judge of that.

Finally, the differences here mask all sorts of variation between different types of conservatives and liberals. Are right-wing libertarians as happy as social conservatives? Are economic liberals more or less neurotic than social liberals? We can't say, because the surveys have never covered that kind of detail.

When it comes to happiness, the bottom line is that politics matter. Conservatives are happier than liberals, a fact you might celebrate or regret. My own reaction to this fact is primarily one of surprise, because virtually everything about the politics of happiness turns out to be at variance with elite intellectual opinion and what I always thought. But the evidence is the evidence.

Politics, however, is only one of the elements that determine whether a person will be happy. The gap between happy Americans and unhappy Americans involves factors other than political ideology per se. We will turn now to some of those other factors, which, as we shall see, hold many more surprises about America's gross national happiness.

CHAPTER 2

HAPPINESS IS A
GIFT FROM ABOVE

Mother Teresa is known throughout the world for dedicating her life to the world's forgotten in the slums of Calcutta. For more than half a century, this diminutive Albanian Catholic nun led the Missionaries of Charity, the religious order she founded in 1950, whose thousands of nuns and priests dedicated themselves to chastity, poverty, obedience, and service to the most destitute members of society—including lepers, AIDS victims, ex-prostitutes, and refugees.

Mother Teresa rose to international prominence in 1968 after British journalist Malcolm Muggeridge profiled her in his best-selling book and accompanying documentary *Something Beautiful for God.* Muggeridge's work demonstrated to the world the power of one person's deep faith and tireless charity to help the poorest of the poor, and Mother Teresa came to be revered among Catholics and non-Catholics the world over.

Mother Teresa was awarded the Nobel Peace Prize in 1979. In her acceptance speech in Oslo, which she delivered in her characteristic simple white and blue sari, she invited her audience to find

"Christ in our hearts, Christ in the poor we meet, Christ in the smile we give and in the smile that we receive." It was a powerful testament to what seemed to be an overwhelming joy she derived from her unwavering faith.[1]

But in 2007, when a series of confidential letters she had written to various people over the course of her adult life was published, it emerged that Mother Teresa's true experience of faith was often not joyful at all. In the letters, she expressed terrible sorrow about her life, describing it in terms of "dryness," "darkness," and "sadness." "Jesus has a very special love for you," she told a priest confidant. "[But] as for me, the silence and the emptiness is so great, that I look and do not see,—Listen and do not hear—the tongue moves [in prayer] but does not speak."[2]

For many prominent secularists, the letters confirmed that just under the surface of religious conviction—even that of a future saint like Mother Teresa—lies bitterness. Christopher Hitchens, author of the bestselling atheist polemic *God Is Not Great: How Religion Poisons Everything,* waxed triumphant: The letters proved that Mother Teresa "was no more exempt from the realization that religion is a human fabrication than any other person, and that her attempted cure was more and more professions of faith could only have deepened the pit that she had dug for herself."[3]

Like Mother Teresa and many others, my own life is bereft of mystical experiences: no apparitions, no voice of God speaking to me in the night, no religious ecstasy. I have witnessed many religious epiphanies—in which people were overcome with joy and, for the first time, saw all things clearly—but have never had one myself. For me, the heavens have always been silent. Yet I have chosen to practice my faith as a Roman Catholic, trusting in the authentic spiritual experiences of people smarter, better adjusted, and more worldly than me. I always thought I experienced happiness as a result of my religion. Am I deluded? Are millions and millions of religious practitioners like me merely fooling themselves, looking for joy where there is only emptiness? That is what the secularist intelligentsia would have us believe.[4]

But that's not what the evidence tells us. We can measure both religiosity and happiness and also their relationship to one another. There is an immense amount of data on this subject, and it indicates conclusively that religious people really are happier and better off emotionally than their secular counterparts. Mother Teresa may have been plagued with doubts, and perhaps she really was unhappy (although her letters are hardly proof of this). But there is no reason to believe that she would have been better off had she abandoned her faith. This may or may not have implications for you personally. But as you will see, it has profound implications for our nation's politics, our culture—and ultimately, our gross national happiness.

————

Let's begin by defining "religious" and "secular." Most social surveys ask people if they have a religion. This is not an especially useful measure, because many people—many Jews and Roman Catholics, for example—strongly identify with a religion, but never practice their faith, know virtually nothing about it, and in many ways behave identically to declared agnostics. What really matters for predicting attitudes and behaviors is not affiliation with a religion, but rather the practice of that religion.[5]

Americans can be divided into three approximately equal groups when it comes to religious attendance. Surveys indicate that a third of Americans attend their houses of worship at least once a week, while another third attend seldom or never. The remaining third attend, but irregularly. (For the purposes of comparison, I call the first group "religious," and compare them with the second group, which I call "secular.") These population dimensions have changed relatively little over the decades: Since the early 1970s, regular attendance at worship services has dropped by no more than 2 or 3 percentage points.[6]

Religious people of all faiths are much, much happier than secularists, on average. In 2004, 43 percent of religious folks said they were "very happy" with their lives, versus 23 percent of secularists. Religious people are a third more likely than secularists to say they are optimistic about the future. Secularists are nearly twice as likely as religious people to say, "I am inclined to feel I am a failure."[7]

The correlation between religion and happiness has little to do with money, age, or education. Religious people are happier than secularists even if they are alike in these ways—as well as in sex, family status, and race. If two people are identical in these characteristics, but one is religious while the other is secular, the religious person will still be 13 percentage points more likely than the nonreligious person to say he or she is very happy.

The connection between faith and happiness holds regardless of one's particular religion. A major 2000 survey revealed that observant Christians (Protestants, Catholics, Mormons, and others) and Jews, along with members of a great many other religious traditions—even esoteric and new age faiths—were far more likely than secularists to say they were happy. It also doesn't matter if we measure religious practice in ways other than attendance at worship services. In 2004, 36 percent of people who prayed every day (regardless of whether they attended services) said they were very happy, versus 21 percent of people who never prayed. In a 2002 study of Protestants and Catholics, researchers found a strong positive correlation between happiness and the intensity of religious belief, level of spirituality, and frequency of coping with life problems through faith.[8]

The only case in which religion positively correlates with *unhappiness* is for those worshippers who have an unhappy image of God. Researchers in 2006 conducted an experiment in which people described their conception of God, and were then asked to rate their level of happiness when prompted to think about Him. They found that believers with a picture of God as loving and uncontrolling tended to be happier than those who saw Him as unloving and more controlling. In other words, if you had a severe religious upbringing full of hellfire, and you think it made you less happy, you're probably right.[9]

But that is the only exception research has identified. In every other case, religion, faith, and spirituality bring happiness.

What about the folks in the middle—neither secular, nor especially religious—who identify with a faith but rarely practice it? Unsurprisingly, the happiness of this group occupies a middle ground between the religious people and the secularists—except in one interesting way. People in this middle group are, toward the end of their lives, much more afraid of death than their counterparts in both the religious and secular groups. This suggests that people suffer when they think their actions are inconsistent with their beliefs. If you believe in an afterlife and practice your faith, you will be secure in your future. If you have no faith and thus have nothing to practice, you don't fear the consequences of your life. But if you have faith but don't practice it—look out.[10]

The obvious question is whether faith merely *correlates* with happiness, or actually *causes* it. It's a chicken-and-egg question: Religion might make people happier, but happiness itself might also lead people to practice their faith. For instance, if I am unhappy—perhaps depressed—I can hardly be expected to go out and worship joyfully. But if I'm happy, and have much to be thankful for, perhaps that will put me in a more religious frame of mind. There are no data that would allow me to answer this question definitively, but I strongly suspect that happiness and faith are in fact mutually reinforcing. Certainly, faith plays a crucial role in our happiness, but we mustn't assume that faith only causes happiness—the reverse is probably also true.

Just as clear as the connection between happiness and faith is the connection between unhappiness and the rejection of faith. Data from 1998 reveal that people who were sure God existed were a third likelier to say they were very happy than those who did not believe in the existence of God. The agnostics were even gloomier than the atheists: Of those who believed there is no way to find out if God exists, a paltry 12 percent claimed to be very happy people. People who stated that there was "little truth in any religion" were only about half as likely to be very happy as people who said there was truth in religion.[11]

Now of course, it is not the case that *all* religious people are happy, or that all secularists are unhappy. Statistics are all about averages, not entire populations, and there are in fact plenty of miserable religious folks and blissful atheists out there. But the huge percentages gaps I've identified do make one thing very clear: If you had to wager about the stranger you saw smiling on the bus on your way to work this morning, the smart bet would be that he is a man of faith.

———

Why are religious people so happy?

One explanation is genetics: Recall that researchers have found, using data on twins, that heredity is responsible for at least half of our baseline happiness. Researchers have also used twin studies to determine if there is a genetic basis to faith. In a survey of almost 15,000 twins born in Virginia between 1915 and 1971, researchers found no evidence that religious affiliation—the actual religion or denomination one belonged to—had a genetic component to it. They did find, however, that between 25 and 42 percent of the variability in how often people attended their houses of worship could be explained genetically. Happy people of faith, it seems, beget happy people of faith.[12]

Another reason religious people are happier than nonreligious people surely has to do with the social integration and support that comes from belonging to a faith community. In his best-selling book *Bowling Alone: The Collapse and Revival of American Community*, Harvard political scientist Robert Putnam drew on huge amounts of data to demonstrate convincingly that voluntary association is a key to American quality of life and happiness. And about half of all voluntary associational membership, which brings great happiness to millions of Americans, is worship-related.[13]

Religion also leads to material comforts. People who live in religious communities—even correcting for other cultural factors in these communities—do better financially than those who live in secular communities. Economists have been interested in this finding for a long time. Noticing that religious communities tended to do well materially, they wondered whether it was only because of religion per se, or some other factor as well—such as the Protestant work ethic famously described by the early twentieth-century social scientist Max Weber—which is not religious in and of itself but rather a social force stemming from religion that builds a culture of hard work and prosperity.

One economist investigated this question ingeniously by looking at the effect on income of the religious attendance of others in one's community—specifically, those outside one's own ethnic group. For example, he measured how income for African American Protestants is affected by the church attendance of the Italian American Catholics in the same neighborhood. His conclusion was that the more your neighbors go to church, the more prosperous you will tend to be. Presumably this is because of the cultural benefits that accrue to the whole community from having members who follow the social norms of religion. For example, people who go to their house of worship regularly might be more likely than otherwise to shun social ills such as divorce and drugs (both of which lower material well-being). This might draw more people like them to their neighborhood and create a good example for neighbors, who thus prosper. So religion isn't just good for religious people—it enriches those around them as well. This conclusion is important for helping us all—even secularists—to understand why we should celebrate the practice of religion in America.[14]

Finally, faith correlates with happiness because many religious traditions uphold the idea of an afterlife, in which many Americans take solace. The early Roman Christian Vibia Perpetua, martyred for her faith in the year 203, put it aptly in a vision of her impending death: "Thanks be to God that I am now more joyful than I was in the flesh." And still today, afterlife believers are about a third more likely than nonbelievers to say they are very happy. Alternatively, people who do not think there is life after death are three-quarters more likely than believers to say they are not too happy. The bottom line is that it is nice to believe you are going someplace wonderful when all is said and done, even if you are not facing death before a crowd of jeering pagans, like Saint Perpetua.[15]

We know that, on average, religious people are happier than secularists. This is indisputable. Many secularists would have us believe, however, that these happy religious people are simply fooling themselves. "Religion is the opiate of the masses," famously wrote Karl Marx, and contemporary atheists cleave to this dogma. Religious people may be exceptionally happy, they argue, but they *shouldn't* be.[16]

To begin with, secularists often argue, there is evidence that religious faith is not based on anything *real*—spiritual impulses are nothing more than a neurological anomaly, a stray spark stimulating some relatively unevolved bit of brain. This argument is not without scientific basis. Researchers over the past decade have noticed that electrical activity in the brain's prefrontal lobes—a very ancient part of the human brain, referred to by some as the "God module"—often stirs people to have religious or mystical experiences. Indeed, this is the part of the brain stimulated by epileptic seizures, perhaps helping to explain why many epileptics report religious ecstasy and visions. One neuropsychologist has developed an electromagnetic device (which he refers to as his "God helmet") designed to stimulate that very part of the brain, and after experimenting on himself, reported actually experiencing God for the first time.[17]

For some, the neurobiological aspect of religious experience offers convincing evidence that God does not exist. He is merely conjured up out of electrical impulses. But this argument is spurious. Scientists have simply found evidence that we possess a physical mechanism for our spirituality. Just as parts of our brains are specially designed to control speech, movement, and imagination, the prefrontal lobes are designed to help us experience things of the spirit. This does not mean that faith—or God—is unreal any more than the fact that happiness is linked to stimuli in the left cerebral cortex negates that we have something real to feel happy about.

Others argue that happiness due to belief in an afterlife is based on a cruel delusion. In a famous article, one economist actually explained church attendance in terms of "expected afterlife consumption." According to this view, Heaven is something like a cosmic pension plan that we take on faith and hope. For some hardened secularists, of course, this is inexplicable, and it seems suspiciously likely that Heaven is a false promise of future riches—an idea created to woo converts, and distract religious believers from the grubby details of their earthbound lives.[18]

What the skeptics overlook, however, is the fact that the majority of *all* Americans—not just the religious ones—believe in some sort of afterlife. It is true that the overwhelming number of religious people—92 percent, to be exact—believe in an afterlife. But it turns out that a large majority of secularists (70 percent) also say on anonymous surveys that they believe in an afterlife, as do even a majority (60 percent) of people who explicitly say they have no religion. Of course, these numbers don't prove that an afterlife really exists—but they do prove that there is nothing uniquely religious about believing in it. It's just that religious folks are slightly more likely to believe (which adds to their happiness edge over secularists).[19]

Dismissals of happiness among the religious are often based—either implicitly or explicitly—on the idea that religious people are unenlightened or stupid. The argument is simple: Ignorant people believe in God; this makes them happy; happiness should not be based on ignorance, but rather on truth. The connection between ignorance and religion is occasionally expressed quite openly, such as after the 2004 election, when Bush won overwhelming majorities among America's most religiously observant voters. One postelection map that circulated widely among academics and on liberal websites included statistics showing that the religious "red states" (which had gone to Bush), vulgarly labeled "Jesusland," had substantially lower education levels than the secular "blue states" (which went to Democratic contender John Kerry). The message was clear: Bush won reelection with the aid of the right wing's most potent weapon: ignorant religious people.

Not only is this offensively intolerant, it is factually inaccurate. Traditionally religious people do not tend to be ignorant or uneducated. Religious individuals today are actually better educated and less ignorant of the world around them than secularists. In 2004, religious adults—those who attended a house of worship every week—were a third less likely to be without a high school diploma, and a third more likely to hold a college degree or higher, than those secularists who never attended a house of worship. The correlation between religion and educational attainment is not due to external factors such as age or income. Imagine two people who earn the same salary and are identical in age, gender, race, and political views—the only difference is that one has a college degree, while the second does not. The college graduate will be 7 percentage points more likely to be a churchgoer than the nongraduate.[20]

Militant atheists go a step further than merely skeptical secularists in dismissing the happiness of religious people, telling us that, while religious people may be personally happy, they lower our national well-being. Once the purview of a handful of cranks, eccentrics, and contrarians, atheism has become fashionable since the appearance of bestselling books in 2004–2007 by prominent authors such as Christopher Hitchens, Richard Dawkins, and Sam Harris. These authors argue that believers, who are inherently superstitious and antagonistic to reason, bring conflict, persecution, and unhappiness to the world. As such, religion is a "public bad," like crime or pollution. We would all be better off if religion were abolished.

Of course it is true that throughout history much evil has been perpetrated under the banner of religion. But much evil has also been perpetrated under other banners—the evils of Stalin and Hitler were explicitly secularist. Evil is a problem with humans, not religions. In fact, the evidence shows that religions generally attenuate natural human badness by encouraging virtuous acts.

There is a huge amount of evidence that religious people, on average, engage in altruistic behaviors that spill over positively onto others far more than secularists do. Religious people are 38 percent more likely than secularists to give money to charity and give about four times more money away each year (even holding incomes constant). They are 52 percent more likely than non-religious people to volunteer. Religious people are even 16 percent more likely than secularists to give money to explicitly *nonreligious* charities, and 54 percent more likely to volunteer for these causes. In other words, your local PTA would not function were it not for religious people in your community. Religious people give 46 percent more money each year than secularists do to family and friends. They are far more likely to donate blood, give food or money to a homeless person on the street, or even to return change mistakenly given them by a cashier.[21]

————

There are a number of organizations in America dedicated to secularizing our public life, such as the American Civil Liberties Union (ACLU) and Americans United for Separation of Church and State. Although these organizations make no attempt to dissuade

Americans from worshipping privately, they do try to root out *public* displays of worship, especially those that have any connection with the government. The ACLU is best known to ordinary Americans for suing municipalities when they display a copy of the Ten Commandments in a courthouse, place Christmas decorations on a public building, or allow children to pray in a public school.

There is no direct evidence quantifying the impact on a community's happiness when, say, the Ten Commandments are removed from the county courthouse by judge's order. We can make some confident assumptions, however, by looking at the public response to such actions. In 2004, the Pew Research Center conducted a large survey in which it asked citizens whether it is proper to display the Ten Commandments in a public building. Nearly three-quarters—including nearly half of all secularists—said they believed it was proper. In 1998, a similar national survey asked whether "the U.S. would be a better country if religion had less influence." More than four times as many Americans strongly disagreed with this statement as strongly agreed. And tellingly, those who strongly disagreed were 78 percent more likely to say they were very happy.[22]

I am emphatically *not* arguing that America should make Christianity, or any other faith, its official religion. America's free market for faith has made American religion—a great engine of happiness—amazingly robust in the face of creeping secularism across the rest of the developed world. The imposition of a particular form of worship is a bad thing for faith. Indeed, one of the reasons for the shocking lack of religious practice in formerly Christian countries like Spain and Italy is the very hegemony of the Roman Catholic Church itself, which consumed the spiritual oxygen in those countries for many centuries. When the church declined along with the nondemocratic regimes it generally supported, it left a colossal void in the Spanish and Italian cultures, and thus a void in Spanish and Italian happiness—which, despite stereotypes of blissful southern Europeans enjoying life a lot more than we do—is strikingly low.[23]

Keeping the market for souls healthy and competitive means that we neither dictate religion nor suffocate it. Organizations like the ACLU do not enhance America's well-being or contribute to the gross national happiness when they try to ban all references to religion and faith from public life. Instead, we need to act in accordance with the U.S. Constitution and Declaration of Independence—"Congress shall make no law respecting an establishment of religion, or prohibiting the free exercise thereof"—and thus allow the pursuit of happiness we deserve. Simply put, the founders saw hundreds of years ago that we should not establish a state religion. But the Constitution does not instruct our leaders to suppress the religious expression of citizens if they touch the public sphere.

Some might argue that allowing the Ten Commandments in the courthouse itself amounts to a kind of de facto establishment of Christianity and Judaism. To this objection I say our government should be only too pleased to add the symbols of justice from others faiths as well, as long as they do no violence to our established laws. For the sake of happiness, our government should promote a heterogeneity of faiths and encourage the reasonable expression of all of them.

Constitutional law is obviously not simple or transparent, and those individuals and organizations calling for the suppression of religion in any context related to government may convince courts and judges they have the Constitution on their side. What is apparent, however, is that they do not have our happiness on their side. The lawyers and activists who look for creative ways to muzzle religious expression in public make life less satisfying for millions of Americans than it could be if, when it comes to our faith, we were truly granted "free exercise thereof."

————

Fortunately, religion in public life is only a small part of the faith experience for most Americans. Religion is far more a part of our private lives, over which lawyers and activists have less control. So to understand the future of faith and happiness in America, it is not necessary to accurately predict how courts will interpret the First Amendment to the U.S. Constitution. We must only develop an understanding of the decisions that people of faith make about their families and other aspects of their lives.

Some predict—some even hope—that in the future Americans will secularize in the same way that Europeans already have. This is not inevitable, however—indeed, it isn't even likely. Religion will most likely grow to be an even greater social force in American culture and politics over the coming decades than it is today. The reason for this is simple arithmetic: Religious Americans create much larger families than secular Americans do, and religious parents tend to have religious kids.

If, in 2006, you had picked 100 adults who attended their house of worship nearly every week or more often, they would have had 223 children among them, on average. Among 100 people who attended less than once per year or never, you would find just 158 kids. This is a 41 percent fertility gap between religious and secular people. Furthermore, according to data collected in 1999, 60 percent of adults who were taken to church at least once per month as children grew up to attend at least this often; only 15 percent never attended as adults.[24]

In order to grow, secular America has to rely on the tough slog of converting people to secular beliefs—which is precisely the objective of the recent spate of books on atheism. In contrast, religious folks only need to keep having babies and bringing them up in the faith. In short, there is no indication that our faith as a nation will shrivel any time in the foreseeable future. For our gross national happiness, this is a very good thing.

CHAPTER 3

Is Happiness a Family Value?

In every preschool class, there is one child known as The Biter. The Biter settles the inevitable toddler conflicts with his or her teeth—leaving marks on the other children, and sometimes on inanimate objects such as furniture.

Who suffers most from The Biter's behavior? You might think it is the bitees—but no. It is The Biter's parents. When dropping off The Biter in the morning, his parents receive reproachful sidelong glances from the parents of the other children. Toddler-counseling is usually suggested by helpful teachers and administrators, to probe the root of the child's aggressive tendencies. The Biter's parents are plagued with fear and self-doubt. Why is my child so violent? Will he grow up to be some sort of criminal maniac, biting his victims like Hannibal Lecter in *Silence of the Lambs*? What have we done wrong in raising this child?

There is tension at home each day as the parents try to explain to the uncomprehending culprit—who seems so normal after school—that his whole future depends on being able to go a whole day without laying his teeth into another person. Each day, the parents stress over every phone call: Is it the school with a report—officially documented for liability reasons—of another biting incident? The parents are *not happy*.

My middle son, Carlos, was The Biter for about a year. He bit boys; he bit girls; he bit siblings; he bit friends. His own fourth birthday party was disrupted by an incident in which he bit three other children, and only continued after he was removed from the scene. My wife and I stressed and worried. We bought books. We argued. We talked to professionals. We lost sleep.[1]

We needn't have worried so. Carlos completely grew out of his biting phase, and laughs when he remembers it today. I doubt his victims, their reproachful parents, or his teachers remember Carlos's biting ways. But his mother and I remember that period, I can assure you.

If you are a parent, you understand. Maybe you didn't have The Biter like we did, but your child is something else: strangely shy, alarmingly extroverted, a late walker, a bed wetter, accident-prone—whatever. Your worries about your kids give you as much anxiety and unhappiness as just about anything else you have experienced.

Family life isn't supposed to be this way. One thing everybody knows is that marriage and kids are the key to a happy life. But maybe, in your weakest moments, you have asked yourself whether it's really true. Could it be that family life doesn't bring bliss, and everything we hear about families being so great is just a bunch of hokum?

This question has implications well beyond our own personal lives. We have designed national policies and based political platforms on the idea that family life is the most crucial element in the high quality of American life. The federal government gives us billions in child tax credits and deductions. We work to make sure our public policies do not create disincentives to marriage, and even scrapped our welfare system partly on these grounds in the 1990s. Private corporations are required by law to protect our jobs when we take time off to have kids, and the most "progressive" firms go even further and give us paid leave to take care of our babies. In short, marriage and kids are sanctified—and indeed *subsidized*—in almost every corner of public life.

Yet, we rarely stop to ask whether family life raises our degree of happiness, as individuals and as a nation. It turns out that these simple questions have some wonderfully complicated answers—and implications for America.

————

I get stuck in airports a lot, like many people these days. Once in the summer of 2007, I had an unplanned overnight layover in Chicago. I was in an endless line to check in at an airport hotel, surrounded by other miserable, stranded passengers who had been badly mistreated by the airlines. Next to me was a married couple having a spat over what they should buy to tide them over during their unplanned nightlong stopover. "Just go to the gift shop and get the things we need," the wife told the husband. This was obviously insufficient instruction for the husband, who no doubt knew that he would buy the wrong things without more specific directions. Irritably, he asked, *"What* things?" "Just get whatever we need—like soap," she told him. "You really suppose they don't have *soap* in a Hilton?" And on it went.

These people were stressed—their control had been stripped away by the airline that had stranded them for the night—and they were barely able to contain their anger. And because there were two of them, they were more miserable than I was under the same physical conditions. I was better off emotionally because I was by myself. In fact, I was able to muster the presence of mind to make note of their conversation for this book.

Every one of us could tell a story much like this one—a tale featuring irritable family members arguing over trivial matters in a stressful moment. We have always heard that marriage brings happiness, yet we've all witnessed—or participated in—episodes in which being with a spouse makes things worse. But that does not mean that marriage is a bad thing overall. Despite spats here and there, presumably people are happier overall with their partners than they would be without them.

Or are they?

Some people do make the argument that traditional marriage is a bad thing for our happiness. In the 1960s and 1970s, it was common to hear that the stable, monogamous marriage was somehow an unnatural state for human beings. Marriage, along with much else, was merely a bourgeois convention—a convention that prevented women and men from truly *realizing* themselves. Gloria Steinem, the leader of the feminist movement at that time, famously quipped that "a woman without a man is like a fish without a bicycle." Free love and sexual promiscuity were promoted as a lifestyle choice leading to liberation.

As we now know, however, the 1960s got it wrong on lots of things—and this includes marriage. For most men and women, matrimony brings far more happiness than the alternatives. The evidence is that humans are designed for long-lasting monogamous relationships, and they are happiest when they are in these relationships—even if they sometimes fight like little children when they're stressed out.

In 2004, 42 percent of married Americans said they were very happy. Only 23 percent of never-married people said this, as well as 20 percent of those who were widowed, 17 percent of divorced people, and 11 percent of those who were separated (but not divorced) from their spouses. Married people were six times more likely to say they were very happy than they were to say they were not too happy. Meanwhile, people who had lost their spouses or had their marriages break up were 2 to 7 percentage points *more* likely to be not too happy than very happy.[2]

Married and unmarried people differ from each other in many ways, of course. Married people are older than singles, on average, and more religious. They have more money and more education. So it's worth trying to isolate marriage to see if it is this institution—or something related to it—that drives the happiness gap between single and married people. It turns out that it's being married itself that makes people happier: If two people are exactly the same but one is married and the other is not, the married person will be 18 percentage points more likely than the unmarried person to say he or she is very happy.[3]

Who is more happily married—men or women? The answer to this question is fascinatingly convoluted. In fact, married women are slightly happier than married men—44 percent of married women say they are very happy, versus 41 percent of married men. Controlling for other factors, including income, women are slightly *unhappier* than men when divorced—20 percent of divorced women are "not too happy," versus 18 percent of divorced men. On the other hand, women are 7 percentage points likelier than men to be very happy after losing a spouse to death. And women are 9 points likelier to be very happy if never married. In other words, women do better than men if they stay single, get more happiness than men when they do marry, and cope better if their spouse dies. They suffer slightly more than men, however, when a marriage dissolves—perhaps because they most often are left with the children (more on that in a moment).[4]

But can we say that marriage *brings* happiness? Research suggests that it does. One study followed 24,000 people over more than a decade and documented a significant increase in happiness after people married. For some of these people, the happiness increase wore off in a few years and they ended up back at their premarriage happiness levels. But for others, it persisted for a long time. This is evidence that marriage does bring happiness—and in some cases, long-term happiness.[5]

Researchers also believe happiness brings marriage. Happy people are more likely than unhappy people to get married. This hardly requires explanation: Who is more likely to end up married—a bubbly, positive person, or someone who is brooding and morose? (I'm talking about averages here, so no fair basing your answers on communities of tortured artists, cynical college professors, or Europeans.) Part of this has to do with extroversion, a largely innate personality trait that promotes relationships and correlates strongly with happiness.

Before you go out and buy the wedding rings, note that it's not clear whether it is the institute of *marriage* that brings happiness, or merely the experience of romantic cohabitation. If it is the latter, then presumably unmarried cohabiting heterosexual and homosexual couples might achieve similar happiness benefits without the legal documentation. We have very little data on which to base an answer to this question, but what evidence there is indicates a slight happiness edge for traditional marriage. One survey from 2000 indicated that nonmarried but cohabiting British people were less happy than those who were legally married, but happier than those who were single, separated, widowed, or divorced. In American data from 2004, married people were more than a third likelier to feel "satisfied with themselves" than unmarried cohabitators were.[6]

But unmarried cohabitation affects the happiness of others besides the partners—especially when there are children involved.

The evidence is overwhelming that unmarried, cohabiting adults give children a worse home life than married parents do, on average. Unmarried parents are less likely to stay together than married parents—indeed, research shows that cohabiting couples have a 90 percent separation rate (although this is among all cohabiting couples; the separation rate might be lower among those with children). And even when cohabiting couples *do* stay together the outcome may be worse than if the parents were married: There is evidence that having cohabiting parents can be dangerous for children. One study found that the incidence of child abuse was twenty times higher in cohabiting biological-parent families than in families with married parents. There are, of course, many wonderful, loving unmarried parents out there. But it seems reasonable to conclude that marriage is generally much better than cohabitation for kids.[7]

I have actually been employing a bit of sleight-of-hand here, in that I have lumped all marriages together and then looked at how they affect happiness, on average. This sort of approach can be misleading, because there is a tremendous range in the quality of marriages, and the evidence indicates a strong correlation between marriage quality and a happy life. People who say their marriage is very happy are four times as likely to say they are very happy people as those who report that their marriage is pretty happy or not so happy.[8]

While a good marriage can make life sweet, a bad one is almost singularly misery-provoking. A bad marriage even degrades the quality of one's health, because the body produces stress hormones in response to constant tension at home. Recent studies have found that people with bad marriages overproduce cortisol, which makes them more susceptible than they ought to be to illnesses, slows the healing time of injuries, and even lowers the effectiveness of vaccines. People in good marriages have lower blood-pressure levels when they are together than when they are apart, but people in tense marriages have higher blood-pressure levels when they are together. "Marriage stress is unique because it basically takes what should be your primary source of support and makes it your primary stress," according to one psychologist.[9]

A bad marriage is like a terrible commute: awful, tense, and constant. That said, while there is no question that you should get rid of your commute as soon as you can, this does not mean that you should divorce immediately if you have a bad marriage: Recall that people do poorly after divorce or separation, which presumably tend to follow a rough marriage. Furthermore, there is ample evidence that marriages can be improved through counseling. We can say one thing, though, with absolute certainty: A bad marriage should never be left unattended.

Enough about bad marriages. What makes for a good marriage? Some might say children, conjuring up the image of a man and a woman joyfully embracing one another as they look down upon their new baby. But in fact many studies have shown that children do *not* make for happier marriages. On the contrary, the evidence shows that marital happiness takes a nosedive as couples move from childlessness to having their first baby; it continues southward until about the time the oldest child starts school. At this point, marriages rebound slightly, until the oldest child is an adolescent, at which point marital happiness falls even further. But this is the nadir: From that point until the kids leave home and beyond, marriages improve. Some studies find that relationships at this stage are happier than before the kids were born, although no doubt that is due to the fact that only the happiest marriages have survived to this point.[10]

Surveys of married couples conducted over the years find that there are many components far more conducive than children to marital bliss. In fact, a 2007 poll found that the top five factors people consider essential to happiness within marriage are, in order: sharing household chores, good housing, adequate income, a happy sexual relationship, and faithfulness. (Parenting comes in eighth on this list.) In 1990, 65 percent of American couples said having children was "very important" to a good marriage. By 2007, only 41 percent agreed with that statement. As American couples have become increasingly aware that having children does not necessarily lead to a happy marriage, fertility has, perhaps predictably, declined: From 1990 to 2004, the average number of children per couple fell by about 9 percent.[11]

We can find some direct explanations for these trends: There are more two-earner couples than ever before, for example, and couples are moving farther away from their extended families because of work. Both of these facts make parenting harder and more stressful than it was in the past.

———

The evidence cited above on the effect of kids on the quality of marriage at different stages arouses suspicion. Children are hard on marriages. Is it possible they have a negative effect on happiness in general?

On the surface, it looks as though kids make people a bit happier: Adults with one or two kids are about 3 percentage points more likely to say they are very happy than childless adults. But this gap is an illusion created by the fact that many happiness-causing things are also correlated with whether one has kids—marriage, age, religion, politics, and so forth. When we correct for these things, the relationship between kids and happiness actually reverses itself, and we see that children make people unhappy. If two adults in 2004 were the same in age, sex, income, marital status, education, race, religion, and politics—but one had kids and the other did not—the parent would be about 7 percentage points *less* likely to report being very happy.[12]

The more children you have, on average, the unhappier you get—up to a point. The average happiness of adults—correcting for all the other factors mentioned above—falls as more children are added to the family. The happiness nadir comes at slightly over four children. But then something surprising happens: Happiness starts rising again. People with eight children report about the same happiness levels as those with just one child.[13]

There is an obvious explanation for this seemingly strange fact: In modern America, where the average number of children per family is around two, the eight kids belong to a different sort of couple than most American couples—they're not necessarily saints and martyrs, but they almost certainly belong to family-loving religious groups. And indeed, while just 3 percent of young secularist families have four or more kids, 23 percent of Mormons have this many, and the percentage is also quite high among some evangelical groups and devout Jews. (Interestingly, it is only 7 percent among practicing Catholics.) In other words, the picture of a large, happy family is probably not distorted, although there's not much reason to believe that just any two parents could have that kind of family if they kept having more and more children.[14]

None of this is to say that people with kids are unhappy people. There are many things in a parent's life that bring great joy. For example, spending time away from their children.

Now, it actually isn't easy to get reliable information about how much people enjoy their families—not because they lie about it, but because they don't remember accurately how they feel over the course of a day. Many studies have shown that people often misremember the happiness and unhappiness that resulted from specific events. For instance, the aggravation people feel when commuting quickly melts away when they get home, and they tend to underestimate that aggravation later. To eliminate this kind of false reporting, several fascinating studies have asked participants to record their happiness levels in real time. The researchers sometimes give people electronic planners that beep every so often, at which point the study participants record what they are doing and how happy they feel. In other studies, they are asked to recreate each day during the study period in fifteen-minute increments and assign positive and negative feelings to the activities.

Using these techniques, researchers have collected data on how people—particularly women—experience life with their children. And what emerges is that they enjoy almost *everything* more than they enjoy taking care of their kids. On a scale of 0 to 6, where 0 is worst and 6 is best, caring for children resulted in an average score of 3.86. Activities that outranked child care in happiness included eating (4.34), shopping (3.95), exercising (4.31), cooking (3.93), praying (4.35), and watching television (4.19).[15]

Of course, we tell ourselves, having young children is difficult—but we will experience the rewards when they are older, right? Probably so—although one British study suggests that senior citizens get more satisfaction from frequent contact with friends than they do from spending time with their grown children. At least once children have grown up, they seem, on average, to stop *lowering* the happiness of their parents.[16]

The obvious question, then, is why we keep having children if they fail to bring happiness. The story favored by many armchair evolutionists is that we are "wired" to have kids. The story goes like this: Our ancestors were those most driven to have offspring, a trait that made them successful in the gene pool—and a trait thus passed on to us. Something deep inside us whispers over and over, "Reproduce." A lower member of the animal kingdom has no occasion to rationalize this biological message, but humans are self-aware, and we examine it in detail. The conclusion we reach is that, if we want kids so much, it *must* be because they make us happy. But this is an error—our genes reinforce inter-generational survival, not happiness.

This evolutionary argument might seem too facile for you. After all, you could probably explain *any* common behavioral phenomenon with this survival-of-the-species argument. Fortunately, there are more satisfying explanations for why we have children.

One reason many people have kids is to avoid future regret. They fear that forgoing childrearing—even though it might raise their current happiness—will result in much lower happiness levels later in life. When people become aware of the ticking of their biological clocks, they generally imagine two opposing scenarios: one in which they are alone, and the other in which they are part of an extended family with adult children they know and like, and grandchildren to enjoy during the day (but who will go home at night). The second scenario sounds a lot better than the first.

The fear of regret is misplaced. It is true that senior citizens who have children tend to be a bit likelier to say they are happy than those who did not ever have any, but this is because seniors who are parents tend to differ in other ways (for example, they are more politically conservative) from those who had no kids. But imagine two senior citizens who are identical in their political views—as well as in income, religion, education, age, sex, race, and marital status. The only difference is that one had children earlier in his or her life, and the other did not. On average, there will be no significant difference between the two in their likelihood of saying they are very happy.

A number of recent studies back up this finding, showing that, correcting for factors such as religious faith, childless seniors are not lonelier or more depressed than those with grown children.[17]

There are far better reasons for having kids than biological clocks and avoiding regret, reasons that go beyond our own psychological happiness. Every parent on the planet knows that kids give their lives *meaning*. Having someone who depends on you affects virtually every other decision you make—from the job you take to the way you comport yourself in public. When a normal parent of young children hates his job, he thinks twice before quitting. He also watches his language and thinks about his smoking and drinking patterns. He does all these things because the meaning in his life is derived not from his own immediate pleasure but from his ability to care for another human being.

Meaning and happiness are not the same thing. Meaning is more akin to the higher definition of happiness—the "moral quality of life," which Aristotle called *eudaimonia*. A life properly lived is full of meaning, and it often involves bringing up a new generation of people who are well-adjusted, have good values, and carry on one's legacy.

People find meaning in providing unconditional love for children. But this unconditional love itself is a source of happiness. Most parents would prefer to suffer rather than allowing their children to suffer, and people who feel this way are more than a quarter more likely to say they are very happy people than those who do not feel this way. What this suggests is that, paradoxically, your happiness is raised by the very fact that you are willing to have your happiness *lowered* through years of dirty diapers, tantrums, and backtalk. Willingness to accept unhappiness from children is a source of happiness.[18]

Indeed, the pain kids cause us may even make us love them all the more. Researchers have found that when people are subjected to discomfort for a cause they care about, they appreciate that cause more. In one experiment, human subjects were exposed to electric shocks of varying magnitudes as part of a club initiation. Those that suffered the strongest shocks were most favorably disposed toward the club afterward. The theory explaining this is that we have defense mechanisms to help us justify suffering—if something hurts a lot, our brains tell us, it must be very worthwhile. And so it goes with kids.[19]

Children also tend to come bundled with a lot of other things that truly *do* make us happy. Having children lowers our likelihood of saying we are very happy by only 6 or 7 percentage points. Meanwhile, practicing a religion—compared with secularism—raises the likelihood by about 18 points, and being a political conservative raises it by about 10 points. Being married by itself raises the likelihood by 18 points as well. In other words, there are many aspects of our lives that totally swamp the happiness effects of kids—aspects that are frequently part of the overall "package" with parenthood. Ponder this: 52 percent of married, religious, conservative people with kids are very happy—versus only 14 percent of single, secular, liberal people *without* kids. Kids are part of a happy lifestyle.[20]

————————

So far, we've been talking about how children affect parents' happiness. But we also need to consider the reverse: how parents affect the happiness of their children. Here too, we find some surprises.

In the 1950s, a psychologist named Harry Harlow undertook a series of famous experiments on rhesus monkeys at the University of Wisconsin. Harlow believed that the relationship between a mother and child had profound and permanent implications for the well-being of the child. He demonstrated this with laboratory research dubbed the "Monkey Love Experiments" by the press. He found that monkeys separated from their mothers at birth and raised in isolation as infants, even if their physiological needs were met, were never able to function normally as adults. They exhibited symptoms of fear and neurosis—unhappiness, by human standards—that had nothing to do with actual physical deprivation.[21]

The results of Harlow's experiments affected entire generations of parenting. Prior to this point, psychologists had adhered to Freudian theories of parenting, which argued that children were attached to their mothers for nothing more than milk, and that people naturally coupled to regularize sexual contact. Harlow believed—and showed with his animals—that primates (like us) need something more: emotional bonds that transcend milk and sex. We are more than the sum of our physical needs, and so good parenting is far more than just providing what children need to stay warm, dry, and fed. If you believe that your job as a parent is to make your child happy, you have Harry Harlow to thank in some part for this insight.

But *do* we make our children happy? Your intuition might tell you we don't. If you have a teenager, you have probably heard many times over what a dreadful parent you are. You shouldn't believe it, though—as long as you work hard to support your child, make her do her homework, and give her lots of love. These are the sorts of things that most determine whether a child will be well adjusted or emotionally damaged. A large set of studies by economists shows that, correcting for socioeconomic conditions such as race, education, and class, parental income is an excellent predictor of a child's economic success: Kids tend to follow their role models in career and life. Similar studies show that a parent's education and involvement in his or her child's education affects the likelihood of the child graduating from high school. In other words, parents who work hard and value education tend to have kids who are more successful by all traditional standards. This will not bring happiness by itself, but it can't help but make happiness that much easier to attain.[22]

In fact, no matter how much they may complain, children do actually recognize what a valuable role their parents play in their lives, at least according to their responses in anonymous surveys. A 2007 poll conducted by MTV (and the Associated Press, for a bit of gravitas) asked more than 1,000 young people between the ages of thirteen and twenty-four what made them happy. The most common answer may have surprised some adults: It was not watching television, playing video games, or driving too fast. It was spending time with family. Almost three-quarters of the respondents actually said their relationship with their parents made them happy.[23]

And here lies the great irony of parenthood. Parents always talk about the joy they get from their kids, while kids complain about their parents. But in fact, there is strong evidence that parents make children much happier, while children make parents slightly less happy. So procreating may in fact contribute to our gross national happiness—just not in the ways we might have always believed. We should think of parenthood as a charitable act, by which parents invest some of their own happiness to create that much more for the next generation. This may be the greatest happiness-related reason of all for having children.

———

All of this talk of marriage and children leaves out the people who are most essential to our happiness: our friends. Friendships matter even more for happiness than family relationships. One study found that the positive feelings from interactions with other people were highest with friends; relatives outside of the immediate family came next, then spouses, and finally children.[24]

In general, more socializing with nonfamilial friends and acquaintances means more happiness. In 2000, a person with more than ten close friends was literally twice as likely to be very happy as someone with no close friends. According to the data, happiness increases dramatically as friends are added to your life. Of course, the reverse causation issue is certainly as present here as it is in the case of marriage—people with more friends are happier, but happier people also have more friends. So this is not just a one-way relationship; it is more like a virtuous cycle. That is why it is so important to live and work in circumstances in which friendships are possible.[25]

For years, scholars have been studying successful communities full of friendships and social networks. On almost every measure—including basic happiness—there is an enormous quality-of-life difference between communities in which people know and trust each other and those in which people don't know their neighbors. You have probably experienced this if you have lived in both a big city and a smaller town. The city has lots of cultural amenities, but you may have found it depressingly anonymous and isolating. The urbanization of modern life is almost certainly a force lowering our happiness as a society.[26]

How do friends and community make us happier? One answer is that they provide us with networks of social support to draw upon in times of need. This is especially important during periods of crisis—the death of a loved one, the loss of a job. In 1981, researchers set out to understand how losing one's job affected depression and then determine what might mitigate or exacerbate this relationship. When people lose their jobs, they experience economic problems, a lower sense of self-worth, and less control over the forces affecting their lives. All of these feelings are highly implicated in the incidence of depression. Using data on several thousand American adults throughout the 1970s, the researchers found that the greater the number of people respondents could "count on for understanding and advice," the greater the sense of control they were able to maintain after job disruptions.[27]

"Hell is other people," wrote the French existentialist Jean-Paul Sartre. This is probably true if the "other people" in question are a bunch of French existentialists. For the rest of us, other people are a secret to happiness.[28]

————————

As individuals, what should we be doing in our family lives to get happier? Some lessons like "get married" are fairly impractical—getting married for the sake of getting married is very unlikely to make you happy in the long run. If you are married, however, you should certainly be working all the time to improve the quality of your marriage. A well-cultivated social life is also a wise investment. Friends may be time consuming, but they are a tremendous source of enduring pleasure—statistically speaking, even more so than your family.

And the recommendation about children? One interpretation of the evidence on kids is that a secret to happiness is avoiding them like the plague. This is a mistake, of course, unless your *only* goal in life is having immediate happiness, which it is not for most people. This strategy is also probably futile, because it may be impossible to disentangle the lifestyle of happiness (marriage, faith, and so on) from one involving kids. Furthermore, while children don't bring happiness per se, happy and optimistic people are the ones most likely to want children in the first place. Conversely, people—and especially societies—who swear off children can't logically be assumed to be very bullish on the future. Individuals and societies looking for happiness in infertility are almost certainly starting with a happiness deficit to begin with.

This is the story of modern Europe. The fact that Europe is euthanizing itself is well-known: Every country in the European Union is well below population replacement, which is about 2.1 children per couple. Instead, most European nations have birthrates around 1.5, and some have rates lower still. (This number is actually an overestimate of native-born Europeans, because it also includes high-fertility immigrant groups, such as North Africans in France.) The European "birth dearth" has led to a series of alarming and frequently cited population facts: The population of Spain will shrink by a quarter between now and 2050; the average Italian at mid-century will have no sisters, brothers, aunts, uncles, or cousins. The European population is declining at rates comparable to those during the Black Plague.[29]

The most common explanations for these facts are economic: In social democratic systems, virtually everyone works—including mothers—which depresses fertility. As secularism has become the European norm, there are fewer religious reasons to have kids. Birth control has made it possible to avoid children while still having sex, and the growing state supports citizens indefinitely, whereas two generations ago they would have relied on children to care for them in their old age. So why have kids at all—especially if they make us unhappy?

To some, these patterns signify enlightenment. Many Europeans (and Americans) see a falling population as a positive phenomenon, because humans are little more than a drain on our planet's resources. Another interpretation is that Europe is experiencing a period of social malaise, of which the infertility is symptomatic. This second interpretation is the one most favored by many Americans; it is also favored by some Europeans, and not just of the exotic, right-wing variety. The chairman of Germany's left-wing Social Democratic Party condemned European infertility in a 2007 interview, saying, "Living for the moment does not help a society develop itself. It is children who give meaning to life. A society without children is a society without a future."[30]

But before we congratulate ourselves on our national optimism, expressed in our still-respectable rate of childbearing, we must note that birthrates are not uniform across the United States: Some population segments have birthrates that are downright European. Commentators often talk about the fact that nonwhites have more children than whites, or that immigrants have more children than nonimmigrants. But the real differences are cultural and—as we saw in the previous two chapters—most prevalent on the planes of religion and politics: Religious people are having more than 40 percent more children than secularists, and religious conservatives are having nearly 80 percent more kids than secular liberals.[31]

Why are religious people—especially religious conservatives—having more babies than secularists, and especially secular liberals? There are many reasons: Secular liberals live disproportionately in cities, where life is cramped and expensive. Secular liberals have a bit more education than religious conservatives, which delays their decision to have kids. Secular liberals are more likely than religious conservatives to belong to two-career couples. Secular liberals are about eight times likelier than religious conservatives to support abortion on demand, which may indicate a greater willingness to terminate an inconvenient pregnancy. In short, there are many reasons why secular liberals are having children at rates so far below the population replacement level.[32]

Like their European ideological cousins, American secular liberals have stepped off the baby train. This fact will have many repercussions for American society and politics in the decades to come. It also holds a powerful implication for American happiness. We know that happiness has strong genetic roots. Religious people and conservatives are the happiest Americans and are also having most of the kids today. Even if their own immediate happiness is slightly mitigated by having kids, this is more than made up for by their religion and politics, and further, they are reproducing kids who possess a genetic proclivity to happiness. The pleasant result of this is that America will probably get happier.

———

Given what we know about families and happiness, what kinds of social policies could we formulate to increase our gross national happiness?

To begin with, it is certainly wise to remove barriers to marriage—and barriers do exist. The arcane, torturous American tax code currently contains what is known as a "marriage penalty" for two-earner couples, especially those in upper income brackets. In a nutshell, total taxes are lower for some couples if they file their taxes as singles instead of filing jointly. The U.S. Congress made an attempt to rectify this in 2003 in legislation called the Jobs and Growth Tax Relief Reconciliation Act, but an increasingly prevalent tax provision called the Alternative Minimum Tax has ensured that upper-income couples still have no incentive to file as couples. In the best-case scenario, policymakers would scrap the entire U.S. tax code and create a simpler, more humane system than the one we have presently—to great cheers of joy from our citizenry. Failing that, they should at least solve the marriage penalty issue once and for all.[33]

The government has created other barriers to marriage through its distribution of benefits. Until a decade ago, marriage actually disqualified many Americans from receiving welfare, which research showed was a major reason why so many poor Americans failed to marry. Besides affecting the quality of life of potential couples, this policy radiated out to affect generations of children with unmarried parents, who had a much higher likelihood than children of nonwelfare families of growing up without a father living in the home. As we have already seen, unmarried parents are hard enough on kids. When fathers are absent altogether, the results are often disastrous. All of the available research finds that the children of absent fathers have more problems than the children of two-parent households, ranging from drug use to low school performance to crime. Clearly, putting up barriers to marriage among the poor lowers the quality of their children's lives.[34]

The American welfare system improved dramatically in the mid–1990s when Congress and President Clinton wisely reformed the system in ways that removed the disincentives to marry. Welfare caseloads fell and there were substantial decreases in child poverty. But such improvements cannot be taken for granted. The welfare reform legislation must be reauthorized periodically by Congress; otherwise, the country will return to the former system. To date, reauthorization has depended mostly on the support of the conservative policymakers who have pushed welfare reform from the beginning. This should not be the case: Reauthorization should be supported by lawmakers of all political persuasions who care about happiness and the other benefits of families. The law should be made permanent if we are truly dedicated to supporting the poorest members of our society. Even the nonpoor should support these permanent reforms, if not just on moral grounds, at least because it will help to lower future crime rates and dependency on the state.[35]

What about nontraditional marriage? What would it mean for American happiness if we as a nation removed, as some states and municipalities already have, the legal barrier against gays and lesbians marrying? The debate over this issue has occupied millions of pages and hours of commentary, but the pundits, scholars, and legal experts virtually never focus on the issue of happiness. Conservatives generally favor a ban on "gay marriage," arguing that sanctioning nonheterosexual unions would be bad for our culture. Liberals usually argue in favor of legalizing gay marriage as a matter of equal civil rights for all citizens. The net impacts on national happiness—including the happiness of homosexuals, as well as the children they might raise as married couples—have never been explored. We need to know these impacts.

The policy implications of the research on children and happiness are poorly understood as well. At present, our government creates some incentives to have kids in the form of tax deductions and credits that only benefit the middle class (because the poor pay no income taxes in the first place, and the rich generally do not qualify for these incentives). We also create incentives to the poor to have children when they receive increased welfare benefits for additional children. Are these incentives smart policy?

Politicians give middle-class citizens tax relief for having kids not because of the benefits kids bring, but because of the goodwill these policies create among middle-class voters. If there is a unifying theme in America's tax code, it is doing favors for certain voters, and this is certainly an example of that. There might be good economic reasons to maintain such policies, however. Economists estimate that the net benefits to society from children are, on average, significant and positive. Balancing the negative and positive socioeconomic impacts from children, one well-regarded academic study from 1990 placed the net present government revenues (that is, the taxes produced minus the value of services the child and his or her descendents will consume, all in 1990 dollars) in excess of $100,000 per American child—and obviously that number would only have grown after two decades. In simple terms, children are an excellent economic investment for our country.[36]

But from the standpoint of gross national happiness, what should we do about children? If the data had indicated that children dramatically increased our happiness, it would mean that the economic externalities underestimate the benefits of children and strengthen the case for more incentives. As it is, children do not increase parental happiness—although the negative effects of parenthood are swamped by things like marriage and religion, and parenting does apparently increase the happiness of kids. On balance, there is no obvious or overwhelming happiness case for or against government incentives to have children.

There is a strong *cultural* case to be made for having children, however, and especially within religious communities. Religious people tend to be our happiest citizens, and thus most prone to have the happiest kids. Religious congregations can improve the happiness and well-being of American society by encouraging and supporting their adherents to have children. This is certainly not costless to religious parents, as we have seen. But then again, no service to others is costless. Having happy children is a service to our nation, and a pro-fertility agenda for houses of worship can be understood as just one more type of stewardship.

————————

The discussion of policies and their impact on family decisions smacks of social engineering, of course. Maybe you are of the opinion that, even if marriage and fertility affect America's happiness, we have no business getting the government into these intensely private matters.

If this is your view, you are probably motivated by the idea that individual liberty is in many cases more important than citizens' happiness—certainly not an unreasonable or uncommon viewpoint. But it begs the question: When are liberty and happiness at odds? The next chapter takes up this question, zeroing in on the relationship between happiness and freedom.

CHAPTER 4

STAYING HAPPY IN THE AGE OF FREEDOM AND INSECURITY

The year was 1960, and after years of suffering under the repressive and corrupt military dictator Fulgencio Batista, Cuba had just fallen to the revolutionary Fidel Castro. Castro proved no more tolerant of political dissent than his predecessor, and in an effort to achieve complete ideological control of the country, Cuba's newest president-for-life instituted a campaign in which public servants were ordered to display a placard on their desks that read *"Si Fidel es comunista, que me pongan en la lista, yo estoy de acuerdo con él"* (If Fidel is a communist, then put me on the list, I agree with him).[1]

A young Cuban postal inspector and committed Catholic named Armando Valladares refused to display the placard. Although he had opposed the Batista dictatorship, he was not, in fact, a communist, he told government agents. This declaration of political independence was not acceptable under the new regime.

Valladares was tried, convicted as a "counterrevolutionary," and sentenced to thirty years in prison—much the same treatment he probably could have expected had he publicly refused allegiance to Batista.

In prison, Valladares suffered hunger, torture, hard labor, and solitary confinement. He witnessed the execution of fellow political prisoners. Any hope of early release depended on him signing a statement that said, "I have been wrong. All my life has been a mistake. God does not exist. I want you to give me this opportunity to join a communist society." While seven out of every eight political prisoners ultimately renounced their former resistance with this pledge, Valladares stood firm in his faith and his beliefs. Ironically, Valladares's demand for true freedom is what kept him imprisoned, year after year.[2]

America had opposed Castro's regime from the beginning, but little help for Valladares came from the United States. Indeed, some Americans—even some Christian organizations in America and Europe—embraced Castro instead of the Christians and other prisoners of conscience in his prisons. In 1976, the National Council of Churches (NCC)—representing a range of mainstream Protestant denominations in America—praised Cuba's social system as one that "sustains dignity" for "every human being, weak or strong, sick or healthy." The Cuban regime used such support from American clergy to weaken prisoners such as Valladares, who later said, "Every time a clergyman would write an article in support of Castro's dictatorship, a translation would be given to us, and that was far worse . . . than the beatings or the hunger. Incomprehensible to us, while we waited for the embrace of solidarity from our brothers in Christ, those who were embraced were our tormentors." But Valladares remained unbowed, even as many American Christian leaders abandoned him and his fellow prisoners.[3]

Valladares was ultimately released from prison after twenty-two years, but only with the help of French President François Mitterrand, who brought international pressure to bear on behalf of Cuban political prisoners. After his release Valladares immigrated to the United States, where President Ronald Reagan appointed him the U.S. ambassador to the United Nations Commission on Human Rights, giving him a stage from which to direct attention to the Cuban gulag. He has since written a bestselling account of his imprisonment, *Against All Hope: A Memoir of Life in Castro's Gulag,* and founded nonprofit organizations dedicated to freedom, the rights of political prisoners, and children.

When it comes to the abridgment of freedom, Valladares's case is an extreme one, and we can say with confidence that a system such as Cuba's would be totally incompatible with any nation's pursuit of happiness. This is an easy call. Where things get more difficult is when we consider less controversial examples of the abridgment of freedom. Every political system on Earth restricts human freedom to some extent, but not all are an obvious human-rights disaster area like Cuba. Even in the United States there are some things our government does not allow us to do: run red lights, smoke in New York City restaurants, shout "fire!" in a crowded movie theater (unless there is actually a fire). Total anarchy is not an efficient or effective way to run a country, and government asserts a responsibility to protect its citizens from others and from themselves—even arguing that this promotes our happiness. Of course, dictators use the same arguments when they implement martial law or send citizens off to communist reeducation camps, as happened in postwar Vietnam, Cambodia under the Khmer Rouge, and China during Mao's Cultural Revolution.

For the sake of happiness, the question is not whether people should be forced to endure *any* restrictions—most people are willing to trade off certain kinds of restrictions in their lives in exchange for a functioning society and state. Different people, and different nations, will weigh these trade-offs differently. Americans are willing to accept speed limits on interstate highways, whereas Germans are not. The British are willing to accept certain limitations on speech and opinion that Americans would find intolerable. Throughout the world, for reasons cultural, philosophical, and historical, people define and value freedom in different ways.

The question for this chapter is this: What is the *right* trade-off between freedom and a functioning society for America? What degree of freedom, and what kinds of freedoms, contribute most to our gross national happiness?

————————

Most Americans believe they enjoy a lot of freedom. Seventy-two percent of adults say they are "completely free" or "very free," and another quarter say they are "moderately free." These beliefs carry through to the freedom we think our fellow citizens possess: About 70 percent of Americans think that Americans in general are completely or very free.[4]

But what exactly is freedom? The earliest American definition—stated frequently by the founding fathers—is all about constraints on personal actions: If I don't hurt anybody else, I should be free from the power of other people or the government to pursue my own will. This comes from an older English tradition summarized in the saying, "The wind and rain might enter the cottage of a poor Englishman, but the king in all his majesty may not."[5]

For some, the definition of freedom has expanded since the Founding era. In his 1941 State of the Union Address, Franklin

Delano Roosevelt famously enumerated the four freedoms due people "everywhere in the world": freedom of speech, freedom of worship, freedom from fear, and freedom from want. While the first two freedoms reflect the earlier, purely negative definition of freedom—the freedom from government coercion, particularly in the areas of speech and worship—the second two freedoms require positive action. In speaking of "freedom from fear," Roosevelt was referring to the goal of meaningful worldwide disarmament. In speaking of "freedom from want," he meant that governments should agree on cooperative economic policies that would keep markets from collapsing.[6]

Roosevelt's speech summed up a broader shift that was occurring over the course of the twentieth century, especially in Europe, in which some came to believe that the mere absence from coercion was an insufficient definition of freedom. Today, most Europeans and some American progressives argue that we are not *really* free unless we possess certain things: high-quality health care, education, housing, and food. The pursuit of such modern "freedom" justifies many claims on each other's resources, claims on the state, and government programs.

Despite these modern attempts to define freedom in the language of our rights to have certain things, most ordinary Americans still harbor simpler, older notions of what it means to be free. When asked what "freedom" means, a large majority of Americans (about two-thirds) explain it in terms of "doing what I want," being able to make one's own choices, or having liberty in speech and religion. Only small percentages define freedom in terms of government guarantees of benefits or economic rights. For the most part, Americans believe that their freedom simply involves the absence of being told what to do in most areas of their lives.[7]

But not all Americans feel equally free. Religious people feel freer than secularists. Unsurprisingly, rich people feel freer than poor people: An extra $10,000 in income raises the chance that a person will say he or she feels free by about 3 percentage points.[8]

And, despite the conventional wisdom, women feel freer than men. Although many argue that the freedom of women is constrained by social convention, lower salaries (women earn about 75 cents for every dollar earned by men), or the demands of motherhood, women don't seem to *feel* shackled at all—at least compared to their male counterparts. Imagine a man and a woman who are identical in income, education, race, religion, politics, marital status, and number of children. The man will be about 10 percentage points less likely than the woman to say he feels personally free.[9]

And there are more surprises. Intuitively, we would assume that the women who felt the freest would be the ones who were least encumbered by restrictive social institutions like traditional religion, marriage, and family. The survey data indicate otherwise: Thirty-two percent of women who never attend a house of worship feel less than "a great deal of freedom," versus just 18 percent of women who attend every week. Women who have children feel slightly less free than those who do not, but married women are 10 percentage points more likely than single women to say they feel free. Republican women are 7 percentage points likelier than Democratic women to say they feel free. And the mixture of gender and politics makes the freedom difference explode: Democratic men are two-thirds likelier than Republican women (29 percent to 17 percent) to say they do not have a great deal of freedom.[10]

————

People who feel free generally also feel happy. Americans who say they are completely or very free are three times as likely as those who don't to say they are very happy about their lives. And this is not just due to the fact that richer people feel freer than poorer people. Holding incomes constant—as well as sex, education, race, religion, politics, and family status—we still find that people who feel free are 18 percentage points more likely than others to say they are very happy.[11]

Freedom *causes* happiness. Experiments have produced profound examples of this. For example, in 1976, psychologists in Connecticut decided to investigate the effects of freedom on senior citizens' happiness and health. They selected a nursing home and applied a simple experiment in the way the residents were treated on different floors. On one floor, residents were given freedom to decide two simple things in their own routines: They could decide what night would be "movie night," and they were allowed to choose and care for the plants on their floor. On another floor of the same nursing home, residents were not given these choices and responsibilities. These tiny differences had huge effects. The first group of senior citizens—no healthier or happier than the second when the experiment began—quickly began to show greater alertness, more activity, and better moods. A year and a half later, they were still doing better; they were even dying at only half the rate that the second-floor residents were.[12]

But this evidence doesn't prove that all kinds of freedom bring equal happiness, or that more freedom is always better than less. Economic freedom—from confiscatory and unrepresentative taxation, for instance—may not have the same impact on individual and national happiness as political freedom, such as being able to protest against the president without fear of being beaten up by the police. Perhaps people derive more happiness from religious freedom—the

right to worship as they choose—than they do from moral freedom—the right to make certain decisions in their lives based on the
judgments of their own consciences, rather than on edicts laid out
by others. Or vice versa. Which of these freedoms are most essential
to our happiness, and how can government best protect them in
order to ensure our right to pursue happiness?

Let's start with economic freedom. Pundits and politicians often
tell us that a free economy makes for an unhappy population. The
vagaries of capitalism make us insecure, and we would prefer the
security of generous welfare programs and national health-care.
But it turns out that, at least for most people, this isn't true.

To begin with, those who favor less government intervention in
our economic affairs are happier than those who favor more. For
example, when asked in 2004 whether it was the responsibility of
the government to improve the living standards of Americans, 26
percent of those who agreed called themselves very happy, versus
37 percent of those who disagreed. When asked in 1996 whether
it should be "the government's responsibility to keep prices under
control," those who said it "definitely should be" were a quarter
less likely to say they were very happy than those who said it "definitely should not be" the government's responsibility.[13]

Furthermore, freer economies mean happier populations, and
this fact is not specific to America. One frequently used measure
scores nations on the freedom citizens enjoy to own and operate a
business, the degree of freedom provided by the country's international trade policies, ease of investment, property rights, lack of
business corruption, and other factors. The result is an aggregate
score from 0 to 100, where 100 means maximum freedom. Near
the top are most of the Anglophone countries (except Canada):
America, Australia, Great Britain, Ireland, and New Zealand, all
of which score above 80. Most Western European countries score

in the 65–75 range; formerly communist countries and developing nations are lower. North Korea sits at the very bottom, with a lowly score of 3; Cuba is second to the bottom. Looking at thirty-five nations together, we see that a 1 percentage point increase in economic freedom is associated with a 2-point rise in the percentage of the population saying they are completely happy or very happy.[14]

If free markets are so great, why do some people complain about them so much? One age-old complaint is that, while markets may distribute goods, services, and incomes efficiently, there is no reason to expect that this distribution will be *just*. A free labor market tends to favor smart people with winning personalities and good teeth, for example—none of which necessarily has anything to do with actual merit. And even when markets *are* just, some people—those treated unkindly by them—hate them still more. Free labor markets also tend to treat hard workers more kindly than lazy ones, but if the lazy workers hold power or seniority, we tend to hear protests about the evils of pay based on market forces or merit. This is a classic problem in public sector workforces.

In other words, free markets can be politically inconvenient. This is why policymakers over the centuries have sought alternative ways to get efficient economies. The results are generally disastrous. The Soviet Union's system of distributing goods and services without free markets is a good example. Under the Soviet ministry known as Gosplan, economic planning and markets were organized to reflect the political and social priorities of the Soviet rulers—not the realities of supply and demand. The result was that shortages and surpluses arose in everything from machinery to food, to the great unhappiness of Soviet citizens. By the late 1960s, things had deteriorated to the point that the economy was barely functioning. Gosplan bureaucrats turned to the West for information about the supply-and-demand conditions in their own country. Using data from American markets and counterintelligence from the CIA on Soviet production, the agency attempted to simulate market realities. Obviously, these attempts failed—the Soviet Union went bankrupt in 1991 and the government collapsed.[15]

The absence of economic freedom was, of course, only one of many problems that beset the Soviet empire. The extraordinary gusto with which ordinary East Germans hacked down the Berlin Wall in 1989 betrayed a deep dissatisfaction with the communist political system, to say the least. Decades of political totalitarianism—in addition to socialism—had produced populations that were arguably unhappier than any found in the West. At the very end of the communist era in 1990, one cross-country survey found that 14 percent of East Germans considered themselves very happy, as did 6 percent of Russians and Czechs and just 2 percent of Latvians. In contrast, in the same survey 41 percent of Americans said they were very happy.[16]

In other words, political freedom matters at least as much as economic freedom. A lot of evidence bolsters this claim, showing that democracy, and participation in the democratic process, are strongly associated with happy citizens. This point was made conclusively by two Swiss economists who in the 1990s compared the levels of happiness across various Swiss cantons. These cantons varied dramatically in the level of participation they afforded to their citizens. It turned out that people living in cantons that allowed citizens more direct democratic rights, and offered meetings with leaders to discuss political and financial matters, were significantly happier than people living in cantons where political access was more restricted.[17]

Political freedom does not occur by itself, though; it is often connected with religious freedom. In America, the two concepts have been inextricably linked since the Founding era. The First Amendment to the U.S. Constitution guarantees that the government shall not prohibit the "free exercise" of religion, nor the "right of the people peaceably to assemble, and to petition the government for a redress of grievances." Religious freedom was known as the "first liberty" for the founding fathers.

Armando Valladares's struggle in Cuba tells us that unhappiness follows restrictions on religious freedom. The plight of Christians in China and other atheist states indicates the same thing. In America, where we enjoy more religious freedom than anyplace else in the world, the assertion that religious freedom brings happiness is hard to test, as no faiths are prohibited and no believers are persecuted. However, we do know that people who support freedom of expression for aggressive nonbelievers are happier than those who do not support this freedom. In a 2006 survey asking if respondents supported the right of people with antireligious views to speak publicly, those who said no were a third likelier than those who said yes to say they were not too happy.[18]

More than just enjoying the freedom to worship as they choose, many of the happiest people in America achieve their happiness *through* their faith. When asked about the experiences in their lives that made them feel the most free, about 11 percent of adults in 2000 put religious and spiritual experiences at the top of the list. These people were more likely than those mentioning any other experience to say they were very happy people.[19]

Most adults understand the value of our economic, political, and religious freedoms. I'm willing to bet, however, that if you asked the undergraduates at my university how they experience freedom, most of them wouldn't talk to you about economics, politics, or religion. They'd tell you what they did at a party last weekend, free from the suffocating oversight of their parents. Not that college students these days are the first to seek freedom in this way. "Turn on, tune in, drop out," urged the iconic 1960s counterculture figure Timothy Leary to the students of his day. In classic utopian style, an army of collegiate Baby Boomers insisted that free sex, drugs, and rock 'n' roll were the secrets to happiness.

The correlation between moral freedom and happiness is not so simple. In point of fact, moral freedom is in a class of its own when it comes to happiness, and the Boomers could have saved themselves and our nation a lot of pain had they done a bit of reading. More than 100 years ago, the father of sociology, Emile Durkheim, looked at moral constraints and happiness in his classic book *Suicide*. Durkheim collected data from various groups of Europeans, comparing their mental states to their social constraints. His shocking conclusion was that people who claimed the most moral freedom were unhappier than those who submitted to moral rules. Durkheim found that this principle was especially true for religious groups: The more morally constrained they were by their religious group, the happier they were, and the less likely to do themselves harm.[20]

How strange to the modern ear! Freedom is freedom, right? Wrong. Unlike economic, political, and religious freedom, moral freedom has *not* brought us happiness. We can see this vividly by comparing people who favor various moral and social freedoms to those who do not. Do you think a woman should be able to have an abortion for any reason? Even correcting for your age, income, education, race, and marital status, you are 9 percentage points less likely to be very happy than those who do not believe in abortion on demand. Do you hate the church's moral strictures and think religion brings more conflict than peace? You are significantly less likely than religion's supporters to say you are very happy. Premarital sex, drug use, you name it—the moral traditionalists have it all over the moral modernists when it comes to happiness.[21]

The link between moral freedom and unhappiness helps to explain the happiness differences between political groups. Moral freedom has been, in fact, a hallmark trait of the political left for decades. Republicans called the Democrats in 1972 under George McGovern "the party of acid, amnesty, and abortion." It was a tacky political slogan, but the underlying idea was correct: Liberals today are 10 percentage points more likely than conservatives to say that religion brings more conflict than peace; they are 40 points more likely to say it is not wrong at all to have premarital sex; and they are 41 points more likely to favor abortion on demand. Without wading into an argument about which side of these issues is right or wrong, we know for a fact that the angles taken by the liberals on these very issues are the ones least associated with happiness.[22]

Why does unhappiness accompany high levels of moral freedom? The answer may well be an uncomfortable excess of moral choice in our lives. Most of us think that choice is a good thing— one of the privileges that distinguishes America from the command economies of the Soviet era. But one recent study concluded with the provocative idea that we have reached a point where we have *too many* choices in our lives, at least as consumers. When we want to buy a car, we have dozens of choices, and the same is true for many other areas of our lives: Selecting a college, choosing a place to live—we are bombarded by choices. Too much choice, the author of the study argued, is actually harmful to our sense of well-being. We are dazed and confused by the dizzying array of options on every matter, from choosing a restaurant to picking a toothpaste.[23]

We can all agree that it's better to have some choice in our lives; it would be dull to eat the same flavor of ice cream our entire lives. Variety is the spice of life—but only up to a point. Researchers at Stanford University demonstrated this point in revealing studies conducted in the mid–1990s. In one experiment, the researchers set up two booths in a supermarket and gave out samples of jam. In one booth there were six types of jam to sample; the second had twenty-four types. Although more shoppers stopped to sample from the wider array (60 percent of passersby versus 40 percent), people who sampled from the limited-choice booth were ten times likelier to buy a jar of jam than the people with the expanded choices. In another experiment, the researchers offered college students the opportunity to write an extra-credit essay in a class. One group was offered six potential essay topics to choose from; the other was offered thirty topics. Those with fewer choices were much likelier to complete their essays—and produced higher-quality work—than those who had the expanded choices.[24]

Why do people prefer less choice to more in these studies? Past a certain point, choice overwhelms us, as the costs of processing information and making a decision outweigh the gains from having more options. Psychologists call this idea the "choice overload hypothesis."

We seem to suffer from a similar overload when it comes to morality. To pose a "freedom overload hypothesis," I suggest that the evidence on happiness shows that too many moral choices leave us insecure and searching, unable to distinguish right from wrong, and thus miserable. Men and women are innately moral beings. As Albert Einstein famously put it, "Morality is of the highest importance—but for us, not for God." A cornucopia of moral options has the same effect as cutting a boat adrift at sea.

It may come safely ashore, but only by sheer luck. More likely, it will drift aimlessly until destroyed by the elements.[25]

————

The unhappiness apparently caused by moral freedom is a difficult problem. In search of a solution, some turn to the law, arguing that we need to legislate morality. No one in America would argue that we need to follow the lead of the Afghan Taliban, which banned singing and kite-flying in the name of morality. However, we still have various "blue laws" on the books—mostly relating to serving and selling alcohol on Sundays—and outlaw certain sexual practices for the express purpose of upholding particular moral standards.

These laws are misguided. From the standpoint of gross national happiness, there are two good reasons government should refrain from infringing on most private, moral freedoms, even if these freedoms are stupid and misery-provoking.

First, the government is better equipped to constrain a person's actions than it is to change his moral outlook. Worldview depends on culture, not politicians. To constrain actions legally affects morality very little. Rather, it entices people to behave in a way that avoids penalties—or to hide their actions from the law. This sort of approach not only fails to increase happiness, but also turns immoral people into criminals. Second, moral licentiousness—from sexual promiscuity to drug abuse—is not the same thing as a little vice, and the law is a blunt tool that can rarely make such a subtle distinction. There is no case here for prudishness. On the contrary, there is a large body of evidence suggesting that there is much virtue—happiness, health, and prosperity—associated with things such as moderate alcohol use and sex within the boundaries of committed relationships. Indeed, the great Saint Augustine taught that moderation is more difficult than abstinence—and hence can be more virtuous. For the sake of our happiness, we need rules in our *private* lives constraining our morality, protecting us from excess in moments of personal weakness, and allowing us to realize our best selves.[26]

In short, the evidence on moral freedom tells us that the recipe for happiness is a combination of individual liberty, personal morality, and moderation. This age-old formula is overwhelmingly supported by the data.

Is it *ever* appropriate to abridge moral freedom legally? Obviously it is, when the moral license of one person unreasonably harms another. If my immorality hurts you, it is no longer a question of protecting me from myself, but a question of protecting you from me. That is why I may drink myself into a stupor and strip down to nothing but a lampshade, but only so long as I do so in private. If I end up in your front yard, I am infringing on *your* freedom.[27]

Of course, the appropriate boundaries between my liberty and your harm are often hard to find. Proponents of smoking bans, for example, believe that smokers cause undue harm to others when exposing them to secondhand smoke, and therefore that smoking should be restricted in public places. Others disagree that the harm to others from secondhand smoke is sufficient to warrant such infringements on smokers' liberty. The disagreement between proponents of abortion rights and those who would criminalize the practice is precisely over whether a fetus is a person who can actually be harmed. Those who are "pro-choice" think abortion is a private moral matter, that their choice does not cause suffering for another human being. Meanwhile, those who are "pro-life" argue that the issue is one of public, not private, morality—specifically, that the fetus is a person who deserves protection from violence.[28]

Other examples of this fuzziness include gay marriage (which some argue affects our culture) and recreational drug use (which affects our communities and families). Even issues as private as disciplining our children, which some localities have sought to regulate in the name of protecting kids' welfare, have come into question. Indeed, lawmakers in California and Massachusetts in recent years have proposed laws making it a crime for parents to spank their children.[29]

In short, on many moral issues we do not have clear or accepted agreement on boundaries between private behavior and public harm. So it is no surprise that matters of private morality produce the bitterest public policy disagreements between otherwise reasonable people.

Not all government policies to change our behaviors and attitudes on moral matters involve making laws. Governments also take it upon themselves to *teach* us what policymakers believe is good for us. Tax dollars are spent on educational campaigns encouraging us to stay in school, not to smoke, to buckle up, and to lose weight.

It is not clear that these public service campaigns are useful—there is good reason to question their effectiveness. The "Just Say No" antidrugs campaign of the 1980s was a source of such general hilarity during my own misspent youth that I have reason to wonder how many of these campaigns have any real effect on personal behavior.

But let's imagine these campaigns *were* effective. Could we justify them on the grounds that they contributed to our gross national happiness? Of course, there is no way the government could possibly address the moral issues *most* relevant to happiness.

Abortion, for instance, is an issue that demonstrably separates happy from unhappy people. But the idea of our government paying for a campaign to tell people to "just say no to supporting abortion on demand" is ridiculous, and probably unconstitutional.

Furthermore, many believe it infantilizes a free citizenry when the government sets a moral agenda, and this cannot help but lower our happiness. When moral suasion is intended to protect us from making the wrong decisions, it affects our sense of personal control and our ability to feel we are earning our own success in life. It is my own view—with which many reasonable people will surely disagree—that the government should not be in the business of judging behaviors and attitudes about private, moral matters, if we can claim they do not unreasonably harm others. So long as we do not create victims, it is the job of individuals, families, communities, and houses of worship to decide what we do to ourselves individually and with others consensually. Our governments serve us best when they protect our economic, political, and religious freedoms, and thus protect us—in the great American tradition of individual will—in our rights to make our own decisions.

I am not defending libertinism in any form. On the contrary, a robust understanding of government protections of freedom tells us we are free as individuals, families, and communities to set our own private standards of behavior—which may be very strict. But for the sake of happiness, this is where restrictions on most moral freedoms should occur—not with government.

———

When it comes to intellectual, political, and religious freedom, as a tenured university professor I have one of the best jobs in the country. Within the bounds of decency and sanity, I can write whatever

I think is correct and valuable, even if others—even the people I work for—disagree with me. Part of the reason I enjoy this freedom (freedom that makes me very happy, by the way) is that I have a high level of job security—it is easier to get rid of fire ants than a tenured professor. My situation is extremely unusual, however: For most folks, and indeed for the nation as a whole, there is a *trade-off* between freedom and security—in their jobs, and in their lives. If we want more freedom, we usually have to tolerate more risk. Conversely, if we want to be safer, we have to give up some freedom.

The right mix of freedom and security differs for each person, and probably across groups of people as well. Some scholars refer to the particular mix of freedom and security people seek as their "entrepreneurial orientation." A higher orientation means a greater ratio of freedom to security, because entrepreneurs seek freedom and are comfortable with relatively high levels of risk in their lives. What affects this orientation? Some studies suggest that it might be innate—that some people are born more tolerant to risk than others. Immigrants, for example, tend to have a naturally high entrepreneurial orientation, as do firstborn children. Furthermore, the freedom and risk people demand changes over the course of their lives, sometimes in unexpected ways: While we tend to seek greater security as we age, there are spikes in our entrepreneurial orientation around monumental birthdays such as thirty, forty, and fifty—when people often take stock of their lives, feel depressed at what they have done (or failed to do) to date, and decide to try something different.[30]

Provocative new research claims that some countries have more entrepreneurially oriented citizens than others. Some nations, the argument goes, have populations that are more freedom-loving than others, while some are more risk-averse. It is fairly easy to witness firsthand these kinds of differences if one travels at all; it takes about a week outside the United States to notice that people in many other places appear to be much more comfortable with the status quo than we are, complaining about their jobs and cities but not actually doing anything about it, like quitting or moving.

But one recent study goes even further and asserts that Americans differ *genetically* from people in most other countries. A simple version of the argument starts with the observation that immigrants tend to be entrepreneurial, willing to give up security and familiarity for the possibility of prosperity and success. This trait is relatively rare—a mutation from the norm. Very few people in Old World communities had it, and those who did were more likely to migrate from their homeland than those who did not. But because America is quite literally a nation of immigrants—or descendants of immigrants—and these immigrants (or their descendants) have married other immigrants (or their descendants), the genetic mutation that leads to entrepreneurial behavior appears with unusual frequency in our citizens. According to this line of argument, America's vast success can be explained by our genetic predisposition to embrace risks with potentially explosive rewards.[31]

The natural ratio of freedom to security in America is high because of our roots and culture. The trouble is that our government, by its very nature, lowers this ratio. Public policies are constantly put in place to protect us from this danger or that—from losing our jobs, from hurting ourselves, from getting sick, or from being threatened or harmed in various ways by others. These policies virtually always come at a cost to freedom. Furthermore, they act as a "safety ratchet": Safety is always increased and freedom sacrificed, but almost never vice versa. This is not good for our gross national happiness.

Consider safety-belt laws. Forty years ago, cars generally did not come equipped with seat belts, although they did exist. After research showed that the likelihood of injury and death in a car accident was reduced by wearing a seat belt, the government implemented regulations that mandated the installation of seat belts in new cars. A few years later, it strengthened the regulations by mandating shoulder belts as well. It was only a matter of time before policymakers realized that making sure people had the option to buckle up would not ensure that we got the safety benefits—so they took the inevitable step of forcing us to wear them, whether we want the extra safety or not. Today, if a police officer sees you driving without a seat belt in most American states, you will be heavily fined. Have these laws enhanced your happiness by making you feel safer? Regardless of your answer, there is little prospect that these laws will be relaxed any time soon.

Another example is airline safety. In the aftermath of the terrorist hijackings of September 11, 2001, the U.S. government began to elevate airport security measures in response to the tragedy. New laws required passengers to forgo all sharp items, because the 9/11 hijackers had used boxcutters to disable their victims. Suddenly, fingernail scissors were illegal on planes, while airline meals—no treat to begin with—could not be consumed with the aid of a metal knife. In addition, passengers were indiscriminately selected for "extra security screening," and we witnessed the excruciating spectacle of old ladies randomly yanked out of boarding lines, frisked like common criminals for weapons, and being relieved of their knitting needles. Since then, we have seen the safety ratchet increase in even more absurd ways, with substantial costs to our freedom—today, after one unsuccessful attempt by an incompetent terrorist to detonate a bomb in his shoe, every passenger on every plane in America must remove his or her shoes while going through security screening. And once again, there is little prospect that these policies will ever be rolled back.

In both of these cases—and you can surely think of dozens more—our government has traded away our freedom for the sake of our safety. And there is every reason to believe that the measures detract from our happiness. Once again, consider airline safety. The U.S. government reports that about 650 million passengers pass through airports in the United States each year, removing their potentially dangerous footwear. It probably only takes about half a minute per passenger to remove shoes—big deal, right? But if you actually add it up, the losses are striking: Calculated at the average 2007 private-sector hourly wage rate, this delay represents more than $90 million in value. The shoe-removal policy costs that much in wage-earners' time, all in mildly unhappy 30-second chunks. One scholar estimated that the loss to American citizens from all airport security measures—the airport bureaucracy, the value of lost time, and other costs—comes to more than $30 billion per year.[32]

To add insult to injury, research indicates that the security measures we have taken cannot legitimately be considered effective or necessary. Even before the measures were taken, the chances of being on an airplane struck down by a terrorist were about one in 20 million, and there is no evidence that this probability has improved as a result of the policies. The government itself advertises that it has intercepted 600 firearms at security checkpoints—out of 7 million items confiscated. That number of firearms, incidentally, comes to less than 0.01 percent of the items surrendered by passengers, most of which were innocuous, like cigarette lighters. (In a rare moment of deregulation, the ban on lighters was rescinded in 2007, after the government was confronted with overwhelming evidence that lighters posed no security threat. In the meantime, security guards had confiscated approximately 6 million lighters).[33]

We can be legitimately angry with our government for its chronic overinvestment in security at the cost of our freedom. The real blame, though, falls on ourselves as citizens in a democracy. Politicians simply react to what they believe their constituents want when they mandate bicycle helmets for children, the use of seat belts at all times in motor vehicles, a choice of certain oils for frying chicken at restaurants, or footwear inspections at the airport.

How is it possible that self-respecting Americans allow—and even ask for—such nanny-state policies? The answer is that we value other people's freedom much less than we value our own. While our own perceived freedom drives up our happiness, the freedom we believe others have does not affect our happiness at all. If two people are demographically identical, and they feel the same amount of personal freedom—but one thinks Americans in general are completely free while the other thinks Americans are not free—they will *not* tend to differ in their levels of personal happiness. Thus, we acquiesce to laws that restrict freedom in the abstract—freedom for others, it seems to us—in exchange for marginal improvements in our security. But when we ultimately suffer the results personally, we find it significantly lowers our happiness.[34]

It works something like this. I am feeling mildly insecure—say, about the threat that some errant terrorist miscreant might attack my local airport in Syracuse, New York (as wildly improbable as that sounds, and no doubt is). I and my fellow citizens around the country express our mild insecurity to our elected officials, telling them in no uncertain terms that we view it as their duty to keep us free from harm. Sweat breaking out on their foreheads as they contemplate reelection, they begin to cast about wildly for something that will satisfy the voters. They consult with some consultants, hold some hearings, and come up with a new ineffective security policy, such as requiring full-body pat-downs of passengers chosen at random. This poses no problem for me—we have to make sacrifices, right?—until I'm the one who gets patted down and delayed just long enough to miss my flight.

The only realistic way that our government could raise our happiness with its promiscuous safety regulations would be to convince people they were effective so that we would *feel* safer—whether it was true or not—and obscure the costs. But we must ask ourselves: Is this a defensible way to promote the happiness of our nation? I believe it is not.

————

From a happiness standpoint, we are too quick to allow government abridgment of our liberties. We are too tolerant of creeping security measures imposed by the state.

I am not suggesting that there is no role for the government in our lives—or recommending that we create some anarchic utopia, in which the only organizing force was the free market. The government *can* help us pursue happiness. But not in the way offered by favor-wielding politicians, ever wheedling for votes and dollars with services and the prospect of income redistributed from others. Rather, what the government can do is to give us control over our own lives as citizens by protecting our freedoms. We are like the senior citizens in the famous nursing home study who were given happiness through control over movie night and their plants. For happiness, a little bit of liberty goes a long way.

The trouble is that frequently, we don't demand this freedom. On the contrary, we find it easier to hand over our decisions to others, most notably our elected officials and their counterparts in the permanent bureaucracies across America. But if we truly care about increasing our happiness, we are making a mistake in stepping back from the freedom that is our birthright. We have the balance wrong, and are erring as a people on the side of giving up our freedom as individuals and citizens.

It is one thing to charge our government with helping us band together as citizens to take care of the most vulnerable. The mentally ill, for example, who do not have strong private support, truly deserve our help in a civilized society, and we cannot realistically rely on private charity to meet that need. It is another thing entirely to demand that the state take care of the rest of us—able-bodied, sound-minded, once-independent Americans—guaranteeing our wages and providing our medicines for free. This is to treat us like children. There is little freedom in the nanny state, and we can expect little happiness there, either.

It is one thing to entrust the government with the financing of massive relief efforts, such as rebuilding a city in the wake of a hurricane. But it is another thing to ask the government to meet every social want and need, from our desire for symphony orchestras to our longing for amateur sports leagues. The attitude is depressingly common that, if something is important to us, the government ought to provide it. The ever-growing social welfare net diminishes our freedom by giving us less power to solve our own problems. It also places our social preferences in the hands of public servants—well-intentioned, perhaps, but with preferences of their own to pursue with *our* dollars.

It is obviously appropriate to invest the government with the responsibility to protect our nation against real dangers, such as the invasion of a foreign army or an attack on our interests abroad. But this is not the same thing as expecting governments—creating new bureaucracies in their earnestness—to pacify us with ineffective security measures or to protect us from ourselves in the course of normal risks in our day-to-day lives. The dignity of the goal of defeating worldwide terrorism is hopelessly degraded when, in the next breath, we declare war on helmetless motorcycle riding and secondhand smoke. Osama bin Laden is a threat to America; trans fats in our food are an annoyance. We need to protest when our government fails to makes these distinctions and uses spurious logic to justify trading away our happiness.

———

Let us suppose that we will insist on remaining a free country, even if our freedom is often compromised. How will we take advantage of the freedoms we still possess? In America, the great frontier of entrepreneurship, we have traditionally used our freedom in incredibly productive ways—hence our extraordinary prosperity. But what's the point of all that prosperity? Does money actually buy gross national happiness? We turn now from the culture of happiness to the economics of happiness.

PART II

THE ECONOMICS
OF HAPPINESS

CHAPTER 5

DOES MONEY
BUY HAPPINESS?

On July 23, 2000, a forty-two-year-old forklift operator in Corbin, Kentucky, named Mack Metcalf was working a twelve-hour nightshift. On his last break, he halfheartedly checked the Sunday paper for the winning Kentucky lottery numbers. He didn't expect to be a winner, of course—but hey, you never know.

Mack Metcalf's ticket, it turned out, was the winner of the $65 million Powerball jackpot, and it changed his life forever. What did he do first? He quit his job. "I clocked out right then, and I haven't been back," he later recounted. In fact, his first impulse was to quit everything, after a life characterized by problem drinking, dysfunctional family life, and poorly paid work. "I'm moving to Australia. I'm going to totally get away. I'm going to buy several houses there, including one on the beach," he told Kentucky lottery officials.[1]

Most state lotteries offer options to take the jackpot either over a twenty-year period or as a discounted lump sum. Metcalf chose the latter, which was $34 million. Forty percent of the money went to his estranged wife with whom he had bought the ticket, and then of course the government took back its share in taxes of what it had just given him, leaving him with a grand total of $14 million—still plenty of money for a man who had never had much money in his life. Metcalf never worked again, but he never moved to Australia either; instead he bought a 43-acre estate with an ostentatious, plantation-style home in southern Kentucky for more than $1 million. There, he spent his days pursuing pastimes like collecting expensive cars and exotic pets, including tarantulas and snakes.

Trouble started for Metcalf as soon as he won the lottery. Seeing him on television, a social worker recognized him as delinquent for child support from a past marriage, resulting in a settlement that cost him half a million dollars. A former girlfriend bilked him out of another half million while he was drunk. He fell deeper and deeper into alcoholism and became paranoid that those around him wanted to kill him. Racked with cirrhosis of the liver and hepatitis, he died in December 2003 at the age of forty-five, only about three years after his lottery dream had finally come true. His tombstone reads, "Loving father and brother, finally at rest."

Did millions of dollars bring happiness to Mack Metcalf? Obviously it did not. On the contrary, those who knew him blame the money for his demise. "If he hadn't won," Metcalf's former wife told a *New York Times* reporter, "he would have worked like regular people and maybe had 20 years left. But when you put that kind of money in the hands of somebody with problems, it just helps them kill themselves." The man who bought Metcalf's mansion (for half of what Metcalf had paid for it) said, "I think things went from bad to worse when he got the money."[2]

So what's the moral of the story? Is money destined to make us miserable?

Of course not. Mack Metcalf's sad case is surely an aberration. If *you* hit the lottery, it would be different. You would give philanthropically and do all kinds of incredibly life-fulfilling things. In short, a thousand flowers would bloom for your happiness. Similarly, if your career suddenly took off in a fantastic way and you earned a great deal of money, you would get much happier. And what is true for the parts must also be true for the whole: When America experiences high rates of economic growth, it gets happier. America is not a nation of Mack Metcalfs, and money is a smart first strategy for attaining a higher gross national happiness.

Right?

———

You've heard the axiom a thousand times: Money doesn't buy happiness. Your parents told you this, and so did your clergyman. Probably the only ones who told you different were people trying to sell you mutual funds. Still, if you're like me, you would just as soon see for yourself if money buys happiness. People throughout history have insisted on striving to get ahead in spite of the well-worn axiom. America as a nation has struggled and striven all the way to the top of the world economic pyramid. Are we suffering from some sort of collective delusion, or is it possible that money *does* buy at least a certain amount of happiness?[3]

Americans have gotten much richer over the past several decades, on average, than they were in previous generations. The inconvenient truth, however, is that there has not been a meaningful rise in the average level of happiness. In 1972, 30 percent of Americans said they were very happy, and the average American enjoyed about $25,000 (in today's dollars) of our nation's total income. By 2004, the percentage of very happy Americans stayed virtually unchanged at 31 percent, while the share of national income had skyrocketed to $38,000 (a 50 percent real increase in average income). If we correct for fluctuations in happiness that have nothing to do with income—from forces such as politics and world events—the data allow us to predict that an extra $1,000 in average income raises the percentage of very happy people by less than 1 percentage point.[4]

The story is the same in other developed countries. In Japan, real average income was six times higher in 1991 than it was in 1958. During the post–World War II period, Japan was transformed at unprecedented speed from a poor nation into one of the world's richest countries. But the average happiness of a Japanese citizen, measured on a scale of 1–4, stayed exactly the same at 2.7.[5]

In some countries, there is even some evidence that economic growth can create *unhappiness*. This is generally the case for nations in the process of rapid and chaotic development, which experience opportunities for great wealth for the first time. The sudden, vast wealth of a few entrepreneurs raises common aspirations to an unreasonable level, the idea goes, leaving the vast majority of citizens deeply dissatisfied with their meager lot. Post-Soviet Russia is an example of this phenomenon. In the 1990s after the fall of the Soviet Empire, a few entrepreneurs made vast fortunes in markets for oil and other primary resources. Yet post-Soviet Russia is a miserable place in which only about one in five citizens say they are very happy about their lives. Some development economists believe that cases of lucky individuals amassing large fortunes raised unreasonable expectations among ordinary Russians, creating a sense of extreme unfairness. And in this way, money created unhappiness.[6]

So individual countries don't seem to get much happier as they get richer. But are rich countries happier than poor countries?

The answer to this question depends on how poor a "poor country" is. People in poor countries where much of the population lives below subsistence level are much *un*happier than people in rich countries, on average. International comparative studies of happiness consistently place the poorest nations of the world—especially the countries of sub-Saharan Africa—at the very bottom. In 2006, one study ranking countries in terms of happiness found that Zimbabwe and Burundi were the unhappiest places on Earth. And this makes sense, of course: It is ridiculous to imagine that illiteracy, high child mortality, and the threat of starvation are any more pleasant or bearable to a Burundian than they would be to an American. But once countries get past the prosperity level that solves large-scale health and nutrition problems, income differences pale in comparison with differences in more important factors—like culture and faith—in predicting happiness.[7]

For example, compare Mexico and France. The cost-of-living difference between the two nations is vast, so economists don't compare raw income; rather, they compare the "purchasing power" of citizens. In Mexico—a nation in which most people live above the level of subsistence but still are much poorer than residents of the United States or Europe—the average purchasing power was about a third what it was in France in 2004. And yet Mexicans, in the aggregate, are happier than the French. In Mexico, 63 percent of adults said they were very happy or completely happy. In France, only 35 percent gave one of these responses.[8]

It might be tempting to dismiss the happiness of Mexicans as delusional or a reflection of the fact that most Mexicans have no idea what life with material wealth is like. But this would be a mistake: There is simply no evidence that Mexicans lack an understanding of true happiness compared to the French. A more reasonable conclusion is that Mexican happiness—and French unhappiness—are caused in large measure by forces other than money.

American communities are like countries when it comes to happiness. Like happy Mexico and unhappy France, the happiness of American communities—all of which are above the level of subsistence—depends very little on their comparative prosperity. Among forty-nine communities across the United States, a $10,000 increase in average household income is associated with just a 3-point rise in the percentage of the population that says it is very happy. Furthermore, there are abundant examples of unhappy high-income communities and happy low-income communities. Take eastern Tennessee (which includes the cities of Chattanooga and Knoxville, but is mostly rural), where people are 25 percent likelier than people living in tony San Francisco to say they are very happy, despite earning a third less money, on average. Obviously, it is more expensive to live in San Francisco than it is to live in Tennessee, but San Franciscans still enjoy more than 30 percent more disposable income.[9]

Like nations and communities, individuals get little or no extra happiness as they get richer—even massively richer. In a classic 1978 study, two psychologists interviewed twenty-two major lottery winners and found that the joy of sudden wealth wore off in a few short months. Further, lottery winners have a harder time than the rest of us enjoying life's prosaic pleasures: watching television, shopping, talking with friends, and so forth. It's almost as if the overwhelming experience of winning the lottery dulls the enjoyable flavors of ordinary life. This chapter opened with the sad tale of Mack Metcalf. In truth, it doesn't necessarily destroy your life to win the lottery, as it evidently did his, but it won't make your life better, either.[10]

Nor will money itself blunt your unhappiness very much. In 2001, about 34 percent of American adults said they had felt so sad at least once in the past month that nothing could cheer them up. How much would a $100,000 increase in annual income lower the probability of saying you were this inconsolable? About 3 percentage points. What about a $100,000 increase in your wealth—say, a big chunk of your retirement portfolio? About 2 percentage points. In other words, it takes lots and lots of cash to make you feel less miserable—which suggests that other strategies (such as working on spiritual or family life, or volunteering for charity) might be more cost-effective than simply striving to get more money.[11]

So it's true: Money doesn't bring enduring happiness for countries, communities, or individuals, except perhaps when people start out in abject poverty. Why not? The answer has to do with what psychologists call "adaptation." Humans tend to adapt psychologically to their circumstances—including their monetary circumstances—and do so very quickly.

Perhaps you've walked into a chain-smoker's home and wondered how on earth he could stand to live with such a stench. The answer, of course, is that he is used to it. For the most part, the same is true of economic gains and losses in our lives: They give us pleasure or pain when they happen, but the effect wears off very quickly. We are excellent at perceiving changes to our surroundings; we're not so good at sustaining any special sensation from the status quo. Adaptation makes money unsatisfying per se because we get used to it quickly. Almost immediately, an increased income becomes the new "normal."

For individuals, communities, and nations, economic life is like being on a treadmill, and getting richer is like speeding up the treadmill: We never get any closer to bliss. According to the great economist Adam Smith, an early proponent of the benefits of pursuing personal economic interests for the common good, "the mind of every man, in a longer or shorter time, returns to its natural and usual state of tranquility. In prosperity, after a certain time, it falls back to that state; in adversity, after a certain time, it rises up to it."[12]

Indeed, economists even refer to our tendency to adapt as the "hedonic treadmill." They have found ingenious ways to illustrate how it works. In 1978, for example, researchers presented a sample of adults with a list of twenty-four big-ticket consumer items (a car, a house, international travel, a swimming pool, and so on). They were asked how many of these items they currently possessed; they were also asked, "When you think of the good life— the life you'd like to have, which of the things on this list, if any, are part of the good life as far as you are personally concerned?"[13]

Inevitably, people felt that the "good life" required more things than they currently possessed. Among the people between thirty and forty-four years old, the average number of items owned was 2.5, while the ideal number was 4.3. The same people were interviewed sixteen years later, in 1994, and presented with the same list. Naturally, most people had more items; the folks formerly in their thirties and early forties (now in the next age category, forty-five to fifty-nine years old) had 3.2 items, on average. They were closer to the good life, right? Wrong. Their requirements for the good life had now shifted, to 5.4 items. In other words, after sixteen years and lots of work, the "good life" deficit had stayed almost exactly the same. The more stuff you have, the more you want.

Researchers have also measured the principle of adaptation using a method called the Leyden Approach, asking people what income levels they would consider to be very bad, bad, insufficient, sufficient, good, and very good. What studies find is that, in general, no matter what income level individuals reach, they will tend to say that their "required income" (the point halfway between insufficient and sufficient) is about 40 percent higher than what they are making at the time. If someone earns $50,000 per year, his or her required income will be about $70,000. But if that same person gets a raise and makes $70,000, his or her required income will very quickly jump to about $98,000.[14]

To relate the principle of adaptation to your own life, remember your last significant pay raise. When did you celebrate it and get the greatest happiness from it—the day you found out it was going to happen, or when the extra money was actually included in your paycheck? If you are like me and answered the former, you were seeing the principle of adaptation at work in your own life.

Adaptation applies to more than just money: Studies show that we adapt to most major events in our lives—the death of a loved one, being fired, moving. What we *don't* adapt to are small, chronic conditions like low-grade pain, a tense marriage, ambient noise, an incompetent coworker, or a frustrating commute to work. Our failure to recognize which factors will lead to long-term happiness or unhappiness, and which will create only temporary joy or discomfort, leads us to commit major errors in the decisions we make about our lives. For instance, let's say that, following a popular formula for happiness, I take a high-paying job in the city and buy a big, expensive, beautiful house in the country. My house and salary will give me enduring happiness, and the only trade-off will be an hour's drive each day to and from my job, which I will get used to—right? Wrong. The evidence shows that I will get used to the high pay and the big house in a matter of months, after which they will no longer make me happier than

I was before I had them. But the misery of my commute will endure, year after gridlocked year. This is actually the near-perfect formula for unhappiness, not happiness.[15]

————

Money may not buy happiness, but there *is* one important way in which money and happiness are related: At any given moment, richer individuals within a country tend to be happier than poorer folks.

In 2004, Americans earning more than $75,000 per year were more than twice as likely to say they were very happy than those earning less than $25,000. One study found that when happiness was measured on a 1–3 scale (where 3 was happiest), Americans in the bottom 10 percent of earners in the mid–1990s had an average happiness score of 1.94; those in the middle of the income distribution had a score of 2.19; and those in the top 10 percent scored 2.36.[16]

This is strange, because we know that money by itself doesn't bring much happiness. Many economists look at these facts and conclude that though we really don't care about having money for its own sake, we do care about having more money than others. In other words, my money only makes me happy when I notice that I am richer than you. Or that you are poorer than me, of course. (Like the old saying goes, "It's not enough to succeed— your friends have to fail, too.")

Some studies appear to back up this idea. In one experiment from the early 1990s, human subjects were presented with two job options, both at magazines. At Magazine A, they would earn $35,000 while their colleagues earned $38,000. At Magazine B, they would earn $33,000 while their colleagues earned $30,000.

Most of the participants chose the higher-paying job at Magazine A—the rational choice. However, two-thirds said that, notwithstanding their choice, they would be *happier* at Magazine B.[17]

In another study involving faculty, staff, and students at Harvard University, participants were asked to choose between earning $50,000 per year while everyone else earned $25,000, or earning $100,000 per year while others made $200,000. The researchers stipulated that prices of goods and services would be the same in both cases, so a higher salary really meant being able to own a nicer home, buy a nicer car, or do whatever else they wanted with the extra money. But those materialistic perquisites mattered little to most people: Fifty-six percent chose the first option, hypothetically forgoing $50,000 per year simply to maintain a position of *relative* affluence.[18]

Could it be that what we care most about is not material comforts, but one-upsmanship? Perhaps out of our primeval past comes the urge to demonstrate that we are better than others. A hundred thousand years ago, it would have given us happiness to have more animal skins than the troglodyte in the next cave; this would help ensure mating prospects, which would keep our genetic lines going. Still programmed in this way, we get unexplainable pleasure from having a bigger house than the guy next door, even if we don't "need" the space, or a better office than our coworkers.

This theory may sound good, and it is quite common to hear it, but it is *not* the explanation best supported by the evidence. Rather, what the data tell us is that richer people are happier than poorer people because their relative prosperity makes them feel successful. Think again for a moment about your last big pay raise. *Why* did you feel such joy over it? Most likely, it was because of what your higher pay represented to you—evidence that you had succeeded, that you had created value. That's why you enjoyed it more when you learned about it than you did when you actually got to start spending it. It is success (not money) that we really crave.

Imagine two people who are the same in income as well as in education, age, sex, race, religion, politics, and family status. One feels very successful and the other does not. The one who feels successful is about twice as likely to be very happy about his or her life than the one who does not feel successful. And if they are the same in perceived success but one earns more than the other, there will be no happiness difference at all between the two.[19]

The upshot: If you and I feel equally successful but you make four times as much as I do, we will be equally happy about our lives. Of course, successful people make more money than unsuccessful people, on average. But it is the success—not the money per se—that is giving them the happiness. This casts a whole new light on the studies just described. Of course I would prefer $50,000 in a world of $25,000 earners—over $100,000 in a world where everyone else earned $200,000—because no matter how the economy values people and rewards success, I want to be one of the successful folks. If the experiment had asked which option the respondents preferred, *given that they were equally successful in either case,* people would choose the higher salary.

I have no doubt that some people do get pleasure from lording their higher incomes over others. But the evidence says this is not the biggest reason that having more than others gives us happiness. Financial status is the way we demonstrate to others (and ourselves) that we are successful—hence the fancy watches, the expensive cars, and the bespoke suits. We use these things to show other people not just that we are prosperous, but that we are prosperous *because we create value.*[20]

There is nothing strange about measuring our success with money; we measure things indirectly all the time. I require my students to take exams not because I believe their scores have any inherent value, but because I know these scores correlate extremely well with how much they have studied and how well they understand the material. Your doctor draws your blood to check your cholesterol not because blood cholesterol is interesting in and of itself, but because it measures your risk of having a heart attack or a stroke. In the same way, we measure our professional success with green pieces of paper called "dollars."

What scholars often portray as an ignoble tendency—wanting to have more than others—is really evidence that we are driven to create value. Wanting to create value is a virtue, not a vice. The fact that it also brings us happiness is a tremendous blessing.

Have you ever wondered why rich entrepreneurs continue to work so hard? Perhaps you've said, "If I had a billion dollars, I'd retire." This is what Mack Metcalf actually did when he won the lottery. But if he had *earned* that money doing something creative and productive, things would almost certainly have gone differently for him. People who succeed at what they do tend to keep doing it. The drive to succeed, as opposed to just having more money than others, explains why the super-rich—who already have so much more than virtually everybody—continue to work.

If there is a downside to success, it is that it appears to work like a ratchet. For a star quarterback who throws twice as many touchdowns each season as the league average, it is a letdown for him and his fans when he has a year that is only a little above average. The more you succeed, the more you *need* to succeed to feel happy.

Take the case of billionaire Larry Ellison, founder of Oracle. The world's eleventh-richest man, he would need to spend $30 million per week, or $183,000 per hour, just to avoid increasing his wealth. Further, he would have to spend it on items with no investment qualities (like real estate), meaning that, unless he sets his money on fire, or (better yet) gives it away, he simple cannot *not* be filthy rich. Yet he continues to slave away, earning billion after billion. Being rich, and having more than the average Joe, simply cannot be driving Larry Ellison. It is the will to succeed and create value at greater and greater heights.[21]

Who enjoys the benefits created from the slavings of Bill Gates (worth $56 billion and counting), Warren Buffett ($52 billion), and all of America's other success-addicted, ultra-rich entrepreneurs? We all do: As long as fortunes are earned—as opposed to stolen, squeezed from governments, or otherwise extorted from citizens—this is good for all of us. Oracle has not made Larry Ellison a rich man without any benefit to society. The firm currently has 55,000 employees, people with well-paying jobs to support their families. The company has introduced technology that has benefited all parts of the economy, and it has paid billions to its shareholders. And we can't forget that Oracle has rendered generously unto Caesar, year after year: In 2005 alone, it paid $810 million in corporate taxes, totally apart from the personal taxes paid by Ellison and his thousands of employees.[22]

If people get happier when they get more successful, then perhaps it makes sense that whole countries should get happier when they get more successful as well. But this appears not to be the case. The astronomical rises in American GDP reflect the fact that, as a nation, we are creating huge amounts of value—we are the most successful nation on earth. Yet we have already seen that happiness *doesn't* follow GDP growth over time. In the United States, our gross national happiness has remained essentially static for the past three decades.

One plausible explanation for this paradox is that people really only perceive and enjoy success at the individual level. Although we might be pleased to be members of a successful nation, it doesn't give us happiness like succeeding personally does. Technological advances for whole nations stem from the individual successes of entrepreneurs. It is the efforts of software moguls and biotech gurus that change technology for the rest of us and make us able to be more productive, and thus richer—but not much happier. To be happier, we have to find our *own* success, however we define it.

————————

Money is a measure of success, and a handy one at that. But there is a dark side to this fact: People tend to forget that money is *only* a measure. Some people focus on money for its own sake, forgetting what really brings the happiness.

This is not really a shocking idea, to be sure: We often mistake indirect measures for the actual phenomena we care about. Take, for example, standardized tests in public schools. The purpose of administering them, at least originally, was to see whether schools were providing an adequate education to the majority of their students. When the students at a particular school perform poorly, on average, the school faces sanctions—thus the teachers have incentives to "teach to the test," focusing on preparing students to take the test instead of teaching the content the test is supposed to measure. There is evidence that this is really taking place. Obviously, it is problematic and ironic if, in order to score higher on the measure of success, we degrade true education.[23]

Just as teaching to the test leads to inferior education, working only for the money can lead to an unhappy life. No doubt you have met people who appear to be trapped in an unsatisfying cycle of materialism and unhappiness. These people confuse money for what it is supposed to measure, and thereby maximize the wrong thing. Among other things, they leave out of the equation all of the kinds of success—in our family lives, in our spiritual lives, in our friendships—that money does not measure. And even their work choices reflect the sad mistake of forgoing what they love doing for what brings in the most monetary compensation. The evidence on happiness is clear that we should avoid the measurement error of materialism.

So why do so many people fall prey to this error? One explanation—a timeless hit for critics of American-style capitalism—is that our commercial culture fosters it: Relying as it does on an unending stream of cash, it creates a cleavage for us between true value creation and the symbols of it: cash, and the stuff it can buy. This is obviously true. We are bombarded day in and day out by marketing that tries to convince us that, if we are successful people, we need a lot of material things.

But before singling out the American free-market system for creating this confusion, note that capitalism is not the only culprit—far from it. Governments encourage this measurement error even more egregiously. Remember Mack Metcalf: There is no doubt that he played the lottery—the government-monopoly-controlled lottery—in the belief that it would enhance his happiness if he won. Almost everyone believes this: How many times in your life have you been asked what you would do if you won the lottery? Have you ever said, "I would start by being exploited by manipulative friends and family, and then maybe go into an alcoholic spiral—and then I'd probably die an untimely and tragic death"? No, you list things you imagine you would like to do: go back to school, take vacations, buy homes in warm places, and so on.

What is going on here? On the one hand, you possess anecdotal evidence about cases like Mack Metcalf's, and I have told you about actual data showing that winning the lottery simply does not make people happier than before. On the other hand, you are being told by those who are ethically and constitutionally bound to represent your interests—politicians and bureaucrats— that easy money will give you happiness. The New Jersey State Lottery's slogan is "Give Your Dreams a Chance." My own state of New York drew in gamblers for years with, "All you need is a dollar and a dream." No doubt your state makes a similar claim.

But easy money will *not* bring you happiness—earned success will (and in many cases that earned success will also bring you money). It is simply inconceivable that your state lottery commissioner does not understand this fact at some level. Yet for the sheer sake of raising money for its own purposes, your government perpetuates this cognitive error. President Franklin Roosevelt once said, "Happiness is not in the mere possession of money; it lies in the joy of achievement, in the thrill of creative effort." How things have changed! Today, government officials eviscerate the very ideal of achievement while exploiting our citizens—some of our most vulnerable citizens at that. In fact, studies of lotteries consistently show that it is the poor who spend the most on state lottery tickets.[24]

I am not advocating an end to legal gambling here. While I personally have no use for it, I understand that gambling is an enjoyable diversion for some. Furthermore, I believe there is a lot of benefit to protecting our freedom to make our own decisions about our resources, even including the freedom to confuse money and success. But it is astonishing that the government—for no other reason than monopolistically vacuuming money out of its own citizens—should abet this confusion and lower our happiness.

————

How could the government make things better for us instead of worse, when it comes to money? Here is an idea: It could tax away our incomes at very high rates so that money and success were no longer so highly correlated. Then, that money (if we still bothered to earn much) could be spent on important public goods and services instead of what we would have spent it on, such as gas-guzzling cars, big houses, and other ostentatious displays of our success. We would be happier if we were forced out of the consumers' arms race that we have (literally) bought into. And as a bonus, we could enjoy all the good things the government would buy. According to one prominent economist, "We could spend roughly one-third less on consumption—roughly $2 trillion per year—and suffer no significant reduction in satisfaction. Savings of that magnitude could help pay for restoring our infrastructure, for cleaner air and water, and a variety of other things." It's so simple![25]

Unfortunately, this idea is misguided. Although consumerism does not buy happiness, government spending does not, either. On the contrary, more government spending makes us *less* happy, in general.

Over the past thirty years, Americans have had increasing levels of money taxed away and spent—at least ostensibly—on them. In 1972, the federal government devoted about $4,300 to each American (in 2002 prices). By 2002, the level of spending had risen to $6,900 per person. Yet we have not gotten any happier. In 1972, 30.3 percent of Americans said they were very happy. In 2002, that percentage was still *exactly* 30.3 percent. Even worse, when we correct for changing household income levels and the passage of time, higher government spending turns out to be pushing average happiness down, not up. Consider that, while a $1,000 increase in per capita income is associated with a 1.24 percent drop in the percentage of Americans saying they are not too happy, a $1,000 increase in federal government revenues per person is associated with a 2.91 percent increase in the percentage saying this.[26]

In other words, private prosperity brings us up, but government spending brings us back down. For every dollar in increased GDP that the government taxes away and spends, there is actually a higher net unhappiness level among the population than if that money had never been earned at all. In order to make up for the unhappiness caused by $1 in extra government revenue per citizen, each person would need an average of $12 in extra income. We demand a growing level of public services in the United States, paid for with a rising percentage of our income and wealth, but there is no evidence that this spending is doing our happiness any good at all. Indeed, some might go so far as to speculate that government spending, financed with taxation, is an "X-factor" helping to explain why growing national prosperity generally does not raise happiness: In virtually every country and era, rising average incomes are matched by rising taxes and government spending. The unhappiness we experience as a result of the taxation mitigates any happiness we might earn as a result of our productivity.

Why does government spending diminish our happiness so significantly? There are a number of possible explanations. First, in some cases the spending goes to things that make us miserable, such as the Transportation Security Administration or the Internal Revenue Service. Second, government spending reminds us of how our economic freedoms are abridged, being paid for as they are with taxes. Third, government spending, for some—the nonworking poor, in particular—creates misery because the people who are supposed to benefit become dependent on government programs.

————

Our market system, which often rewards success with dollars, can create the tendency to confuse success itself with money. But giving more money to the government will not fix this; on the contrary, our government tends to exacerbate the problem with its money-making schemes (like the lottery), and it would only make things worse for us if it tried to adjust our values through taxation and redistributive spending. The moral confusion of materialism is one best left to ourselves, our families, our communities, and our faiths to resolve.

This is hardly an original observation on my part. Alexis de Tocqueville wrote in his 1835 classic *Democracy in America* about the tendency toward "excessive individualism" in an atomistic, hard-driving American society. Tocqueville noted, however, that the remedy lay not in a reordering of the free American system, but in the institutions of civil society: families, churches, charities, and friendships, which are the connective tissue between people that help us to avoid errors in our values. In other words, *markets* are not enough—we need *morality* as well, and the institutions that make it possible to express this morality.[27]

Free markets allow us to live the way we want to live—giving most people maximum buying power, and allowing citizens to find jobs that match their skills and passions. How we use this power and freedom is up to us and depends on our values: We can make decisions that lead to happiness, or we can make decisions that make us miserable. But to throw out free markets because capitalism does not bring happiness directly would be senseless: It would be like getting rid of your computer because it didn't make your coffee.[28]

What about the losers in a capitalistic economy? Doesn't a competitive market system make it harder for people unable to participate effectively in the market system to pursue happiness like the rest of us? The answer might be yes, but only if we are bereft of our core values of charity and caring for others. The fact that some sick or handicapped or otherwise-challenged people are miserable because they cannot provide for themselves in a free-market system does not mean there is something wrong with our system—it means there is something wrong with our morals. In a moral society, these people should be aided by the rest of us in a way that preserves dignity and avoids dependence.

The fact that money doesn't buy happiness is no indictment of capitalism. On the contrary, capitalism is the best system to allow people to succeed on their merits in the economy—and we know that it is success that truly *does* bring happiness. Capitalism, moored in proper values of honesty and fairness, is a key to our gross national happiness, and we should defend it vigorously.

————

One of the most important conclusions in this chapter is that the pleasure we get when we have more than others is not evidence that we are somehow venal and greedy. Rather, it is evidence that we naturally strive to succeed and create value. True, measuring our success by looking at our money and possessions relative to others' can lead us in the wrong direction in terms of happiness. Materialism is a common and grave error in which we substitute the symbols of success for success itself. Properly understood and personally managed, however, our acquisitive nature is nothing to be ashamed of.

But there is still a major problem. Just as having more denotes success and brings happiness, having *less* suggests failure and brings unhappiness. In the game of comparison, there are never just winners—someone has to lose. This fact has led generations of intellectuals and politicians to conclude that economic inequality is the primary force behind our gross national *unhappiness*. Could they be right? We will see in the next chapter.

CHAPTER 6

INEQUALITY AND (UN)HAPPINESS IN AMERICA

The United States is a rich nation and is getting richer. According to the U.S. Census Bureau, over the decade ending in 2003 the top quintile of earners in America experienced an average inflation-adjusted income increase of 22 percent. But prosperity didn't end with the top earners. The middle quintile saw an average 17 percent real increase, while the bottom quintile enjoyed a 13 percent rise. In the thirty years leading up to 2003, earners in the top quintile saw their real incomes increase by two-thirds, versus a quarter for those in the middle quintile and a fifth among the bottom earners.[1]

This may seem like reason to celebrate—even if money doesn't buy happiness. Yet, some find within these numbers something to regret: the fact that the rich are getting richer much faster than the poor are getting richer. Income inequality in the United States is rising, according to most responsible estimates. For example, in

1973, the average family in the top quintile earned about ten times what the average bottom-quintile family earned. By 2003, this differential had grown to fifteen times. The U.S. Census Bureau measures economic inequality using what is called a Gini coefficient, in which 0 indicates no inequality (all incomes are the same) and 1 is perfect inequality (one person has all the income). Over the past four decades, the American Gini coefficient has increased by nearly a third, from 0.36 in 1965 to 0.44 in 2005. In European countries, the coefficients generally hover below 0.30, indicating much more economic equality than we see in the United States.[2]

Liberal politicians have placed special emphasis on the fact that economic inequality in America is rising. In particular, North Carolina Senator John Edwards, who rose to prominence when he sought the Democratic nomination for president in 2004 and again in 2008, has based his campaigns almost entirely on the idea that we are "two Americas"—rich America and poor America. In his own words: "Today, under George W. Bush, there are two Americas, not one: One America that does the work, another America that reaps the reward. One America that pays the taxes, another America that gets the tax breaks. One America that will do anything to leave its children a better life, another America that never has to do a thing because its children are already set for life. . . . One America that is struggling to get by, another America that can buy anything it wants, even a Congress and a President."[3]

Edwards must believe that economic inequality is a source of unhappiness to lots of Americans, or he wouldn't use it as his principal campaign theme. Other politicians agree with him. Democratic Senator Barack Obama complained that "the average CEO now earns more in one day than an average worker earns in an entire year." Democratic Senator Hillary Clinton characterized today's economy as "trickle-down economics without the trickle." She declared that a progressive era is at hand because of "rising inequality and rising pessimism in our work force."[4]

But it is not just the Democrats who worry about income inequality in America. Indeed, 2008 Republican presidential contender Mike Huckabee has decried the widening gap as strenuously as any liberal. Conservative populists such as Huckabee are as alarmed as any on the left about the vast fortunes earned by the lucky few in America and the unhappiness it supposedly causes for those who remain behind.

Many intellectuals and scholars have built whole careers around the subject of income inequality. It is practically an academic article of faith that inequality per se is socially destructive and should be avoided wherever and whenever possible. The prevailing view is that the fairest, least envious societies—that is, the *happiest* societies—are the most economically equal ones. And thus, if we want a happier citizenry, we need less economic inequality.

Perhaps they're right—after all, equality appears side by side with happiness in the U.S. Declaration of Independence: "We hold these truths to be self-evident, that all men are created equal, that they are endowed by their Creator with certain unalienable Rights, that among these are Life, Liberty and the pursuit of Happiness." To be sure, most people understand this sentence as referring to political equality, or equality before the law. But a loose interpretation that includes income equality doesn't necessarily make someone a utopian leftist.

But there are good reasons to question the supposed link between inequality and unhappiness. For one thing, the prevailing intellectual view on inequality doesn't seem to match the views expressed by most normal, nonacademic folks. Although some ordinary people of my acquaintance might complain about the enormous compensation of CEOs, I rarely have heard them express any shock or outrage at the great wealth of America's richest people: successful entrepreneurs. On the contrary, they say they hope their *kids* might become the next Bill Gates or Warren Buffett. Most people I know actually admire those successful folks and don't begrudge them their success.

More convincing than my personal experiences are the data showing no link at all between rising inequality and unhappiness. If inequality were so depressing for us, we would expect to see American happiness falling. Yet average happiness has *not* fallen. Remember that, in 1972, 30 percent of the population said they were very happy with their lives. In 1982, 31 percent reported this level of happiness; in 1993, 32 percent; and in 2004, 31 percent. This total lack of significant change in average reported happiness occurred over the same period in which income inequality increased by nearly half. Statistically, income inequality does not explain any of the fluctuations in happiness or unhappiness over the past three decades.[5]

Nor does income inequality explain happiness differences between American communities. Looking at 30,000 households in forty-nine American communities in 2000, we see that the variation between income levels in communities explained nothing about how many people in each stated that they were very happy. Take two very different communities: the Latino community in Cleveland, Ohio, and the city of Boulder, Colorado. Boulder is characterized by far higher income inequality than Cleveland's Hispanic community, yet its citizens are more than twice as likely—45 percent versus 18 percent—to say they are very happy. Income inequality does not lie anywhere behind this happiness gap.[6]

So is this inequality bad for our nation's happiness, or not? Despite all the rhetoric from populist politicians and egalitarian academics, a good hard look at the best available data tells us that, in fact, inequality does *not* cause unhappiness in America. And efforts to diminish economic inequality—without creating economic opportunity—will actually lower America's gross national happiness, not raise it.

If you ask an American whether we have "too much inequality" in our society, you are about as likely to hear "yes" as "no." In 2005, 55 percent of U.S. adults believed that income differences in our society were too large. Forty-nine percent thought income inequality was a "serious problem." And 53 percent thought the government should "do more to try to reduce income inequality." Taken on its face, as politicians and some scholars do, this is a major public concern and one worth addressing, even if these percentages are nowhere near as high as the concern expressed about other issues such as crime, education, and national security.[7]

There are several common explanations for the consternation that many Americans evidently feel about economic inequality. The most common is a concern for basic *fairness*. No matter how much you may study or how hard you may work, some believe it is simply unfair for you to be rich while others lack basic health care or worry about making their rent. In fact, even if others don't lack these basics, some say, the obscene income differences in the United States are unfair because they simply *cannot* be attributed to merit differences. Bill Gates has a net worth that is hundreds of thousands of times higher than mine, and millions of times higher than that of many poor Americans. Is Bill Gates really

250,000 times more productive than I am? Is he a million times more productive than the average lower-middle-class fifty-year-old? If he is not, some believe, the income and wealth differences between us are not legitimate. They are immoral. They make us unhappy, if we have any conscience at all.[8]

Perceived unfairness can lead to envy. Envy used to be condemned as a sin; today it is dignified in policy proposals. One prominent British economist—in a book entitled *Happiness*—argued that we should tax higher-earning individuals not just to get their money for public services, or even to redistribute it to those who have less, but because in earning a lot these individuals make others feel bad. This is an extraordinary argument for lowering the incentives for higher earners to work. It runs contrary to millennia of moral teaching that valued hard work and actually compares it instead to a destructive vice like tobacco, which we tax or otherwise penalize in order to curtail an undesirable behavior.[9]

Such arguments may sound dubious to you, but history suggests that too much envy can be a dangerous thing. Plutocrats and oligarchs throughout history have found out the hard way that the envy of the masses can cost you your head. Income inequality during the Industrial Revolution is a conventional explanation for the rise and flourishing of communism. Roman emperors coined the term "bread and circuses" to signify the policy of giving free grain and entertainment to the poor masses in order to avoid social strife, and there is an ancient Chinese saying that states the problem succinctly: "Inequality, rather than want, is the cause of trouble." Some today reach the conclusion that equalizing income a bit would be a smart investment to placate the less fortunate.

Academics argue against income inequality in a slightly more sophisticated way than simply complaining that it isn't fair. They assert, instead, that it is inefficient, advocating income equalization on the belief that transferring money from the rich to poor people hurts the rich less than it helps the poor. This argument relies on what economists call "diminishing marginal utility," which works something like this: Imagine you have two bowls of ice cream and I have none. You eat both and don't share. The first bowl gives you 10 units of happiness, while the second—still tasty but not as delicious as the first, because the first *always* tastes best—gives you 5 units. I get 0 units—or maybe even negative happiness as I sit and watch you enviously. Together, we have 15 units of happiness, at best. Now imagine that you give me your second bowl (or we pass a law taking it away from you). Assuming you and I have the same preferences, our total happiness will be 10 plus 10, or a total of 20 units. According to this logic, equalizing income, like equalizing ice cream, will increase our gross national happiness.

There are lots of problems with this concept as a guide to policy. It might be expensive to redistribute income. If we care about liberty, taking from the earner by force might do disproportionate harm to our society's happiness. And probably most importantly (and in fact a demonstrable truth—more on this later), I might gain far less happiness from getting *your* money than I would from earning money myself. Still, despite these issues, for many, especially political liberals, the concept of diminishing marginal utility justifies income redistribution to rectify income inequality.

Another academic argument against income inequality concerns public health. Some social scientists claim there is an association between bad health outcomes (such as shorter average life spans) and high levels of income inequality. Some have interpreted this association as evidence that inequality *causes* poor health. The implications of this hypothesis can be quite radical. Free markets tend to emphasize the productivity differences between individuals by connecting them to differences in pay. Some believe that the result of this is ill health. In other words, capitalism leads to inequality, inequality makes us sick, and thus unhappy.[10]

In sum, in an effort to explain why income inequality brings unhappiness, some argue that it is unfair, inefficient, and maybe even unhealthy. Each of these arguments is problematic. But there's one big reason to reject all of them: The evidence shows that it isn't income inequality that leads to unhappiness at all, but something else entirely.

———

About half of all American adults think economic inequality is a major problem, and about half of them do not. Do these two groups differ in some way that might explain the contrasting attitudes? As it turns out, their opinions cannot be explained by income, class, race, or education. Instead, what best predicts an individual's views on income inequality is his or her beliefs about income *mobility*—that is, about whether Americans have opportunities to get ahead economically. And it is these beliefs about mobility, not beliefs about income inequality, that lie directly behind much happiness and unhappiness. Those who believe that they and other Americans can get ahead with hard work and perseverance—that America offers paths to success—are generally happy and unfazed by economic inequality. Those who think that economic mobility in the United States is an illusion are relatively unhappy and tend to complain about income inequality.

In other words, some Americans are unhappy because they don't believe they have opportunities to succeed, but they complain about income inequality, as if this were the root cause of their problem. If our leaders focus on getting rid of income inequality, however, the underlying problem—lack of income mobility—will not improve, nor will happiness. (In fact, it will get worse, because the treatment for inequality exacerbates problems with mobility.) They are mistaking a symptom for a root cause.

People mistake symptoms for root causes all the time. If I am an alcoholic, my relationship with my spouse will probably suffer, and that will make me unhappy. I might complain about the bad relationship, even though my drinking is the real problem. I can work on the relationship all I want, but as long as I keep drinking, things probably won't get better. In fact, the longer I ignore the root cause, the worse it will get and the less likely I am to get back the happiness in my relationship.

And so it goes with inequality, immobility, and happiness. Let's look at the evidence.

First, feelings about mobility and inequality go together. Imagine you are asked the following question: "How much upward mobility—children doing better than the family they come from—do you think there is in America: a lot, some, or not much?" If you think there is not much upward mobility in America—you are not a big believer in American opportunity—you will be 46 percent more likely than people who believe there is a lot of mobility to say that income differences in our society are too large. In addition, you will be 63 percent more likely to say that income inequality is a "serious problem," and you will be 71 percent more likely to say that the government should do more to reduce inequality. Perceived immobility is what drives concern about income inequality, pure and simple.[11]

Or take the following statement: "While people may begin with different opportunities, hard work and perseverance can usually overcome those disadvantages." Imagine two people who are identical with respect to income, education, race, sex, religious participation, and family situation. The only difference is that the first person agrees with that statement, while the second disagrees. The optimist about work and perseverance will be 31 percentage points less likely than the pessimist to say inequality in America is too high. He will also be 39 points less likely to say that inequality is a big problem, and 32 points less likely to advocate for more government intervention to lower inequality. Note that this difference is *not* due to the fact that the optimist is more economically successful, better educated, or is of a different race than the pessimist—the two are identical in these ways. This is purely a difference in views about opportunity.[12]

This pessimism about opportunity is clearly linked to unhappiness. In 2004, 700 American adults were presented with a statement about opportunity and asked whether they agreed or disagreed. The statement was: "The way things are in America, people like me and my family have a good chance of improving our standard of living." Those who agreed were 44 percent more likely than those who disagreed to say they were very happy in life. The optimists were also 40 percent less likely than the pessimists to say they felt like they were "no good at all" at times, and they were 20 percent less likely to say they felt like a failure.[13]

As we have found again and again, happiness follows earned success (not money) and a sense of control in our lives. Indeed, people who feel they do not have control over their own successes are generally miserable. In 2001, people who said they did not feel responsible for their own successes—whether they enjoyed successes or not, mind you—spent about 25 percent more time feeling sad than those who said they did feel responsible for their own successes.[14]

Pessimism about mobility and worries about income inequality are both associated with unhappiness. But only the former is the *cause* of unhappiness. Imagine two demographically identical people who have the same beliefs about mobility. The inequality they personally experience—the difference between their own incomes and average incomes in their communities—is uncorrelated with their happiness. But what happens when one person believes that his family has a chance of improving its standard of living while the other person does not? The believer in mobility will be 12 percentage points more likely to be very happy than the nonbeliever.[15]

In other words, people who feel economically immobile are generally unhappier than those who feel more mobile. If we ask them about income inequality, they will say they don't like it. But it is not inequality that is driving their unhappiness—it is their perceived immobility. To confuse the two is to commit what economists call the "association-causation fallacy." It is like saying that height leads to intelligence just because, on average, we see that tall kids in developing countries do the best in school. (The real reason is that taller kids, on average, have better nutrition than shorter kids, which leads to both height and intellectual ability.)

It works something like this. Imagine you have a job at a factory, and have no other realistic employment opportunities. Seventy-five percent of the workers, like you, earn a low wage, although enough to get by. The other quarter are no more talented (in your opinion)—nor do they appear to work any harder than you do—yet they earn twice as much as you and live in relative luxury. What would you like? Obviously, the opportunity to make it into the privileged class. But since this is impossible, you instead complain about the unfairness of the difference between your wage and theirs. But if there were a clear path to the upper class and a realistic prospect of making it there if you worked hard enough, you wouldn't complain about inequality. In fact, you might even like inequality, because it would demonstrate what you could attain.

British researchers have found this to be precisely the case: People's happiness rises when the average income increases relative to their own income, if they believe they have opportunities to succeed; they interpret the income average as a measure of their own potential. The fact that Bill Gates is so rich probably raises the happiness of America's optimists, because it demonstrates to them what somebody can do with hard work, good ideas, great luck, and a system that protects free enterprise. Gates is not a duke or a prince; there is no evidence that God especially likes him. He simply had a lot of opportunities and made the most of them.[16]

In contrast, it is depressing to think that no matter how hard you work or how clever you are, you can never get ahead. This is why, when people feel there is a lack of opportunity to advance at their workplace, they often quit their jobs. Indeed, 70 percent of those who say their chances for promotion are good are very satisfied with their jobs, versus just 42 percent who say their chances for promotion are not good. We need clear paths to success, not guarantees of income equality, to be happy. Guarantees of equality actually take us in the wrong direction.[17]

The true relationship between mobility and happiness explains why happiness levels in America have not fallen over time, even though income inequality has risen. Unequal as it is, economically speaking, America is still a happy land of opportunity.

———————

Those who are unhappy about income inequality favor public policies that redistribute resources. Seventy percent of people who feel that income inequality is a serious problem say the government should do more than it is doing at present to reduce the income gap. Only 33 percent of those who believe it is less than a serious problem think the government should do more.

There are a number of ways that government can do more to bring about greater equality—by instituting, for example, the kinds of policies advocated by Senator Edwards. Funding welfare programs and other kinds of income support for the poor is one way. Another type of redistributive policy seeks to mandate minimum wages for the poor, placing the burden (policymakers believe) on private companies. And since equality can be achieved not just by giving to the poor, but also by bringing the top down, we can get greater equality by increasing income taxes on the rich, a redistributive policy we will no doubt see after 2008 if a Democratic candidate is elected. Democrats are also generally enthusiastic about increasing the estate tax, which limits the amount of wealth passed on from one generation to the next.

A major problem with all these policies is that they tend to have dramatic unintended consequences that hurt those they are intended to help. Welfare programs have a long history of inducing misery—provoking dependency among beneficiaries, for example, and disengaging money from earned success. Minimum wages create unemployment disproportionately among the least skilled, most at-risk members of the workforce. At the same time, policies that bring the top down change the incentives of the wealthy in ways that hurt the poor as well. Punitive income taxes reduce entrepreneurship, meaning fewer jobs created, less economic growth, less in tax revenues, and less charitable giving—all to the detriment of those left behind.[18]

Ironically, these inequality policies don't even address our main problem, if a happy society is our goal. We know that inequality per se simply does not lie directly behind life satisfaction. In some cases—even among people of modest means—inequality can actually raise happiness by holding out the promise of rewards for future success. Rather, what makes people unhappy, either intrinsically or by way of social strife and ill-health, is immobility. Those left behind in the economy will almost certainly *not* become happier if we simply redistribute more income.

This is why egalitarian policies always hold out the promise of happiness but never deliver on that promise. Every movement to stamp out economic inequality has looked toward, as George Orwell termed it in *1984,* "our new happy life." Yet that happiness is always out in the future, never in the present. Stalin called himself in Soviet propaganda the "Constructor of Happiness"—a moniker that would be comical today were it not for the tens of millions of Soviet citizens who died as a result of the repression that accompanied his pursuit of egalitarian projects such as the push to collectivized farming.[19]

Furthermore, policies to redress income inequality hardly affect *true* inequality at all. Policymakers and economists rarely denounce the scandal of inequality in work effort, creativity, talent, or enthusiasm. We almost never hear about the outrage that is America's inequality in time with friends, love, faith, or fun—even though these are things most of us care about more than we do money. We know that married people, for example, tend to have much happier lives than singles, but no progressive politician I know of is out there declaring war on bachelor life. To believe that we truly redress inequality in our society by moving cash around is to take a materialistic—and totally unrealistic—view of life. To focus on income redistribution is to profess a mechanistic and impoverished understanding of the resources Americans truly value.

If policymakers who care so much about inequality *did* focus on non-money resources, they would find much more equality in America than they typically think exists. Recall that the American Gini coefficient—the typical measure of income inequality—is a rather-high 0.44. For other, more valuable resources, the coefficient is much lower. For example, the inequality of the frequency of prayer is 0.34. The inequality in the willingness to sacrifice for another person is 0.25. The inequality of optimism is 0.20. Last but not least, the coefficient for the inequality in American happiness is a rock-bottom 0.18—lower than the level of income inequality seen anyplace in the world. The average happiness level in America has not changed since the early 1970s, but inequality in happiness has actually fallen.[20]

So why don't policymakers who denounce economic inequality so strenuously focus on these nonfinancial items? There are two plausible reasons. First, egalitarians might actually believe that money truly *is* the most important or relevant thing for American society. If they're right, the European caricature of the shallow, money-obsessed American is actually accurate, and we can solve a major problem simply by moving some cash around with redistributive policies. Second, they might believe that making people equally happy is less important than trying to help those who are unhappy to get happier. That is, it might make more sense to help depressed people than it does to worry because some folks are enjoying a disproportionate share of our nation's happiness.

But if happiness inequality is irrelevant, it begs an obvious question: Why is income inequality so different? If greater income equality is our end goal, it means that bringing the top down is as useful as bringing the bottom up. This makes about as much sense as depressing the happy for the sake of the sad—which reminds me of the old Spanish proverb, *Mal de muchos, consuelo de tontos*

(The misfortune of the many is the consolation of fools). It does nothing for the living standards of the poor simply to confiscate the resources of those at the top.

It is absolutely true that there is economic inequality in America—in fact, the gap between the richest and poorest members of society is far wider than in many other developed countries. But there is also far more opportunity, which is what is fundamentally important to both our personal happiness and our gross national happiness. Hard work and perseverance *do* hold the key to jumping from one economic class to the next. While it is true we must solve the problems of absolute deprivation, such as hunger and homelessness, we must also recognize that the promise of rewards for hard work render the remaining inequality benign at worst—and a positive stimulant to achievement at best. Redistribution and taxation, beyond that necessary to pay for some key services, can weaken America's willingness and ability to progress.

Knowing this, we should direct our policies not at wiping out economic inequality, but at enhancing economic mobility. This means improving educational opportunities; aggressively addressing cultural impediments to success; enhancing the fluidity of labor markets; encouraging the investor revolution, which reaches further and further down the income-distribution chain every decade; and stimulating the climate of American entrepreneurship.

Many people, particularly on the political left, will call me a Pollyanna for claiming that Americans can really get ahead with hard work and perseverance. They will point out that those who reject the idea of opportunity and mobility might be *unhappy*—but that doesn't necessarily make them *wrong*. They will even point to some oft-cited research to show that not everyone enjoys equal access to the American Dream. For example, one famous study from the early 1970s looked at the economic success of schoolchildren as they grew up and concluded that school quality could not do much to redress inequalities in income. The author of the study asserted that deeper factors—such as discrimination and cultural problems—were largely to blame for ongoing economic gaps. If schools don't bring the bottom up in America, many have thus argued, isn't equal opportunity really just an illusion? And if the disease is incurable, shouldn't we just move right to the symptoms and lower economic inequality? [21]

Subsequent studies have greatly weakened such arguments, however. Whatever the limitations of our education system for improving the lives of the underprivileged, there is in fact an amazing amount of economic mobility in America. Research from the U.S. Census Bureau, the Federal Reserve, and the U.S. Treasury Department have all shown that, as a general rule, about one-fifth of the people in the lowest income quintile will move to a higher quintile within a year, and about half will rise within a decade. To be sure, this tells us that about half will *not* have risen, and the research also says that a significant proportion of people will fall to a lower quintile over the same period (which must be true, mathematically). But all in all, it puts paid to the claim that economic mobility is in any way unusual in America. Millions and millions of poor Americans climb out of the ranks of poverty every year.[22]

————

While there are a few prominent conservatives who complain about income inequality, it is an issue owned primarily by the political left. Rank-and-file liberals are more than twice as likely as conservatives to say income inequality is a "serious problem."

This is not just because of income differences: Seventy-seven percent of liberals with above-average incomes think inequality is a serious problem, but only 40 percent of conservatives with below-average incomes agree with them.[23]

This is not to say that liberals care *only* about inequality and not about opportunity. Liberals do worry about social mobility. But they're far more pessimistic about it: Even liberals who have themselves succeeded are less convinced than conservatives—including poorer conservatives—that economic mobility is actually possible in America. And this difference is one of the biggest reasons American conservatives are happier than American liberals today. Forty-eight percent of lower-income conservatives believe there's a lot of upward income mobility in America, versus 26 percent of upper-income liberals. And 90 percent of the poorer—but optimistic—conservatives said that hard work and perseverance can overcome disadvantage, versus just 65 percent of richer liberals. If a liberal and a conservative are identical in terms of income, education, sex, family situation, and race, the liberal will be 20 percentage points less likely than the conservative to say that hard work leads to success among the disadvantaged.[24]

These attitudes are exhibited every day in egalitarian policies promoted by the Democratic Party, which broadcasts the message that there is little opportunity for certain groups, who must instead fight for redistributive policies. According to the Democratic National Committee, "The federal minimum wage is so disgracefully low that now, during a period of extraordinary prosperity for the nation's corporations and wealthiest families, the average CEO earns as much in just a few hours on the first workday of the year as a full-time minimum wage worker earns the entire year."[25]

Democratic officials no doubt only want to help the poor when they make such statements. But these statements are nonetheless depressing—and not just to me. Research shows that messages have an effect not only on those they reach, but also on those who deliver them. In one provocative study, researchers found that when they asked normal, happy human subjects in an experiment to repeat depressing sentences, the subjects quickly began to show signs of depression. It requires no stretch of the imagination to conclude that an unhappy message about America's lack of opportunity and mobility will make the proponents of this message unhappy.[26]

In contrast, the happy political right in America reinforces its good mood whenever conservatives express faith in the American promise that anyone can get ahead with hard work and perseverance. This view is evidence of a light heart, not a hard one. What our nation must do is work tirelessly to ensure that this promise never becomes hollow.

CHAPTER 7

HAPPINESS IS A FULL-TIME JOB

Marienthal is a small Austrian village about half an hour from Vienna by train. In the 1920s, it was dominated by one textile factory, which employed the majority of the town's residents. As the firm fell on hard economic times, it pulled the fortunes of Marienthalers down with it: When the factory closed in 1929, 75 percent of the town's 478 families lost their earnings.

Unemployment was not unusual in Austria and Germany at the time. The economic depression that gripped America in the late 1920s and early 1930s was mild compared to what occurred in much of Europe. A group of Austrian sociologists seeking to study the effects of this sort of unemployment on society identified Marienthal as a typical case and went there to observe and conduct interviews with the residents. They expected to find dislocation and unhappiness, but what they found exceeded their worst expectations and became a classic case study on the social importance of work.[1]

The Marienthalers were not starving—Austria in those years had unemployment insurance that covered the better part of a factory worker's wages. But the townspeople languished none-theless. There were no regular jobs to replace their old positions, and to qualify for unemployment support, workers were strictly prohibited from doing any part-time work. Indeed, the researchers mentioned one poor soul who lost his benefits after he was turned in to officials by his neighbors for taking a little money for playing his harmonica on the street. Economic circumstance and government policy conspired to guarantee that the Marienthalers had nowhere to go and nothing to do.

Marienthal had previously been an active community with many social clubs and political organizations (including, alarmingly in retrospect, the National Socialist Party, which was quickly forming among those with German ethnic roots). Paradoxically, after the factory closed and people had all day to participate in leisure and social activities, these organizations withered. People couldn't seem to find the time or energy to do much of anything. In the two years after the factory closed, the town library lent out only about half the number of volumes per person as before. According to one woman, "It used to be magnificent in Marienthal. . . . During the summer we used to go for walks, and all those dances! Now I don't feel like going out anymore." Another man said, "I often used to go dancing with my wife. There was life in Marienthal then. Now the whole place is dead." This comment was typical: "I used to have less time to myself but do more for myself."[2]

In fact, people felt they had no time because their sense of time seemed to warp. Men stopped wearing watches, and wives complained that their husbands were chronically late for meals—even though they were not coming from anyplace. The researchers observed that it took people longer and longer just to walk down the street. People slept for more hours each night than they ever had before. Most strangely, people could not recall how they spent their days; they in fact spent far more time sitting at home or standing around in the street than they did doing anything else.

The researchers logically concluded that what had destroyed life in Marienthal was not the loss of wages, but the loss of the ability to earn them. As they left the village at the conclusion of the study, their pessimistic words were these: "As conditions deteriorate, forces may emerge in the community ushering in totally new events, such as revolt or migration. It is, however, also possible that the feeling of solidarity that binds the people of Marienthal together in the face of adversity will one day dissolve, leaving each individual to scramble after his own salvation." We all know our history well enough to remember what indeed happened to hard-hit towns across Germany and Austria in the ensuing decade and a half as Adolph Hitler rose to power.[3]

——————

The Marienthal story seems vaguely surreal to most Americans. Why on earth would people endure such misery rather than migrate out immediately? Why didn't people leave Marienthal—maybe even leave Austria—as soon as their factory closed? This is typically American thinking: If you lose your job in the United States and you are a reasonably motivated person, you will move someplace else and start over. As a matter of fact, many people pick up and move across the country just because a better-sounding job comes their way.

For Europeans, the idea of leaving one's home just for a nicesounding job is practically anathema, as it is predicated on the notion that work is the center of life. You've heard it a thousand times: Americans *live to work,* while Europeans—those happy Europeans—*work to live.* You have the image of an American staying late at the office or writing an e-mail on his Blackberry at the beach, stress-lines etched into his forehead. Meanwhile, a Spaniard or a Frenchman sips coffee with friends on a Wednesday afternoon, his office dark and abandoned. These images aren't far off the mark, actually. By almost every measure, Europeans work less, and relax more, than Americans. We work 25 percent more hours each year than the Norwegians or the Dutch. Our average retirement age is 64, whereas European men, on average, only work until they are 60.5, and European women retire at even younger ages. And our vacations are pathetically short by comparison. The average American worker takes just 16 days of vacation each year, less than half as many as the Germans (35 days), the French (37 days), and the Italians (42 days).[4]

Americans look at these differences with a mix of contempt and admiration. On the one hand, *37 days of vacation?* Not to be indelicate, but that sounds suspiciously like sloth. On the other hand, we wonder if the French are on to something: They really know how to live, it seems. American elites—who enjoy sipping café au lait and can probably even pronounce it properly—inform us that we're living in the puritanical past for working so hard. According to *Time* magazine, "In the puritanical version of Christianity that has always appealed to Americans, religion comes packaged with the stern message that hard work is good for the soul. Modern Europe has avoided so melancholy a lesson." If and when we throw off our religious shackles, we will guiltlessly enjoy the delights of long vacations, thirty-five-hour workweeks, and early retirement—right?[5]

Wrong. The evidence tells us that, exactly as the Marienthal story teaches, work is an authentic source of happiness, and idleness—especially involuntary idleness—is a source of pure misery. When it comes to our gross national happiness, hard-working Americans have nothing to apologize for, and our policymakers should certainly not look across the Atlantic for any advice. According to the data on the connection between work and happiness, we're doing just fine, for the most part.

Americans *like* to work. *Dilbert* cartoons, the sitcom *The Office*, and Barbara Ehrenreich's bestselling book *Nickel and Dimed* notwithstanding, Americans like or even love their jobs. Among adults who worked ten hours a week or more in 2002, an amazing 89 percent said they were very satisfied or somewhat satisfied with their jobs. Only 11 percent said they were not too satisfied or not at all satisfied.[6]

You might think this is only true for those of us with rewarding white-collar jobs. Surely there are bound to be big differences between people with "good" jobs and those with "bad" jobs, right? Many of us find it hard to imagine that all those people with modest incomes and without college degrees—post office clerks, factory workers, the people who sell you your groceries and serve you your lunch—find their work satisfying.

This assumption is both condescending and incorrect. It turns out that job satisfaction is not solely a privilege of the elite. People of all classes and job types are satisfied with their work. There is no difference at all in job satisfaction between those with below- and above-average incomes: Eighty-nine percent are satisfied in both groups. Similarly, 88 percent of people without a college education are satisfied. And people who specifically call themselves working class, those "nickel-and-dimed" folks? Eighty-seven percent. The middle class, who television pundits and politicians say are so increasingly dispirited, are satisfied with their jobs as well, to the tune of 93 percent. The percentage is also almost exactly the same among people working for private companies and people working for nonprofit organizations or government.[7]

People who do not like their employment situation do make up a small slice of the population, to be sure. But any claim that hating your job is somehow typical is, simply put, pure nonsense. People get a lot of happiness from their work.

Even if we like our jobs, we might still get even more pleasure from leisure. Indeed, one study of people's happiness throughout the day showed that "relaxing" gets a higher average happiness rating from people than "working." What if we were able to substitute leisure time for *all* our work—wouldn't that make us even happier? One way to test this hypothesis is to ask people something like this: "If you were to get enough money to live as comfortably as you would like for the rest of your life, would you continue to work or would you stop working?" Surely the vast majority of people would stop working, right? Wrong again: In 2002, that number was just 31 percent. Sixty-nine percent of American adults said they would continue working even if they didn't need to. And there is no difference at all between those with below- and above-average incomes. Similarly, 66 percent of people without a college education would keep working, as would 69 percent who call themselves working class.[8]

Many other statistics reinforce these patterns. "Very happy" people work more hours each week than those who are "pretty happy," who in turn work more hours than people who are "not too happy." Happy people work more in their free time than unhappy people. And having more hours to relax is not related to higher happiness.[9]

Furthermore, there is no indication that Americans wish they had more vacation time than they have already: In 1998 (the year for which the most recent data are available), only 11 percent of

American workers said they wished they could spend much less time on their paid work—versus 12 percent who said they could spend much *more* time on it. In 2001, people who reported that they had *not* felt so sad that nothing could cheer them up in the past month took, on average, one more day of vacation time per year than people who said they had felt inconsolably sad. Obviously, vacation per se had nothing to do with the happiness difference between the groups.[10]

For most Americans, job satisfaction is nearly equivalent to life satisfaction. Among those who say they are very happy in their lives, 95 percent are also satisfied with their jobs. Only 5 percent say they are not satisfied with their work. Imagine two workers who are identical in every way—same income, education, age, sex, family situation, religion, and politics—but the first is satisfied with his or her job and the second is not. The first person will be 28 percentage points more likely to say he or she is very happy in life.[11]

This is not just coincidental. Job satisfaction actually *increases* life happiness. We can show this statistically by predicting job satisfaction with something unrelated to overall happiness: the answer to a question on whether someone's "main source of satisfaction in life comes from work." If the predicted value of job satisfaction is still related to happiness, it means the former is increasing the latter. Indeed, the statistical analysis shows that this is precisely the case.[12]

Obviously, there is a point where excessive hours of work lower health and quality of life. Some people work themselves so much that they get sick, their marriages fall apart, and they are miserable. But within the bounds of normal worklife, the data are overwhelmingly clear that for most Americans, work in and of itself brings happiness—regardless of how much income it generates.

We can deride or denounce this finding if we want to—and some do. But if gross national happiness is our goal, the American formula of hard work appears to function pretty well.

————

Given the clear evidence that Americans love their work, it might appear odd that some continue to claim just the opposite. Europeans and even some Americans cling to the view that market work brings us down and that social progress inevitably means more hours of leisure. As strange as it seems, this misapprehension about work has been fueled by 200 years of economic theory.

If you have ever studied economics, you have been exposed to what we call the "economic problem": how to meet unlimited wants with scarce resources. In a nutshell, economists start their entire social science with the plausible assumption that, if goods and services were free, there would not be enough to go around. Instead, we have to ration things of value by giving up resources of value and making choices among all the things we'd like. You do this every time you go to the supermarket and decide how to spend your money. You don't just go and say, "Give me one of each thing"; you make choices based on how much money you have and the food you most want to eat.

We solve the economic problem every day with more than our money, however. We make choices on how to spend everything of value in our lives. We apportion our energy among projects ("I don't have time to work on this today"), and decide how to divide up the attention we give to people (some people get an immediate e-mail response; others never get a response at all). We even solve the economic problem with our appetites ("I'm hungry, but if I eat these cookies it might spoil my dinner" or "I can't afford the calories").

So economics is really the study of choices, not money. Money is just one currency of value—and not even the most common (or important) one. There is one form of currency where there is no inequality; we all have the same amount of it, and we all make decisions on how to spend it every minute of every day of every year of our lives: It is, of course, *time*. You have twenty-four hours a day, no matter who you are, and you have to figure out how to spend them. Should you get up and exercise, or should you sleep an extra hour? Should you stay at work an extra hour, or go home to your family? These decisions don't feel like "economics," but they are. They are all examples of the economic problem and represent the trade-offs we all face in our day-to-day life. The fact that economics is fundamentally about these interesting, ubiquitous choices (as well as the boring, grubby choices involving whether we should buy the name brand or the house brand) makes it the most powerful of all the social sciences and explains why its methods have largely colonized the others (such as sociology and political science).

Using this conception of choice, economists frequently refer to the "labor-leisure trade-off," in which people have to decide whether to work or not, and if so, how much. It is true enough that these decisions exist. But economists usually make the further assumption that time spent in leisure gives us pleasure, while time spent in labor gives us pain—and that we only work because it is necessary to earn money, which we want in order to meet other desires. In other words, if it were not for pecuniary necessity, we wouldn't seek gainful employment. We would choose leisure instead.

Of course, few economists are naive enough to believe that we all hate our jobs and would prefer to goof off all day. But this assumption is nonetheless inconspicuously embedded in a lot of economic policy. A wealthy society, we are given to understand, would inevitably tend to have shorter workweeks, longer vacations, and earlier retirements than a not-so-wealthy society. Why? Because when we're rich we can afford these things. What else are we working for, after all?

According to this theory, work should define the difference between happy and unhappy people: People work less if they can afford to, and this brings happiness; people who work more would generally prefer not to (unless they have pathological preferences), and thus they are made less happy. An easy conclusion, to be sure—but, as evidence has shown, an incorrect one. On the contrary, work brings happiness. But why?

————

Work brings professional success, and—all else being equal—working harder brings more success. As we have seen in detail, success is rocket fuel for our happiness. This is a plausible explanation for why billionaire Larry Ellison continues to work his tail off, and it is certainly part of the reason that I am writing these words in the middle of the night when I really should be sleeping like everybody else.

Work also brings happiness because it gives our lives meaning—and meaning brings happiness, sooner or later. Work allows us to create value in an easily measurable way. As long as we do not lose sight of the fact that compensation for our efforts is only a symbol of this value, work reminds us that we are creators—that the world would be less valuable if we were not here. It is something that makes us feel like our lives are worth living. In terms of meaning, work is similar to parenting, which is also generative and creative. But unlike parenting, work has the added bonus of being, for most people, pleasant in the short run, so that it can bring us happiness in the present moment (whereas with parenting, the happiness is often greatly delayed).

Viennese psychiatrist Victor Frankl believed that a search for meaning motivated men's entire lives, and that a lack of meaning was the root of much mental illness. He built an entire school of psychotherapy around the concept, which he called logotherapy. In his aptly titled memoir *Man's Search for Meaning,* Frankl wrote of his own experience finding meaning through work in a Nazi concentration camp, where he was an inmate during his late thirties.[13]

> On my fourth day in the sick quarters I had just been detailed to the night shift when the chief doctor rushed in and asked me to volunteer for medical duties in another camp containing typhus patients. Against the urgent advice of my friends (and despite the fact that almost none of my colleagues offered their services), I decided to volunteer. I knew that in a working party I would die in a short time. But if I had to die there might at least be some sense in my death. I thought that it would doubtless be more to the purpose to try and help my comrades as a doctor than to vegetate or finally lose my life as the unproductive laborer that I was then.[14]

Success and meaning can create happiness through work even if the work is difficult, wearisome, or even dangerous, as it was for Victor Frankl. Indeed, the thrill of success and the poignancy of meaning might even be all the greater when work entails a difficult sacrifice for something we believe is of great value. After all, as we saw in the case of children, there is evidence that the more we endure, the greater we love. This is an insight that has motivated entire religious movements.[15]

Striving for success and finding meaning in work reminds us once again that remuneration, while necessary to support ourselves, is not the secret to happiness, but rather just a symbol of the value we create. It is no surprise to find that money and benefits matter far less to people than success and meaning-related rewards, such as recognition and evidence that their work is valued. People who believe their work allows them to be productive are about five times likelier to be very satisfied with their jobs than people who don't feel they can be productive. And those who are proud to work for their employers are more than ten times as likely as those who are not proud to work for their employers to be very satisfied with their jobs. In fact, pay increases and bonuses matter far less than pride and perceived productivity when it comes to job satisfaction, and the amount of leisure time each day has no significant effect on satisfaction at all.[16]

There is a considerable amount of evidence that compensation such as pay and vacation—so-called "extrinsic rewards" for working—can actually have a negative effect on job satisfaction because they can crowd out the "intrinsic rewards" that people care about so much. Many studies have illustrated this, such as a famous experiment in which college students were given puzzles to solve. Some of the students were paid, and others were not. The researchers observed that the unpaid participants tended to continue to work on the puzzles after the experiment was finished, whereas the paid participants abandoned the task as soon as the experiment was over.[17]

Work produces happiness in more direct ways than through success and meaning. Perhaps you've had the experience while working of "losing yourself" for long periods when you are deeply engrossed and completely focused. This happens to me sometimes when I am working on a book. It is a special kind of bliss; writing the book you are holding in your hand was professional nirvana. This state is called "flow" by the prominent psychologist Mihaly Csikszentmihalyi.

In his research, Csikszentmihalyi found that people in many walks of life attain this state when lost in their work. He interviewed people from numerous professions, from writers to athletes, and found they had a remarkably similar experience when deeply engrossed: Time and the world around them seemed to disappear as they became somehow "one" with their task. Csikszentmihalyi found that experiencing this phenomenon predicts incredible satisfaction from one's job—or any activity.[18]

What leads to flow? There is a zone in any activity in which challenge is balanced with ability. If a task is beyond our ability, it is frustrating and disconcerting, making flow impossible. But if an activity is boring, we cannot become engrossed. Aristotle said, "People enjoy the realization of their capacities. The more complex the capacity or the greater the development of it, the more it can be enjoyed." The concept of flow puts a finer point on this, suggesting that task complexity and development of capacity must be in balance. This balance, and thus the bliss of flow, might come from hitting fastballs, driving nails, or teaching economics—depending on one's skills and abilities.[19]

———

"Happiness belongs to the self-sufficient," said Aristotle. Control over our circumstances is yet another way that work can bring happiness. To the extent that work gives people a sense that they are in charge of their lives, it will bring them joy. If work—or the lack of work—strips people of control, it will bring misery.

The misery is compounded when people are reliant on the state for support because they cannot take care of themselves.[20]

In 2002, a sample of adults was asked, "At any time during the last ten years, have you been unemployed and looking for work for as long as a month?" Their answer to even this fairly mild question predicted enormous happiness differences. Middle-aged adults who had experienced unemployment in the past decade were a third less likely to say they were very happy than those who had not been unemployed. A bout of unemployment predicts happiness deficits even after correcting for income, education, race, religion, and many other demographic characteristics. In 2001, people who had missed any work at all during the past year because of involuntary unemployment were two-thirds more likely than other people to say they felt hopeless, and more than 50 percent more likely to say they felt worthless.[21]

Economists have found that unemployment in a country even lowers the happiness of people who *are* working, because the prospect of unemployment—even when benefits are generous—is so dire. People hate the very idea of being out of work. In fact, people who say their job security is not good are more than six times likelier than those who say their security is good to be unsatisfied with their jobs. One economist looked across a large sample of nations and found that higher unemployment makes a country unhappier, especially among older people and those with the least education—that is, those who have the hardest time recovering after they lose their jobs. In contrast, those who can recover best— the young and the educated—are more concerned about price inflation. The lesson is that policies that destroy jobs lower happiness among the most vulnerable members of the workforce.[22]

What about retirement? Does voluntarily separating from work at an appropriate age have the same negative influence on happiness? It appears not. In 2002, retired people were 2 percentage points less likely than nonretired people to say they were very happy. And this difference disappears entirely when we correct for income, education, and other personal characteristics.[23]

Involuntary unemployment is a disaster for happiness, because—beyond the economic misfortune it creates—it strips away the sense of control people need in their lives. But it gets even worse. What is the most common policy solution when people cannot find work and support themselves? In Western countries, it is public support—welfare. This is a sensible response on its face, and may combat the material deprivation that comes with unemployment. But this kind of policy does nothing to combat the unhappiness problem. In 2001, people receiving public assistance were more than twice as likely as those not receiving it to say they felt hopeless or worthless.[24]

Receiving government assistance appears to have special unhappiness-provoking properties, even apart from the fact that people on welfare are generally not earning their living through work. Holding constant all of one's personal characteristics, including income and whether one is actually unemployed, we find that receipt of public assistance by itself pushes up the chance of the recipient saying he or she has felt inconsolably sad at some point over the past month by about 16 percentage points. No other single factor—not income, age, education, or anything else—comes close to predicting this much of one's unhappiness.[25]

The misery from welfare may be compounded if it teaches helplessness, which is quite plausibly the case. Researchers have discovered that people quickly begin to behave as if they were helpless when they believe circumstances are beyond their control. In one famous experiment conducted by Japanese researchers, participants in two groups were subjected to loud, disagreeable noises. The first group had no way of turning the noises off, while the second could switch the noises off by pressing a button. Next, the researchers took both groups to a room with the same noises, but in this room there was an on-off lever that was unmarked. The people who had experienced being able to turn the noise off in the first part of the experiment were far more likely than the others to figure out how the unmarked lever worked and to shut off the noise. Even more interestingly, people in the "helpless" group later performed far worse on simple word puzzles than those who had experienced a sense of control, and were less likely to try to win in simple games. In this experiment, it took only minutes for people to learn to be helpless.[26]

————

The data on work and happiness hold some lessons for private employers seeking to improve the job satisfaction and life happiness of workers. The stakes in getting this right are more than just ethical—they actually mean lots of money, too. American firms have been bemoaning the costs of high employee turnover for years, and nothing predicts attrition better than job satisfaction: People who are not at all satisfied with their jobs are about seven times likelier to quit within a year than those who are very satisfied.[27]

Workers need to work for something meaningful. Believing in the job is critical to satisfaction. Consider this: In 2002, among those workers who strongly agreed that they were proud to work for their employers, 10 percent planned to quit their jobs. If they strongly disagreed, however, the number planning to quit rose to 53 percent. Among younger workers (so-called Generation-Y workers, born after the mid–1970s) who strongly disagreed, this number skyrocketed to 68 percent.[28]

Workers, especially young workers, don't just need jobs; they must also have pathways to succeed. Thirty-four percent of all Generation-Y employees had plans to quit their jobs in 2002, but 76 percent of those who felt they had few chances for promotion in their present employment had similar plans. "Dead-end" jobs bring little happiness, even if they do not involve low-paid, low-skilled work. People need to know they are progressing in the value they create.[29]

Aspects of work unrelated to meaning and success are relatively unimportant to workers. For example, despite all the interest in compensation innovations that enhance "work-life balance," there is little evidence that they really matter. One major study of worker preferences asked employees to rank various aspects of their total compensation, where "1" meant unimportant and "5" was very important. As we might expect, vacation time ranked far below money in importance (3.2 versus 4.6). But the more faddish compensation strategies mattered still less: Flex-time was rated 2.7, telecommuting 2.2, and on-site child-care a measly 1.92. Enlightened employers are less focused on compensation fads and more keyed into the core values that bring happiness through work itself.[30]

Remember the differences between the worklives of Americans and Europeans: We work longer hours, take shorter vacations, and retire at a later age. The lesson Europeans (and some Americans) take from this comparison is that our system is exploitative. According to one British newspaper, the heavy U.S. work effort is due to the fact that Americans are "terrified of losing their jobs." The implication is that we could improve happiness by attaining a higher level of job security through enhanced labor laws that would allow us to work less with impunity, and thus abandon the brutal rat race we are in of working long hours to stay employed. The evidence cited in this chapter, however, demonstrates that this explanation for the difference between European and American attitudes toward work is incorrect. On the contrary, we choose to work hard, and the European model of legally protected leisure is not what we want or need, if happiness is our goal.[31]

In fact, the evidence suggests that most of Europe is in a vicious cycle of low job satisfaction and rigid labor markets. Across Europe, job security is significantly higher than in America: It is hard to lay off workers or even fire people for just cause. Although this model might sound ideal to some, it has in fact led to a real scarcity of employment. If I cannot fire a worker, I will be reluctant to hire her in the first place—especially if she is young and untried. This rigidity has led to significant unemployment, especially among the young. Indeed, in France, upward of a quarter of the adults under age twenty-six are unemployed because employers are so reluctant to give what amounts to lifetime tenure. The effect this has on the people who *do* have jobs is probably quite substantial. If finding a new job is a difficult or impossible task, I will hold on to my old job for dear life, even if it is a bad match for my interests, skills, and tastes—in which case, I can bid adieu to flow, and probably to meaning and a sense of success as well.[32]

Not surprisingly, job satisfaction is generally much lower in Europe than it is in the United States. A 2002 international survey showed that, while 51 percent of American adults reported being completely satisfied or very satisfied with their jobs, only 36 percent of the Dutch gave this answer, as well as 35 percent of the British, 33 percent of the Spanish, and 32 percent of the French. (The only European countries with higher job-satisfaction levels than the United States were Switzerland, Austria, and Denmark.) People who are dissatisfied with their jobs tend to make their lives outside of work. Europeans have supported and implemented policies that shorten their workweeks and lengthen their vacations with no legal reprisal from employers, and ship them off to retirement while still in the prime of life—so they still have plenty of years and good health to enjoy without going to work.[33]

And so it goes: Mandated job security ratchets up unemployment and the difficulty of finding jobs, workers stay in jobs they dislike, voters demand laws that give them more time away from their unsatisfying jobs while protecting their job security, and so on. The American labor system is better for happiness on balance, which is one reason that Americans tend to be happier people than most Europeans.

Still, there is the nagging reality that job security does matter—the threat of unemployment makes people unhappy, and some Americans suffer as a result of it. Is there a middle way between the wild, wild west of the American workforce and the French Ministry for the Lifetime Protection of Incompetent Workers?

Some policymakers and economists advocate a policy whereby companies would be allowed to lay off workers only if they committed to retraining them. After this retraining period—which would be heavily subsidized by the government—workers would be obligated to accept an employment offer (if there was one) and get off the unemployment rolls. This, in theory, would enhance happiness by removing the threat of job insecurity while also minimizing permanent government assistance and the helplessness it creates.

This approach is close to current practice in Sweden and was accepted as a policy goal in 1997 by all of Europe's heads of state.[34]

America should not follow Europe down this primrose path, at least for the majority of the workforce. Setting aside the obvious problems of practicality and expense to taxpayers, this kind of mandate would be unlikely to create greater national happiness; although it would provide a guarantee of a job, it would not promise a job with any sort of personal meaning for the worker or any prospects for success. In addition, being obligated to take any job offered would deprive workers of any sense of control.

A better solution is to maintain sufficiently free labor markets such that workers and employers can decide the level of risk they're willing to take in their professional lives. Free markets are good at producing an assortment of jobs that appeal to our varied tastes and needs. If you have an especially strong desire for freedom and adventure, America provides entrepreneurship opportunities that are risky but offer the possibility of explosive returns. If you prefer lots of security, there are jobs that offer just that. In government work, for example, once you are established you can generally hold your job until you retire or die.

This argument produces howls of protest from those who believe that reliance on free labor markets is an invitation for firms to exploit workers. But this is 2008, not 1908. We no longer have a manufacturing-based goods economy in which factory jobs are the norm and employers can bust unions with impunity. Most Americans are in service professions where tasks are variegated, skills and education are prized, and unionization is legally protected (but declining). Firms compete with each other for good employees just as much or more than employees compete for good jobs.

To be sure, there are workers left behind in our brave new world—those with skills no longer needed by employers, from backgrounds in which work is culturally underemphasized, or with mental or physical problems that prevent them from meeting job requirements in the modern economy. It is appropriate for the state to assist these people. Instead of mandating minimum wages, which tend to destroy jobs for the most at-risk workers, we should reward workers willing to take low-wage positions with an expansion of the Earned Income Tax Credit, which augments low earned wages from private jobs with government subsidies. And to give more people better opportunities in line with their interests and skills and the economy's needs, public policymakers need to turn back to the idea of meaningful vocational education, instead of propagating the peculiar notion that a liberal arts college education is the right path for all Americans.

Of course, implementing these proposals would require money. Policymakers generally like to deal with labor markets by mandating things to be paid for by others: Minimum wages and job protections, which must be covered by private firms, are a classic case. The problem is that these policies have terrible unintended consequences—they do nothing to improve jobs, to match people to satisfying work, or to stop the process of job destruction affecting underprivileged individuals and communities. Bad policies are no bargain at any price. Instead, we should be willing to pay for policies that work, especially if they increase our gross national happiness.

————

Now we have completed a tour through the economics of happiness. The main conclusions are all related: Money by itself does not bring us happiness; money equality is a mistaken goal, based on either materialism or envy; and happy people don't primarily work for money.

You might be tempted to conclude that money has no important place in the search for happiness. But you would be wrong. Money can make us incredibly happy if we use it in the right way. In the next chapter, I'll explain how.

CHAPTER 8

THE SECRET TO
BUYING HAPPINESS

A few days before Christmas in 1999, a poor, elderly man by the name of Jerry Brooks was shopping in a thrift store in Kansas City for some warm winter clothing. He had only 75 cents, which doesn't go far even for a secondhand coat. A man approached Brooks and unexpectedly wished him a Merry Christmas, handed him a $100 bill, and disappeared. Stunned, Brooks said, "I don't even know that man. He gave me $100 . . . if he doesn't live to be 500, I'll eat my hat."[1]

This was not the first time the generous stranger, known for years only as "Secret Santa" to the citizens of Kansas City, had helped someone in need, nor would it be the last. Over the years he ended up giving away more than a million dollars in Christmas cash to strangers, including about $100,000 during the 2006 holidays alone. In addition, he built a YMCA, gave generously to the Salvation Army and a number of health charities, funded scholarships for the poor, and supported sports programs for inner-city kids.

"Secret Santa" was actually Larry Stewart, an entrepreneur who had made millions in cable television and long-distance telephone service. But he hadn't always been rich. He grew up poor in a small town in Mississippi, raised by his grandparents. The family got by on $33 a month and welfare food support. He didn't get his first break until one day in 1971 when, hungry and with no money, he sat down in a diner. After eating, he pretended to have lost his wallet in an attempt to get the meal for free. The diner's owner came to him, said "You must have dropped this," and pushed a $20 bill into his hand. He never forgot that kind man and the experience of receiving that gift, and it set him on a path to his own giving—and happiness.[2]

Secret Santa's true identity became known when he was diagnosed with terminal cancer in 2006 and decided that he wanted to pass along his message of joyous giving. Before he passed away, he wanted to tell people about the generosity that had given his life so much joy and meaning. Explaining why he had given so much to so many, he said: "I'm just doing what the Lord is directing me to do. I'm just a pair of hands and feet. He's using me. He's lightened my path. . . . Part of my daily prayer was 'Lord, let me be a better servant.' I had no idea this is what he had in mind, but I'm happy. I'm so thrilled that he is able to use me in this way." [3]

Larry Stewart's life illustrates a powerful secret to a happy life. The true way to buy happiness is by giving away what we value. Although most of us will not become millionaires and give away $100 bills on the street, all Americans can enjoy great happiness like Mr. Stewart did by practicing the act of giving.

———————

People who give charitably are happier than people who don't. The data prove this point overwhelmingly. Survey data from 2000 show us that people who give money to charity are 43 percent more likely than nongivers to say they are very happy. Volunteers are 42 percent more likely to be very happy than nonvolunteers. It doesn't matter whether the gifts of money go to churches or symphony orchestras—religious and secular giving both leave people equally happy, and far happier than people who don't give. And the more people give, the happier they get. If two people are identical in terms of income, education, age, religion, politics, sex, and family circumstances—but one volunteers once more than the other each week—the one who volunteers more will be half again as likely to say he or she is very happy.[4]

People who give are also less likely than nongivers to experience sadness and depression. People who gave money away each year in 2001 were 34 percent less likely than nongivers to say they had felt "so sad nothing could cheer [them] up" in the past month. They were also 68 percent less likely to have felt "hopeless" and 24 percent less likely to say that "everything was an effort." Those who did *not* give money away were nearly twice as likely as givers to say they felt worthless. These differences persist even if givers and nongivers earn the same amount of money and have the same personal characteristics. Imagine two people—a giver and a nongiver—who are identical in income as well as in age, race, family, and education. The giver will be about 15 percentage points less likely than the nongiver to report feeling inconsolably sad.[5]

The happiest communities in the United States tend to be those in which people give and volunteer the most. For instance, the citizens of Minneapolis–St. Paul, Minnesota, give and volunteer at exceptionally high rates (86 percent and 65 percent, respectively), and an unusually high percentage (44 percent) say they are very happy. Compare this with Houston, Texas, where giving and volunteering rates are more modest (74 and 48 percent) and

34 percent say they are very happy. This is typical. Comparing communities in the United States, we find that a 10-point increase in the percentage of the population that gives money to charity corresponds to an 8-point rise in the percentage who say they are very happy. In fact, the extra 10 points in giving even correspond to a 6-point increase in the percentage of *nongivers* in a community who say they are very happy—suggesting that even those who don't give benefit from living in the happy places where most people *are* charitable.[6]

Giving goes beyond formal gifts of money and time, of course. Many of the ways in which we serve others are less formal and involve other resources of value in our lives. Donating blood, for instance, is one particularly personal kind of giving. Slightly more than 15 percent of Americans donate at least once each year. And there's evidence that this form of giving brings even greater rewards than financial charity. In 2002, 43 percent of the people who gave blood two or three times during the year said they were very happy, versus only 29 percent of those who did not give blood. We see the same pattern with many informal and nontraditional types of charity: Giving to a homeless person on the street, giving directions to a stranger, and so forth—it is all associated with higher levels of happiness and life satisfaction.[7]

There are many studies that demonstrate this link between charity and happiness. Researchers have looked at a vast array of population groups, historical periods, and geographical regions and always find that charitable people are happier people. For example, researchers in 2003 looked at a sample of 115 poor American senior citizens and measured how their charitable acts predicted their moods. They found that even after correcting for differences in income, health, education, age, and the number of children and grandchildren respondents had, people who gave and volunteered were significantly more likely than those who didn't to report "positive affect": a state of high energy, concentration, and engagement.[8]

The same types of effects occur among the young. Several studies have shown that teenagers who give and volunteer have higher self-esteem and optimism than those who don't give. In one study researchers followed 1,000 teenagers over five years and measured the extent of their charitable attitudes and behaviors through such questions as, "For the job you expect to have in the future, how important is helping people?" and, "How often do you spend time performing community service outside school?" The teenagers who were the most giving were least likely to be involved in street violence and teen pregnancies. They were also least likely to experience stress and negative feelings. Provocatively, the investigators found that charity and faith tended to interact for extra benefit: Religious, giving teens had higher self-esteem, confidence, and optimism than nonreligious, giving teens.[9]

The link between giving behavior and happiness is not limited to the United States. A study of British neighborhoods in 2004 found that communities with more volunteerism had lower crime rates, better schools, and higher levels of happiness among their residents than communities with less volunteerism. In fact, the connection between happiness and volunteerism is easy to see as we compare whole countries. In one international survey from 1998, 51 percent of the American respondents said they volunteered and 37 percent said they were very happy. In Germany, in contrast, only 19 percent volunteered and 18 percent were very happy; and in Russia, 20 percent volunteered but only 5 percent were very happy. Obviously, there are many forces at work influencing the happiness of citizens besides their volunteering (especially in a country like Russia); still, the correlation is striking. A comparison of volunteerism and happiness levels in thirty-two countries shows that a 10-point increase in the percentage of people who volunteer corresponds to a 3-point rise in the percentage saying they are very happy.[10]

Givers are happier than nongivers. This is not the same thing, however, as saying that giving *causes* happiness. In all likelihood, the charity makes people happy *and* happy people tend to be the most charitable. Further, it may well be that factors such as culture, faith, education, and family values affect both happiness and the propensity to act charitably. To prove that charity actually *causes* happiness, we need a different kind of evidence than the research results we have looked at so far. We need to study how people change *after* they give to others *because* they have given. A large body of this sort of evidence, in which researchers have documented enormous positive life changes that can be directly attributed to giving, does in fact exist.[11]

One way to find out whether giving makes people happy is to expose them to charity experiences and then measure to see whether their happiness levels change as a result of these experiences. In one study of several hundred senior citizens in the Detroit area, researchers asked the subjects about their happiness and then presented them with a set of volunteering opportunities they could choose to engage in according to their interests. Six months later, the researchers asked the seniors whether they had volunteered for any of the causes and then measured their happiness again. As it turned out, a tremendous increase in happiness was attributable to the volunteering experiences. The researchers found that volunteering for just six months significantly increased the seniors' morale, self-esteem, and sense of social integration. In general, the researchers found that volunteering for nonprofit organizations was even better for senior citizens' happiness than helping out their families or their neighbors.[12]

————

So we know that happiness and charity are strongly correlated, and that charity actually *causes* at least some of the happiness that givers experience in their lives. The real question is: *Why?*

Perhaps surprisingly, there seem to be actual physiological explanations for at least part of the correlation between giving and happiness. There is evidence that giving affects our brains in pleasurable and beneficial ways. Starting in the 1980s, researchers began to accumulate evidence that people who volunteer experience feelings of euphoria. Psychologists have referred to this as the "Helper's High" and believe it is due to endorphins—natural opioids in the brain that produce a mild version of the sensations that occur with the use of artificial opiates like morphine and heroin.[13]

Charity also lowers the stress hormones that cause unhappiness. In one charming experiment, adults were asked to give massages to babies—the idea being that giving a baby pleasure is a compassionate act with no expectation of a reward—even a "thank you"—in return. After they performed the massages, the seniors were found to have markedly lower stress-hormone levels—cortisol, epinephrine, and norepinephrine—in their brains than before. In fact, researchers discovered that the subjects enjoyed more stress-lowering effects from giving massages than they did from *getting* them.[14]

Even *thinking* about charity brings demonstrable physical benefits. In one study, college students were shown a film about Mother Teresa's work with the poor in Calcutta. Strangely, during the film, the students produced more of the protective antibody immunoglobulin A than when they were shown a film that did not feature charity.[15]

In an attempt to understand more about the physiology of charity, researchers have looked directly at the brain while people are engaged in giving activities. In some studies, the methodology involves functional magnetic resonance imaging (fMRI): Strange as it sounds, test subjects are put into narrow, hollow tubes and asked, via an interactive computer, to make decisions about whether they want to give to various charities or not—all while scientists look at images of their brains. Subjects in one such study were given a certain amount of money and then asked whether they wanted to give some of it to charitable organizations. Researchers found that the part of the brain activated when people designated gifts was the same part that lit up when people received money themselves.[16]

Meaning seems to play an important role in the neurological link between charity and happiness. Scientists have actually discovered a part of our brain (the posterior superior temporal cortex) associated with the experience of meaning—which they define as the connection of an activity with intent or purpose. For example, imagine an apple sitting on a counter, close to the edge. If it falls off by itself, our brains will not experience meaning in this. But if someone *pushes* the apple off the counter, our brains perceive *meaning:* Somebody meant for the apple to fall. In one 2007 fMRI study at Duke University, subjects watched a computer game win money for themselves or for a charity of their choice. When the money went to charity, the "meaning center" in their brains was activated the most.[17]

Interestingly, the most meaning was perceived by the people who said they regularly gave and volunteered. And this raises a number of questions. Do people develop an ability to derive meaning—and thus, probably, happiness—from charity when they practice giving? Or do some people naturally experience more meaning from giving than others (due to a "charity gene," perhaps), which is why some people are better givers than others? The first explanation is supported by evidence that giving is habitual, and—like good manners, good taste, and other fine things in life—the earlier people are exposed to the joys of charity, the more likely they are to practice giving throughout their lives and enjoy its amazing benefits.[18]

Charity also brings happiness for psychological reasons. First, it gives us a sense of *control*. We have seen again and again that people are happier when they feel in control of their lives, and charity is one way to achieve a measure of control in a chaotic world. It offers individuals a way of solving problems proactively—whether by giving money for disaster relief, donating a coat that will be used by someone who needs one, or becoming a mentor to a teenager in search of a role model. When people are able to solve problems, they feel empowered. And when people feel empowered, they are happier.

Giving money and volunteering time can also provide an important way to mentally "reboot." Psychologists have found that giving "crowds out" unhappiness because our brains tend to focus on just one problem at a time. In particular, the challenge of helping someone else tends to displace the challenge of facing our own demons. Giving and volunteering are thus highly effective ways to redirect our energies away from our own problems.[19]

Is it healthy to run away from negative emotions through distractions, albeit highly beneficial ones like charity? Indeed it may be, contrary to what we have often been told. We are frequently advised to let our emotions out; mental health professionals have created a massive industry based on the principle that bottling up anger or sadness will harm us psychologically, and that distracting ourselves from our problems will only lead them to fester within us and get worse. But this is not right, for the most part: Research has not shown that letting off steam through tears and anger usually does much more than reinforce our bad feelings. For the sake of happiness, it is best to turn our attention away from our anger and sadness, and toward healthy, happy activities like serving others.[20]

Giving delivers direct psychological and physiological benefits. But it also benefits us in an indirect way: It makes other people like us more. There is evidence that we are held in higher esteem and rewarded when people see us behaving generously.

In 2006, two British researchers set out to see how charitable behavior affected social status. They started with a laboratory experiment on cooperation in which subjects were brought together in small groups, given an equal amount of money, and asked individually to decide whether to keep it all or donate some part of it to a "group fund." The researchers then counted the money in each group fund, doubled it, and distributed the total (the original contributions plus the amount they added) equally among each group's participants. The optimal strategy for a group was to put in all the money and thus double each person's earnings. But since contributing to the group fund was optional, each individual had the incentive to "defect" (and not contribute) while selfishly hoping the other group members would cooperate—so that he or she could keep all his or her own money and also get a chunk of what the others had contributed plus a share of what the researchers had added.[21]

The researchers found that most groups were fairly cooperative, especially if each individual's cooperation decision was made in front of the others. Some people gave more than others, however—donating more to the fund than they got back in return. The researchers wanted to know how the others felt about these generous members and investigated this question with a second phase of the experiment. This time, the individuals in each group were asked to vote for a group leader. More than 80 percent of the groups elected their most generous member. The researchers concluded that when people have a choice, they prefer to deal with altruists over selfish people. But even more importantly, the results imply that generosity and faith in others can be good for a person professionally: People believe that an unusually giving person deserves leadership, and they reward or look up to such a person accordingly. It is hardly surprising that givers tend to be happier than nongivers, if they are more successful in life because of their giving.

————

All together, the research on giving puts paid to a common cynical claim about humans: that we are naturally selfish. On the contrary, our brains, minds, and bodies experience equilibrium and pleasure when we give. We are actually *un*naturally selfish: We are wired to serve.

It clearly follows that we should try to maximize charity in America if we are concerned about our gross national happiness. Obviously, each and every one of us should be giving as much as we can individually, teaching our children about the benefits of giving, and defending charity as a social good. But is there anything the government should be doing on the level of social policy to maximize charitable behavior?

When we think of the role of the government in charitable giving, we generally think about tax breaks. Both the U.S. federal government and our state governments make gifts of money to nonprofit organizations tax-deductible: In other words, the money given to charity does not count as taxable income, so long as the taxpayer "itemizes deductions." The amount a person saves in taxes in this way can be calculated by multiplying the total amount of the donations by the tax rate. So if someone gives $1,000 and falls into a tax bracket where he or she will be paying 35 percent on his or her last dollar of income, the donation saves that individual $350 in taxes.

This policy is obviously worth keeping—the tax deduction induces a small amount of charitable giving. But tax deductions aren't the best way to promote giving in America—for the simple reason that tax-deductibility is totally irrelevant for most people. Internal Revenue Service records show that only about a third of people who file tax returns itemize their deductions—which means that most Americans (those who are middle class and below, in particular) don't even claim the deductions to which they are entitled. Even among households earning over $120,000 per year, only about 40 percent itemize their deductions. Furthermore, research shows that virtually nobody is motivated meaningfully to give only because of our tax system. I've been doing research on charity for many years, and I've never seen a tax break that can warm up a cold heart.[22]

The most productive focus for the government is not to create incentives for people to give, but to figure out how to avoid *dis*incentives to giving. The government gets in the way of giving behavior all the time, sometimes making it difficult or even impossible to behave charitably. Take, for example, a 2006 policy adopted by Fairfax County, Virginia, that barred residents from giving food to the homeless unless it was prepared in a kitchen approved by the county. This disqualified the food that was being produced by approximately half the operating shelters and churches that had previously fed the hungry in that county. It also made it illegal for someone to share a homemade sandwich with a homeless person. Why did the government pass such a law, you might ask? To prevent food poisoning, officials argued—despite the fact that food poisoning had never been reported from donated food in the history of the county. Of course, the result was that the homeless became more likely than before to eat out of Dumpsters instead of church kitchens—and individuals were deprived of the opportunity to help.[23]

Government barriers are not always so egregiously obvious, however. The government can discourage giving in more subtle ways as well. For example, when governments fund nonprofits, this tends to displace private donations. This effect is most pronounced in assistance to the poor and other kinds of social welfare services: When the government gives your local soup kitchen $1, it drives off up to 40 cents in private donations. When the state gives $1 to your favorite theater company, it lowers private giving to the theater by about 30 cents—and so on. The reason for this may have something to do with the behavior of donors—there is less perceived need when a nonprofit gets a government grant. But even more, it is related to the behavior of nonprofits themselves, which tend to put less effort into fundraising when they receive government subsidies.[24]

There is a barrier even more insidious than displacing private giving with public subsidies, however. It turns out that people give less when they *think* the government should redistribute income between rich and poor. In 1996, people who disagreed that "the government has a responsibility to reduce income inequality" gave four times more money to charity than those who agreed with this statement. This was true for every type of charity, from religion, to aid for the poor, to environmental protection, and was not due to people's income, race, or age. This pattern also extends to nonmoney giving. In 2002, people who said the government was spending "too much money on welfare" were a third likelier to donate blood than those who said the government was spending "too little." Ironically, welfare opponents were also more likely than welfare proponents to give food or money to a homeless person on the street. Note that this charity difference was not due to anything the government was actually doing; rather, it was due to what people thought the government *should* be doing. In other words, for many Americans, a mere belief about what the government should be doing substitutes for private giving.[25]

————

Charity is a great virtue; thus, we should work to make sure we are not suppressing it. This seems like an obvious proposition. And yet there are a great many people who disagree, claiming that private charity represents all that is *wrong* with America. They argue that we wouldn't *need* charity if the state adequately met the needs of American citizens. Nobody should be reduced to waiting in line for free food or medicine, or have to beg for a college education—and have to show gratitude on top of it. In a wealthy society, food, medical care, education, and many other services should be expected as *rights,* not privileges. This is why so many throughout history, especially on the political left, have contended that private charity degrades us and creates an excuse to abdicate our responsibilities as a society.

But there is no actual evidence that charity degrades anybody. On the contrary, it is beneficial to givers and receivers alike. As we have seen, those who give to others gain a sense of meaning and happiness in their lives: The "joy of giving" is real. Recipients benefit as well, and there is no evidence that charity degrades them. Indeed, virtually all of us are recipients of charitable giving in one form or another, and few of us suffer violence to our self-esteem as a result. If you went to college, the chances are about one in two that it was a nonprofit that was highly dependent on philanthropy—above and beyond your tuition payments—to educate you. If you like classical music, the chances are nine in ten that the last concert you attended was presented by a nonprofit dependent on private giving.[26]

Even in the case of aid to the needy, charity is less corrosive to recipients than government welfare is. Charity is seldom an entitlement, so it is much less likely than welfare to create dependency. Nor is charity associated with welfare's antisocial behavior. Indeed, one study showed that welfare aid suppresses the tendency of recipients to be givers themselves, while private charitable aid to people encouraged their own giving. This was true even when the people who received charity aid were just as poor as those on welfare.[27]

The bottom line is that charity is good for givers, good for charities, and good for the people it is intended to help.

None of this means that the state should have no role in providing goods and services in our society—that would be an outlandish claim. Governments cannot be entirely replaced by philanthropy, realistically speaking. In 2002, various levels of government provided more than $200 billion in funds to the American sector as well as more than $40 billion in tax revenues not collected because of the tax-deductibility of charitable contributions. This puts government money at a roughly equal level with private giving. And in some areas, such as social welfare, government money greatly exceeds private giving as a source of support. There's no telling how much damage it would do to our gross national happiness if we were to dismantle all our government programs for the poor, disabled, and elderly.[28]

My claim is simply that government aid to individuals and nonprofits comes at a steep price. We should be working to expand private giving as much as possible, recognizing that, while tax-based funding can never be completely replaced by private giving, the more it is, the better off we will be as a society.

————

One of the reasons America is a happy country, by international standards, is that we are a giving country. Americans privately gave nearly $300 billion to charity in 2006—more than the entire GDP of some of our allies in Europe. In the late 1990s, the average American gave three and a half times as much to charity as the average Frenchman; seven times as much as the average German; and fourteen times as much as the average Italian.[29]

The average American is a giver. More than three-quarters of our total charity comes from private individuals, as opposed to foundations, corporations, or bequests. Surveys consistently find that between 65 and 85 percent of U.S. families make charitable donations each year. Among the families that gave, the average amount donated to charity in 2003 was more than $1,800. And contrary to what one might assume, it is not the case that this giving goes all—or even mostly—to churches. Only about a third of individual gifts go toward religion, such as support for houses of worship. The rest go to secular activities such as education, health, and social welfare.[30]

Still, not everyone in America gives: Approximately 30 million American families decline to give away money each year. And these families tend not to make up for it with other, nonfinancial forms of giving, either. On the contrary, people who give formally to charity are the ones who give informally as well: Money donors are nearly three times as likely to give money informally to friends and strangers as nondonors are. People who give to charity at least once per year are twice as likely to donate blood as people who don't give money. They are also significantly more likely to give food or money to a homeless person.

Not surprisingly, the fault lines between charitable America and uncharitable America lie very close to the fault lines between happy America and unhappy America. Politics are one factor in both divides: Conservatives are both happier and more charitable than liberals. In the year 2000, households headed by a self-identified conservative gave, on average, 30 percent more dollars to charity than households headed by a liberal (even though the average conservative family had a slightly lower income than the average liberal family). Volunteering levels are virtually the same between conservatives and liberals, but in most other nonmonetary ways, conservatives outpace their liberal and moderate counterparts. For example, if liberals and moderates gave blood like conservatives do, the blood supply in the United States would increase by nearly half.

Religious faith is important for happiness, and it plays an even greater role than politics in both happiness and charitable behavior. In 2000, people who attended a house of worship weekly were 21 percentage points more likely to donate money each year than those who did not attend, and they gave away 3.5 times more money (despite having the same average incomes). They gave significantly more to both religious and secular charities, and also gave far more in informal ways such as volunteering and donating blood. These facts favor conservatives not because something about right-wing politics makes people generous, but because there are nearly four times as many religious conservatives as there are religious liberals. In truth, religious liberals are every bit as generous as religious conservatives are—there are simply fewer of them in America today.[31]

But no matter what a person's political views or religious affiliation, charity by itself makes one happier. Even when two people are identical in religious attendance and political views (as well as marital status, income, education, race, age, and everything else that might be relevant), if one gives money or volunteers while the other doesn't, the giver will be significantly happier than the nongiver, on average. This fact is essential for understanding the full transcendental power of charitable giving for our lives, regardless of how we vote or worship.[32]

If you asked me how you could be happier and I told you to vote Republican or go to church, you might justifiably tell me to go jump in a lake. But if I told you to give to charity, I would be giving you excellent advice. Everybody can give, and give more, *today*. Each and every one of us can afford to dig a little deeper—whether into our wallets or into our free time. So *give*—write a check, volunteer, donate the things you no longer need (or even better, things you still do need). And remember: I'm not trying to lecture you on how to be a better person—just a happier one.

CONCLUSION

Happiness Lessons for Our Leaders

I remember a Sunday school story I heard when I was about eight years old. It was about a young boy in an orphanage who dreamt day after day about how wonderful it would be to be adopted by a rich family. He imagined all the nice things he would have and how much he would enjoy them. But no prospective parents—rich or poor—ever came.

Then one day, an unthinkable thing happened: *Two* families came to the orphanage, and somehow it came to pass that *both* wanted to make him their son. The first couple was the boy's dream family—rich, good-looking, and promising to shower him with gifts (including, I remember, a pony). But they were also morally a bit loose, by Sunday school standards: Their language was rough, they loved money, and they were nonbelievers. The second couple was poor, but they were goodhearted, upstanding religious people. They told him that they would take him to church every week, that they would expect him to be honest, and that they would not tolerate cursing.

After spending his childhood with no family at all, the boy now had to choose between these two very different couples. In the end, the boy chose the poor but religious parents, and in the story he grew up happy and healthy. (To be honest, I remember thinking, "That kid is nuts to pass up a pony.")

You might be chuckling to yourself about the corniness of that story, or disapprove of its silly assumption that secularists naturally would be worse parents than religious people. Fair enough. Consider instead this parable: A woman has just finished law school and receives two offers of employment. The first is from a private firm that specializes in defending companies accused of polluting the environment, a mission she dislikes, given her environmentalist sentiments. But the job pays a lot of money. The second offer is from a nonprofit organization that advocates on behalf of the environment. She loves the idea of the second job, but it pays little. After thinking it over, she opts for the money and goes with the first firm. She regrets this decision for the rest of her career.

If one (or both) of these stories makes intuitive moral sense to you, it is because you know that having and practicing good values is what matters most for acquiring happiness. Imagine I asked you this: What is better for raising a happy child—to be raised with lots of *things,* or to be raised with good *values?* My money says you would vote for good values, because you know that the child who is armed with a strong moral sense will be able to pursue his or her happiness successfully.[1]

When it comes to values, what is true for each of us as individuals is also true for America. The lesson in every chapter of this book is that our gross national happiness depends on the way we teach and live our values. These values are faith, family, freedom, nonmaterialism, opportunity, hard work, and charity. These values make up the ecosystem of happiness in America. They were also the vision of our nation's founders, who took happiness very seriously.

Most Americans still understand how important values are to the health of our nation. When pollsters asked voters in the 2004 presidential election what the most important issue facing America was, the issue chosen more than any other was "moral values." Moral values beat out the economy, terrorism, the Iraq War, education, and health care as voters' primary concern. Critics scoffed at this fact—noting in particular that eight in ten of the voters who chose moral values as first in importance were Bush voters. They interpreted this as evidence that ordinary Americans—and especially conservatives—were hopelessly puritanical and out of touch with the truly important things facing our nation, such as the economy, education, and health care.[2]

But the critics are wrong. According to the research and evidence—as opposed to elite opinion—we know exactly what is important to us. Without proper values, our jobs and our economy will bring us soulless toil and joyless lucre. Our education will have little meaning. There will be no reason to fight—or make peace, for that matter—to protect our way of life. Our health-care system will keep us healthier—for what? The founders knew this, most Americans still understand it, and today's policymakers should take it to heart. The point is this: The pursuit of happiness is central to everything we do, and our values are what make this pursuit possible.

Maybe you are inclined to argue that our values will take care of themselves, and we don't need to do much as a nation to "protect" them. After all, average American happiness has fallen almost imperceptibly over the past thirty-five years. But this argument is specious. It is like the argument that, since you feel fine right now, there is no reason to eat right and exercise. Your health will be fine, until it's time to pay the piper for eating all those French fries and skipping the gym—at which point, it's too late. We *do* have a relatively happy country, but we need to tend to our values constantly to ensure that this happiness endures.

———————

America will elect a new president in 2008, and we face continuing ideological realignment of our government. We will have many new leaders in this country in the coming years. What should these leaders know about happiness? This book has reached a series of conclusions about values that could benefit our country. These conclusions hold nine main lessons for increasing our gross national happiness, and I submit that they could serve as the outline for a "happiness platform" for our nation.

1. Right or left, political extremism is bad for our nation's happiness.

Regardless of who is right or wrong on the political issues of the day—you have your opinions and I have mine—conservatives consistently come out on top over liberals in the happiness game. When combined with certain other personal traits—such as religion and family life—the conservative advantage explodes. You can interpret this as a prescription for our leaders to become more conservative in order to enhance our national happiness, or you can take it as a challenge to liberals to figure out just why happiness eludes them, and what to do about it, without abandoning their core political principles.

But as for political extremism, both the Left and the Right must admit that it lowers our quality of life. The rhetoric on both the far left and far right makes the rest of us unhappier. Furthermore, there is evidence that those with extreme views behave poorly as citizens compared to others. They tend to be less empathetic, less compassionate, and even less honest than people with more moderate political beliefs.

Our political leaders must stop catering to the extremes. The extremes are obviously useful—they can attack a political opponent by proxy, they can get out the vote, and they can create very entertaining books and documentary films. But they don't represent the vast majority of Americans; instead, they pull us apart as a country and coarsen our political debate. And worst of all, they make us less happy as a nation.

2. America must defend its tradition of religious faith.

America has a long tradition of faith, and it is the source of much felicity. George Washington himself said, "I humbly implore that Being on whose will the fate of nations depends to crown with success our mutual endeavors for the general happiness." It took 200 years to show it, but the link between faith and American happiness is even more direct than just "our mutual endeavors." We are happy in no small part *because* we "implore that Being." America is a religious country, and happily so. Secularization along the lines followed by our European allies would be a grave error, and we would pay a heavy price in happiness for it.[3]

Religious people will surely like and agree with this lesson. Ironically, this lesson is *least* pertinent to them. People of faith already know that it is a key to their happiness, and few are contemplating secularization. I know no religious people who are thinking, "Now that things are going pretty well with my life, I think it's time to get modern and stop doing all this praying." Rather, this is a lesson for secular people of goodwill—those who want the best for America, even if religion does not hold a place in their personal beliefs. I am arguing in this book that it is not just in the interest of religious folks to protect our religious traditions, but also in the interest of *secularists*. You may not go to church—you may be an atheist. But if you enjoy living in a happy country, you can thank—well, you can thank your lucky stars—that so many of your American compatriots are religious.

Our leaders must cultivate—not weaken—religious communities and public expressions of faith. This does not mean establishing an official religion, which would be blatantly unconstitutional. Nor does it mean that discrimination against nonbelievers is acceptable. Rather, it means cherishing the concept of faith in a higher power, respecting its many manifestations among our citizens, and resisting policies that make it harder for citizens to worship freely and openly.

3. Family life must be protected.

This precept is not as hackneyed as it sounds, because it's a very complicated truth. Marriage is strongly associated with happiness. Children, in contrast, represent a big personal sacrifice for us, and even psychological unhappiness for many, at least in the near term. However, children usually come "bundled" with the other dimensions of a happy, well-adjusted life—marriage, stable work, religious faith, and so forth. Furthermore, the sacrifice of parenting may be an ultimate source of happiness through the deep meaning we derive from it.

But whether kids bring us up or down, whatever destabilizes families will deliver a hard and swift blow that brings unhappiness. When marriage falls, happiness will fall behind it. And a child without two parents is simply disabled in his or her right to pursue happiness. If we make it harder for families to succeed, we fail to live up to what our founders demanded when they declared our independence.

Some of our country's worst social policy failures have involved unintended consequences for our most vulnerable families. Most notably, the poverty-relief programs of the Great Society—well intentioned, obviously—created disincentives to marry, driving up the rates of fatherless families, child poverty, crime, and dependency on the state. Nobody knows how much misery among America's poor could have been avoided if we had known then what we know now about the impact of welfare on families. Whether we avoid future calamities like this, with all their attendant misery, will depend on the wisdom of our leaders. They must assess the impact on families from every social and economic policy proposed and enacted.

4. We should be quick to defend freedom, but slow to abridge it.

Political, economic, and religious freedoms are crucial to our happiness. If this sounds painfully obvious to you, it is because you are an American. I suggest you go to Saudi Arabia, and loudly proclaim that religious freedom is a key to gross national happiness. Not only will people disagree, but you'll probably end up in jail. Or go to Bhutan—enlightened little Bhutan of *gross national happiness* fame—and assert that political freedom will make the country happier. One hundred thousand ethnic Nepalis, stripped of their Bhutanese citizenship fifteen years ago and currently residing in refugee camps, might help make your point. Go to many countries in Western Europe, and try to assert your economic freedom by opening a pharmacy during hours when the others are closed by law. A healthy fine will be bestowed upon you for violating ordinances designed to make sure nobody ruins anyone else's leisure with "unhealthy economic competition."

In truth, America is an oasis of happiness-producing freedom in a world that generally doesn't believe citizens can handle freedom—and doesn't trust them to try. But the truth is that freedom brings happiness, and so we must guard it jealously and fight against its abridgment. Furthermore, the idea of freedom is America's gift to the world, which is why we must not only promote it aggressively, but also use it in our own country in a responsible way—a way that demonstrates why it makes us a happy nation.

Using freedom responsibly means that we must, both as individuals and as a nation, balance our abundant private liberty with healthy personal morality. The failure to do so brings moral ruin, which is why, even though having certain moral freedoms is important, exercising them does not always lead to happiness. The paradox of freedom that our leaders need to grasp is that, for our national happiness, excess and depravity (except that which does violence to others) must be our legal prerogative, and we need to forgo them voluntarily. This depends on the restrictions that we as individuals and families—not through our governments—impose on ourselves.

When it comes to our security as a nation, protecting freedom also requires substantial courage from our leaders. It is much easier to bend to our short-term safety demands as citizens than to give us the freedom that—while unnerving—delivers the best environment for pursuing happiness in the long run. This may mean that leaders dedicated to happiness have to rethink many of the security policies that have been put in place since 9/11.

5. For happiness, our national priority should be success, not just economic growth.

Contrary to the old axiom, money is *not* the root of all evil. The root of all evil (or at least, the root of a lot of misery) is our tendency to forget what money—beyond basic subsistence—really is: a way to mark our success and measure the value we are creating.[4]

We are a privileged nation, having largely moved beyond the point where a few dollars means the difference between starvation and survival. In a country where the average household has an annual income of more than $66,000, most people could get by on less. We don't because, happily, we don't have to. The reason other nations don't consume like we do is not because they don't want to, but because they *cannot*.[5]

There is still no more entrepreneurial a nation than the United States. No nation is more comfortable with risk, more creative in its view of the future, or more confident that it can conquer what troubles it. The financial return on this national characteristic is fantastic wealth, and the nonfinancial return is happiness. But the wealth is not *causing* the happiness—the value we successfully create is causing it.

But our leaders have to remain ever vigilant against the error of confusing success and money. In the policy world, there are many who would narrow our national objectives to focus more on economic growth. As an economist, I adore economic growth. But for an already-rich country, economic growth is important only because of what it indirectly provides: the opportunities for people to work, to support themselves instead of relying on the state, to serve others, and to succeed in their personal and professional lives. Economic growth is not, and can never be, a direct measure of our national happiness. A narrow focus on gross domestic product, without a conversation about how it meshes with and enhances our culture and values, will not necessarily enhance our gross national happiness. It may, in fact, take us in the wrong direction altogether.

6. We must look for ways to promote opportunity, not economic equality.

Materialism is not just the fatal flaw of those who make economic growth their only priority. It is also the Achilles' heel of economic egalitarians, those who complain that the money gap between rich and poor is getting too large.

Egalitarians, from populist politicians to mainstream intellectuals, make two major errors. The first is confusing economic inequality for social inequality; the second is believing that economic inequality is the real problem just because that is what many people complain about. Both of these errors betray materialism—a belief that money is intrinsically valuable and motivating to people. Not only is this inaccurate, but it reduces us as human beings. People tend to start to believe they really are how they are characterized—for better or for worse. Policymakers therefore degrade us when they characterize us in materialistic terms.

Egalitarians always promise a happier future—but never deliver, because the world they create is rife with unhappy consequences. By trying to force greater equality in the rewards to our toil, they reduce our ability and incentive to toil in the first place. Rigid labor laws make it harder for companies to hire employees, affecting especially the most vulnerable workers. Punitive taxation makes it less worthwhile to start a business and work hard—once again hitting those at the bottom the hardest. And history has shown that in the long run, all this will lower the ability of governments to raise the very tax revenues that the unemployed poor will increasingly need.

Our leaders do not owe us the rewards earned by people richer than we are. They owe us a system that fosters real opportunities to succeed. This was the philosophy of the great philanthropist Andrew Carnegie, who built thousands of libraries so that motivated men and women could attain some education without charge. Carnegie's philosophy should still inspire our policies today. Leaders should ignore calls to equalize income, but search assiduously for ways to equalize opportunity.

7. We should celebrate our work, not impose greater leisure.

Most Americans are happy with their work. Only about one American worker in ten is not satisfied with his or her job. Amazing as it may seem, most people would continue working at their current jobs even if they became independently wealthy. More Americans regret that they can't work *more,* not that they can't work *less.*

It is unclear whether the American model of happiness with work is applicable to Europe—perhaps we have peculiar values, or different policies have led us to this state of affairs with regard to our jobs, or both. But we can say with assurance that importing European labor-leisure models to the United States would be a big mistake. Mandating vacation time, limiting work hours, and retiring us when we were still fairly young would have to be based on the assumption that we were being exploited by employers, or that we didn't know what was best for us. Neither argument is plausible for the vast majority of American workers.

Some critics of the American system believe we are suffering from some sort of "false consciousness"—that we have been deluded by the "American dream" into thinking that we will be happier if we work harder and make more money. This argument betrays a crass materialism on the part of those who make it, and a crude naïveté about what really motivates most of us to work. When we are matched with a job in which we create value, we earn success and gain a sense of meaning in our lives—money aside—and thus find happiness. It would be a mistake to force leisure on Americans—for there is no evidence that the majority of us want it.

Our leaders should be concerned not with those who choose to work a lot, but rather with the small minority who are unsatisfied with their jobs—or worse yet, who can't find work. We need to discover ways for more people to be matched to their skills and interests, to be free to work as much as they would like, and to find success in whatever personal way they define it.

8. A happy America must continue to be a giving nation.

There is one exception to the rule that money doesn't buy happiness. If you want $100 in authentic happiness, give that money away to your favorite charity. You will experience a "Helper's High," lower your stress hormones, and maybe even identify yourself as a leader to others and become more successful as a result. Given the price of therapy and prescriptions these days, this is about the best deal in town.

America was built as a nation of givers. Religious pilgrims were some of our earliest ancestors. Thousands of miles away from their homes and governments, they were confronted by a vast frontier that could only be managed if private individuals took the needs of their community into their own hands. This has led to the simple and enduring fact that no country gives and volunteers privately like America does. This fact is more than just a curiosity or source of national pride. It is part of the reason we are generally happier than people in other developed countries.

Leaders need to take our giving seriously. It is not a dalliance, or an expendable substitute for government spending. The day we displace our gifts with expanded state funds for services is the day we get unhappier. Our nation needs a serious conversation about what private giving can and will deliver—and a commitment from our leaders to keep the long arm of the state out of these areas. Our leaders must also look for ways to topple policy barriers to giving, like the regulations and threat of litigation that keep people from serving others.

9. Happiness is easiest to find in limited government.

As the developed world has grown rich over the past fifty years, two competing theories of the role of government in our happiness have emerged. The first, derived from classical economics, argues that governments tend to play a positive role in our lives, providing the services we want, need, and thus demand as a democratic society. A more modern view, from a field called *public choice*, argues that governments tend to become intrusive and hyperactive based on the motivations of the few—those with access to political power and those in government jobs, most notably—and we are made worse off as a result. The data support this latter view.

Economists have studied the impact of public expenditure on happiness by comparing the cost of government in nations around the world to the self-reported happiness levels of their citizens. They find that as government grows—measured in the percentage of GDP it soaks up—the percentage of the population that is satisfied with life shrinks.[6]

The bottom line is this: Much government activity depresses people. Why? There is ample evidence that the government wastes money in most countries and that it tends to provide public goods inefficiently. Look around you and you might find evidence of this—bridges to nowhere, special-interest, pork-barrel spending, and services that seem more expensive than they need to be. Worse yet, government often creates services that leave some people dependent on the state and miserable. This is frustrating and lowers our happiness.[7]

But government may even lower our happiness when it does things well. When the government expropriates resources and uses them to provide the things it believes we want and need, whether it is correct or not, we give up a measure of control. Of course, we elect leaders who are supposed to represent our interests. But taxation is inherently coercive: You pay your taxes or you talk to the judge; it's that simple. We know that anything that strips away our sense of control will lower our happiness. Government, as important as it is, has inherent happiness-lowering tendencies. This is why it is critical for government to limit itself to what we can clearly see is a worthwhile trade-off: While we will never *enjoy* handing over a chunk of our paychecks by force, for most of us it is worth it to pay for the army, the police, the roads, the schools, and other services that don't simply reward a few winners in our population or crowd out private alternatives.

As citizens, we tend to demand more and more from the government, and this invites the state to capture and redistribute more and more of our resources. This lowers our long-term happiness because government works like a ratchet: It is easy to grow it, but nearly impossible to shrink it. For the sake of our happiness, our leaders should remember this fact and always be looking for ways to give us more private responsibility as citizens. Our leaders should always ask these questions: "Will citizens still want the government to be doing this in ten years?"

————

These nine lessons are much easier for me to present than they would be for our leaders—including our next president—to implement. Politicians face acute pressures that are completely contrary to following these lessons. Liberal politicians are selected by overwhelmingly secular—sometimes militantly secular—activists, who expect secularist policies. They are asked to support welfare initiatives that weaken incentives to marry. They are expected to raise taxes in ways that equalize incomes but frequently not opportunities, and to lower the rewards to market work. They are expected to spend government money in ways that displace private giving. Conservative politicians face similar pressures. They are often asked to curtail personal moral freedoms, and they enact security measure upon security measure to ensure our safety, while impinging upon our freedom. Even worse, they sometimes blindly follow an agenda for economic growth because it is expected of them. And *all* politicians receive some of their most generous and energetic support from the radicals and political activists who, by all rights, should be ignored.

Leadership is hard. But the pursuit of happiness is not just another right, like a public education. It is our birthright, enshrined in our Declaration of Independence by the courageous Americans who struggled to start an experiment in democracy that blossomed in less than 200 years to become the strongest, freest nation the world has ever known.

Our leaders can't be expected to do it all, however. Happiness also depends on us as citizens—the owners of America and bosses of our politicians—and what we do to pursue it. We must select and enthusiastically support leaders who are committed to following the principles of American happiness. Furthermore, we have to resist our desperate urge to demand the expanding government services, nanny-state regulations, and abridgments to our freedom that seem so appealing in the short term—but that ultimately strip us of our ability to chase our felicity.

Our forefathers fought and died to defend our right to the pursuit of happiness. Our responsibility as citizens today is to continue to exercise that right—in the way we vote, in the leaders we select, and in the values manifest in our lives. This is the key to ensuring and growing America's gross national happiness, both for ourselves and for many generations of happy Americans to come.

APPENDIX

The Data on Happiness

In this book, I reach virtually all of my conclusions on the basis of statistics—those generated by my own analysis as well as those compiled through the empirical work of other scholars. A huge number of studies, and literally gigabytes of data, are lurking behind the preceding chapters.[1]

For the work of others, I rely mainly on studies from psychology, economics, and other social sciences. I have based my conclusions on the studies I judged to be the best executed according to standards of good research and methodology, regardless of whether they supported any preconceived notions I might have had at the outset. In general, these studies come from the most reputable peer-reviewed academic and scientific journals in their respective fields.

Where there are unanswered questions in the existing literature, I rely on my own data analysis. Some of the statistical details (particularly on modeling procedures) are outlined in the endnotes. Many of the goriest details I have skipped for the sake of brevity and readability, this being a book for humans (not academics). However, for those curious about some of the empirical procedures, or researchers keen on reproducing any of the results in this book, this Appendix discusses the datasets I employed most intensively in this project. I introduce each dataset, describe how I used it, and present some of the most salient results that appear in the text.

This Appendix is not exhaustive. To describe every statistical test that went into the analysis in this book would make for an appendix as long as the book itself. Therefore, I have selected here the data summaries and statistical tests that were particularly important for building the book's arguments.

Virtually all the data I use come from surveys conducted of individuals over the past decade. I did not design or field these surveys myself; rather, they were undertaken by some of the most reputable nonpartisan research organizations in the world. All the data are publicly available to any and all researchers.

The surveys I used generally involved asking people (in person, on the phone, or through the mail) some variant of this question: "Taken all together, how happy would you say you are—very happy, somewhat happy, or not too happy?" These surveys provide a tremendous resource for understanding psychological happiness because they generally look at large numbers of individuals (instead of aggregating across groups of people) and get the information anonymously straight from respondents. With these data, we can match up self-reported happiness with people's personal characteristics: their political views, religious beliefs, family circumstances, and demographics, for example.

The Introduction to this book tells why we can trust self-reported happiness data to gauge actual happiness. These data are, however, far from perfect, and are beset by four problems. The first problem is that the way questions are asked sometimes biases the way people answer the questions, potentially leading to a systematic over- or underestimate of happiness. For example, some surveys ask people if they are happy *right now,* and others ask if they are happy *in general.* These two types of surveys will probably not generate the same types of responses. The second problem is that a lot of people either refuse to answer certain questions or answer "don't know." This is called "nonresponse." If certain people tend to answer this way, or tend to give this response instead of more revealing answers that they don't care to give, the data may not reflect reality. The third problem we often face is that a survey might not really represent a population. For example, if I were to conduct a survey about happiness and religious beliefs in Utah, it might not reflect beliefs across the United States as a whole. Finally, whenever a survey asks people about happiness, we have to worry about the honesty of their answers. It may in fact be hard for people to admit that they are miserable.

Empirical researchers (number crunchers) like me meet these threats primarily with the force of replication. It is a bad idea to base all one's conclusions on a single dataset. That is why the data-gathering stage for this book involved assembling so many large databases—in which different surveyors at different times asked different populations similar questions (but in different ways). Although individual surveys and populations might produce inaccuracies and biases, a large body of evidence on a topic is more trustworthy than a more limited one. I am confident in the findings in this book because multiple data sources told more or less the same story.

When studying the relationships between happiness and other forces, a problem that often arises is one of controlling for alternative explanations. For example, in this book I find that political conservatives are a lot happier than political liberals. Does this mean that politics per se are the only key to happiness? Of course not. Politics play some role, and it is important to note the happiness difference between political groups, but the demographic differences between conservatives and liberals, beyond political views, also matter.

Statisticians have techniques for getting to the truth of these kinds of relationships, and these techniques are called *regression analyses*. When I find a relationship between two variables—say, between political views and happiness—I usually go an extra step and isolate this relationship by holding all other relevant factors constant. Regression analysis allows me to do this, telling me the true association between happiness and politics, even if other characteristics between two people are the same. The technical details of the specific regression analyses I use in this book are contained in the notes. I also provide the details on a few key regressions in this Appendix.

One of the ways that researchers deal with nonresponse is to weight the survey data they use so that it "looks" representative of the population. For example, if more women than men answer a survey—which is quite typical—we might weight men's responses slightly more heavily than women's, so that the survey sample looks fifty-fifty. The problem with this technique is that it makes data analysis less transparent, and the weighting scheme can be controversial. In my empirical work, I choose not to weight my data, but rather to work with "raw" survey responses. This rules out the argument that an esoteric weighting scheme, which is opaque to the reader (and maybe even the researcher), lies behind any of my results. I ensure that the raw data are not *too* unrepresentative by frequently checking to make sure that the weighted and unweighted results are close to the same (and statistically insignificant in their differences). For example, I find in an early chapter of this book that, using the raw data from the 2004 General Social Survey, 44 percent of conservatives say they are very happy, versus 25 percent of liberals. Using the survey's weights, these percentages change to 46 percent and 28 percent, a net difference of just a point.

Below are the datasets I used most intensively and an outline of some of the key analyses leading to this book's conclusions.

The General Social Survey

The General Social Survey (GSS) is a nationwide survey that has been administered through the National Opinion Research Center (NORC) most years since 1972. It asks a sample of about 2,000 respondents different subsets of about 4,000 questions on a wide variety of topics. The GSS is one of the only repeated surveys in the world to ask people about their happiness, and as such, it has been used in countless happiness studies over the years. The GSS collects a large amount of sociodemographic information on each respondent. Each year, it features batteries of questions on special topics, such as freedom (2000), attitudes about work (2002), and religion (2004).

The GSS asks respondents about happiness with the following question: "Taken all together, how happy would you say you are these days—would you say that you are very happy, pretty happy, or not too happy?"

The trends in American happiness, measured in the GSS from 1972–2004, are used in several chapters. Table 1 displays these trends, compared with average American income as well as the Gini coefficient of income inequality.

TABLE 1 **Trends in Happiness, Average Income, and Income Inequality, 1972–2004**

Year	Percentage of Adult Population Saying They Were "Very Happy"	Percentage of Adult Population Saying they Were "Pretty Happy"	Percentage of Adult Population Saying They Were "Not Too Happy"	Real GDP per Capita	Gini Coefficient
1972	30	53	17	$25,421	0.401
1973	36	51	13	$27,126	0.397
1974	38	49	13	$26,657	0.395
1975	33	54	13	$25,785	0.397
1976	34	53	13	$26,666	0.398
1977	35	53	12	$27,916	0.402
1978	34	56	10	$29,212	0.402
1980	34	53	13	$27,884	0.403
1982	31	55	15	$26,328	0.412
1983	31	56	13	$27,333	0.414
1984	35	52	13	$28,923	0.415
1985	29	60	11	$29,709	0.419
1986	32	56	11	$29,966	0.425
1987	29	57	13	$31,088	0.426
1988	34	57	9	$31,884	0.427
1989	33	58	10	$32,427	0.431
1990	33	58	9	$32,251	0.428
1991	31	58	11	$31,122	0.428
1993	32	57	11	$31,769	0.454
1994	29	59	12	$32,520	0.456
1996	30	58	12	$33,249	0.455
1998	32	56	12	$34,717	0.456
2000	32	58	11	$36,468	0.462
2002	30	57	12	$36,316	0.462
2004	31	55	13	$38,191	0.466

NOTE: Income levels are corrected for inflation using the Consumer Price Index and reflect 2004 prices. In some years, percentages do not sum to 100 because of rounding.

SOURCES: James A. Davis, Tom W. Smith, and Peter V. Marsden, *General Social Surveys, 1972–2004* [machine-readable data file] (Chicago: National Opinion Research Center [producer]; Storrs, Conn.: The Roper Center for Public Opinion Research, University of Connecticut [distributor], 2004); *Statistical Abstract of the United States* (Washington, D.C.: Government Printing Office, various years); U.S. Census Bureau, Consumer Price Index.

Table 2 shows the differences over time between liberals and conservatives in the likelihood of saying they are "very happy."

In chapter 5, I use the GSS time series on happiness levels to see how average income and government spending affect the tendency for people to say they are "not so happy." Using Ordinary Least Squares, I regress the percentage of American adults who say they are not so happy (expressing the percentage between 0 and 100) on a time trend, real

TABLE 2 Percentages of Liberals and Conservatives Saying They Were "Very Happy," 1974–2004

Year	Percentage of Liberal and Extremely Liberal People Saying They Were "Very Happy"	Percentage of Conservative and Extremely Conservative People Saying They Were "Very Happy"
1974	35	42
1975	34	34
1976	30	39
1977	29	35
1978	32	47
1980	27	43
1982	27	35
1983	24	44
1984	32	46
1985	33	34
1986	34	44
1987	26	40
1988	32	41
1989	30	40
1990	34	38
1991	32	40
1993	28	42
1994	30	35
1996	26	38
1998	33	40
2000	26	39
2002	28	36
2004	25	44

SOURCE: James A. Davis, Tom W. Smith, and Peter V. Marsden, *General Social Surveys, 1972–2004* [machine-readable data file] (Chicago: National Opinion Research Center [producer]; Storrs, Conn.: The Roper Center for Public Opinion Research, University of Connecticut [distributor], 2004).

GDP per capita (in 2004 prices), and real federal government spending per capita (in 2004 prices). The results are summarized in Table 3.

Chapters 1 and 2 use the 2004 GSS data intensively to look at happiness, religion, and politics. Table 4 summarizes the relationships between these factors.

TABLE 3 Variables That Individually Affect National Unhappiness

Dependent Variable: Population percentage saying it was "not too happy"

Independent Variable	Regression Coefficient	Standard Error
Constant	32.39**	7.48
GDP per capita (1,000s of 2004 dollars)	-1.24**	0.40
Real federal government spending per capita (1,000s of 2004 dollars)	2.91*	1.15
Year (time trend)	0.11	0.11

N=25. Adjusted R^2=0.31.

* Coefficient is significant at the 0.05 level or higher.

** Coefficient is significant at the 0.01 level or higher.

Sources: James A. Davis, Tom W. Smith, and Peter V. Marsden, *General Social Surveys*, 1972–2004 [machine-readable data file] (Chicago: National Opinion Research Center [producer]; Storrs, Conn.: The Roper Center for Public Opinion Research, University of Connecticut [distributor], 2004); *Statistical Abstract of the United States* (Washington, D.C.: Government Printing Office, various years); U.S. Census Bureau, Consumer Price Index.

TABLE 4 Percentages of the Population Saying They Were "Very Happy," 2004

Political Orientation	Religious	Secular	All Religious Participation Levels
Liberal	31	22	25
Conservative	50	35	44
All political beliefs	43	23	31

N=1,306

Source: James A. Davis, Tom W. Smith, and Peter V. Marsden, *General Social Surveys*, 1972–2004 [machine-readable data file] (Chicago: National Opinion Research Center [producer]; Storrs, Conn.: The Roper Center for Public Opinion Research, University of Connecticut [distributor], 2004).

Table 5 presents the results of probit regressions of a dummy variable for saying one is "very happy" on measures of religion, politics, and other demographic characteristics.

TABLE 5 Variables Affecting the Probability of Saying One Was "Very Happy," 2004

Independent Variable	Model 1 (full model) Coefficient (standard error) [marginal effect]	Model 2 (no politics) Coefficient (standard error) [marginal effect]	Model 3 (no religion) Coefficient (standard error) [marginal effect]
Constant	-1.29*** (0.29) [-0.45]	-1.18*** (0.28) [-0.41]	-1.39*** (0.28) [-0.48]
Religious[1]	0.15 (0.1) [0.05]	0.21** (0.1) [0.07]	
Secular[1]	-0.24** (0.1) [-0.08]	-0.25*** (0.1) [-0.09]	
Liberal[2]	-0.001 (0.128) [-0.0004]		-0.03 (0.13) [-0.01]
Conservative[2]	0.29*** (0.1) [0.1]		0.36*** (0.1) [0.13]
Household income ($1,000s)	0.004*** (0.001) [0.001]	0.004*** (0.001) [0.001]	0.004*** (0.001) [0.001]
Age	0.0003 (0.0028) [0.0001]	-0.0005 (0.0027) [-0.0002]	0.0007 (0.0027) [0.0003]
Education (years)	0.01 (0.02) [0.004]	0.01 (0.02) [0.004]	0.01 (0.02) [0.005]
Male	-0.09 (0.08) [-0.03]	-0.09 (0.08) [-0.03]	-0.13 (0.08) [-0.05]
Black[3]	0.33* (0.19) [0.11]	0.29 (0.19) [0.1]	0.38** (0.19) [0.13]
White[3]	0.28* (0.16) [0.1]	0.28* (0.16) [0.1]	0.24 (0.16) [0.08]
Married	0.54*** (0.09) [0.19]	0.55*** (0.09) [0.19]	0.59*** (0.09) [0.2]
Children	-0.07** (0.03) [-0.02]	-0.07** (0.03) [-0.02]	-0.06** (0.03) [-0.02]

N=1,152

NOTES:

1. Reference group: Those who attended religious services, but irregularly.

2. Reference group: Political moderates.

3. Reference group: Nonblack minorities.

  * Coefficient is significant at the 0.10 level or higher.

  ** Coefficient is significant at the 0.05 level or higher.

  *** Coefficient is significant at the 0.01 level or higher.

SOURCE: James A. Davis, Tom W. Smith, and Peter V. Marsden, *General Social Surveys, 1972–2004* [machine-readable data file] (Chicago: National Opinion Research Center [producer]; Storrs, Conn.: The Roper Center for Public Opinion Research, University of Connecticut [distributor], 2004).

Chapter 3 uses the 2004 GSS to look at happiness as it relates to marriage and parenting. Tables 6 and 7 show the percentage of adults in different marital situations who said they were "very happy" and "not too happy."

TABLE 6 Population Percentages Saying They Were "Very Happy," 2004

Marital Status	Men	Women	All
Married	41	44	42
Widowed	15	22	20
Divorced	18	16	17
Never married	19	28	23

N=1,290

SOURCE: James A. Davis, Tom W. Smith, and Peter V. Marsden, *General Social Surveys, 1972–2004* [machine-readable data file] (Chicago: National Opinion Research Center [producer]; Storrs, Conn.: The Roper Center for Public Opinion Research, University of Connecticut [distributor], 2004).

TABLE 7 Population Percentages Saying They Were "Not Too Happy," 2004

Marital Status	Men	Women	All
Married	9	6	7
Widowed	35	25	27
Divorced	18	20	19
Never married	20	10	15

N=1,290

SOURCE: James A. Davis, Tom W. Smith, and Peter V. Marsden, *General Social Surveys, 1972–2004* [machine-readable data file] (Chicago: National Opinion Research Center [producer]; Storrs, Conn.: The Roper Center for Public Opinion Research, University of Connecticut [distributor], 2004).

For chapter 3, I created a nonlinear predictive happiness model based on an Ordinary Least Squares regression of a 0–2 happiness index (where 0 is unhappiest and 2 is happiest) on the number of children and a full vector of demographics. The resulting fitted equation for predicting happiness is

$$(1) \quad \hat{H} = 1.267 - 0.062C + 0.0069C^2,$$

where $\hat{H}$ is predicted happiness and C is the number of children a person has. All other regressors are held at their mean values in generating the constant. The results produce a convex relationship between happiness and children, as summarized in Table 8. The happiness nadir occurs at 4.48 children. Notice that people with one child experience about the same happiness, on average, as those with eight children.

Chapter 4 uses the 2000 GSS, which contained a module of questions on people's attitudes about freedom. Table 9 shows the relationship between the perception of freedom and happiness.

TABLE 8 **Happiness Predicted by Number of Children, 2004**

Number of Children	Predicted Happiness Score
0	1.27
1	1.21
2	1.17
3	1.14
4	1.13
5	1.13
6	1.14
7	1.17
8	1.21

N=1,136
SOURCE: James A. Davis, Tom W. Smith, and Peter V. Marsden, *General Social Surveys, 1972–2004* [machine-readable data file] (Chicago: National Opinion Research Center [producer]; Storrs, Conn.: The Roper Center for Public Opinion Research, University of Connecticut [distributor], 2004).

TABLE 9 **Happiness and Perceived Personal Freedom, 2000**

Person Feels He or She Enjoys ...	Population Percentage Giving This Response	Percentage Saying They Were "Very Happy"	Percentage Saying They Were "Not Too Happy"
Complete freedom	17	42	10
A great deal of freedom	55	35	6
A moderate amount of freedom	24	19	18
Not much or no freedom at all	4	12	49

N=1,372
SOURCE: James A. Davis, Tom W. Smith, and Peter V. Marsden, *General Social Surveys, 1972–2004* [machine-readable data file] (Chicago: National Opinion Research Center [producer]; Storrs, Conn.: The Roper Center for Public Opinion Research, University of Connecticut [distributor], 2004).

Table 10 presents the results of a probit regression of a dummy variable for saying one is "very happy" on measures of religion, politics, and other demographic characteristics.

The 2002 GSS featured a module of questions about work, which provided much of the data for chapter 7. One technical finding in this chapter is that job satisfaction actually causes general happiness. This claim is based on a full-information maximum likelihood (FIML) tobit model in which a 0–2 measure-of-happiness scale (where 2 is happiest)

TABLE 10 Variables Affecting the Probability of Saying One Feels "Complete Freedom" or "a Great Deal of Freedom," 2000

Independent Variable	Coefficient (standard error) [marginal effect]
Constant	0.16 (0.29) [0.05]
Household income ($10,000s)	0.09*** (0.02) [0.03]
Education (years)	0.01 (0.02) [0.005]
Male	-0.29*** (0.08) [-0.1]
Married	-0.19** (0.09) [-0.06]
Children	0.002 (0.026) [0.001]
White[1]	0.16 (0.18) [0.05]
Black[1]	-0.24 (0.2) [-0.08]
Liberal[2]	-0.1 (0.12) [-0.03]
Conservative[2]	-0.13 (0.11) [-0.04]
Religious[3]	0.32*** (0.11) [0.11]
Secular[3]	-0.09 (0.1) [-0.03]

N=1,133

NOTES:

1. Reference group: Nonblack minorities.

2. Reference group: Political moderates.

3. Reference group: Those attending religious services, but irregularly.

  * Coefficient is significant at the 0.10 level or higher.

 ** Coefficient is significant at the 0.05 level or higher.

*** Coefficient is significant at the 0.01 level or higher.

SOURCE: James A. Davis, Tom W. Smith, and Peter V. Marsden, *General Social Surveys, 1972–2004* [machine-readable data file] (Chicago: National Opinion Research Center [producer]; Storrs, Conn.: The Roper Center for Public Opinion Research, University of Connecticut [distributor], 2004).

is regressed on a 0–4 measure of job satisfaction (where 4 is most satisfied). The instrument is a measure of agreement with the claim that work brings a person's greatest satisfaction in life, a measure that is strongly, positively correlated with job satisfaction (as one would expect), but not directly related to general life satisfaction. This model is detailed in Table 11.

TABLE 11 FIML Tobit Model Testing Whether Job Satisfaction Causes General Happiness

Independent Variable	Coefficient (standard error)
Constant	0.2 (0.46)
Job satisfaction	0.36*** (0.14)
Income ($1,000s)	0.002 (0.002)
Education (years)	0.002 (0.014)
Age	-0.006** (0.003)
Male	-0.0334 (0.0795)
Married	0.28*** (0.08)
White[1]	0.19 (0.2)
Black[1]	0.05 (0.21)
Religious[2]	-0.01 (0.09)
Secular[2]	-0.12 (0.09)
Liberal[3]	0.14 (0.1)
Conservative[3]	0.13 (0.11)

N=313

NOTES:

1. Reference group: Nonblack minorities.

2. Reference group: Those attending religious services, but irregularly.

3. Reference group: Political moderates.

  * Coefficient is significant at the 0.10 level or higher.

 ** Coefficient is significant at the 0.05 level or higher.

*** Coefficient is significant at the 0.01 level or higher.

SOURCE: James A. Davis, Tom W. Smith, and Peter V. Marsden, *General Social Surveys, 1972–2004* [machine-readable data file] (Chicago: National Opinion Research Center [producer]; Storrs, Conn.: The Roper Center for Public Opinion Research, University of Connecticut [distributor], 2004).

The International Social Survey Program

The International Social Survey Program (ISSP) is a research collaboration project that began in 1983. The ISSP group develops modules dealing with specific topics, which it adds to the regular national surveys of some thirty countries worldwide (including the GSS in the United States). The countries sampled change somewhat from year to year but always include Europe and North America. One of the survey topics in 2002 was happiness. In additional to the topical modules, the ISSP collects full data on the sociodemographic characteristics of respondents.

The ISSP asks respondents about happiness with the following question: "If you were to consider your life in general, how happy or unhappy would you say you are, on the whole?" The possible answers to this question are "completely happy," "very happy," "fairly happy," "neither happy nor unhappy," and "fairly unhappy."

The book's Introduction ranks countries by the stated happiness levels of their citizens. Table 12 summarizes this comparison.

TABLE 12 **Countries Around the World Ranked by the Population Percentage Saying They Were "Completely Happy" or "Very Happy," 2002**

Country	Percentage "Completely Happy" or "Very Happy"
Mexico	63
Brazil	58
Cyprus	57
Chile	57
United States	56
Northern Ireland	55
Japan	53
Switzerland	53
Austria	52
New Zealand	52
Great Britain	48
Australia	47
Philippines	47
Denmark	44

continues

TABLE 12 *continued*

Country	Percentage "Completely Happy" or "Very Happy"
Ireland	43
Norway	43
Israel	42
Sweden	39
Taiwan	38
Portugal	38
Netherlands	36
Finland	36
Spain	36
France	35
Western Germany	31
Slovenia	29
Hungary	29
Slovak Republic	29
Eastern Germany	26
Czech Republic	24
Poland	22
Russia	21
Latvia	18
Bulgaria	10

$N = 45,800$

SOURCE: International Social Survey Program (ISSP), Zentralarchiv für Empirische Sozialforschung, *International Social Survey Programme*, 2002.

Thirty-three of the countries in Table 12 appear in the *Wall Street Journal* and Heritage Foundation's Index of Economic Freedom.[2] Regressing the happiness measure (H, measured as a percentage between 0–100) on each country's freedom score (F, also measured as 0–100 percent) using Ordinary Least Squares produces the following result.

$$(2) \quad \hat{H} = -74.92 + 1.75F$$

The standard error on the coefficient on freedom is 0.17, so it is significant at above the 0.01 level.

The Maxwell Poll on Civic Engagement and Inequality

Each year, the Campbell Public Affairs Institute at Syracuse University's Maxwell School undertakes a national poll of about 600 American adults, randomly selected, on issues of civic participation. Called the Maxwell Poll, the survey asks respondents approximately eighty questions about their beliefs concerning the conduct of government, their involvement in governmental affairs, and their attitudes about income equality and mobility in America. The poll also collects data on respondent demographics.[3]

In chapter 1, I look at the political activity of people who never attend worship activities. Table 13 summarizes the results.

TABLE 13 **Political Activity of People Never Attending Worship Activities, 2005**

Group	Percentage of People Never Attending Worship Activities in This Group
General adult population	11
Self-described political liberals	21
Liberals who attend political meetings	33
Liberals who contribute to political causes	27

N = 609

Source: Campbell Public Affairs Institute, Maxwell Poll on Civic Engagement and Inequality [dataset] (Syracuse, N.Y.: Maxwell School of Citizenship and Public Affairs, 2006).

Chapter 6 compares views about the existence of economic mobility in America with beliefs about inequality and the government's role in decreasing it. The findings are summarized in Table 14.

Using the 2005 Maxwell Poll data, chapter 6 investigates the relationship between political ideology and beliefs about economic mobility, finding that conservatives are approximately 20 percent more likely than liberals to agree that, "While people may begin with different opportunities, hard work and perseverance can usually overcome those disadvantages," even correcting for other demographics. This is found with a probit regression (see Table 15) of a dummy for agreeing with the preceding statement on dummies for political ideology and a vector of personal characteristics.

TABLE 14 Views on Economic Mobility and Income Inequality, 2005

Belief	Percentage of Those Who Think There Is a Lot of Economic Mobility Who Believe the Given Statement	Percentage of Those Who Think There Is Not Much Economic Mobility Who Believe the Given Statement
Income differences are too large	44	64
Inequality is a serious problem	38	63
The government should do more to reduce inequality	40	68

N=596

SOURCES: Campbell Public Affairs Institute, Maxwell Poll on Civic Engagement and Inequality [dataset] (Syracuse, N.Y.: Maxwell School of Citizenship and Public Affairs, 2006).

TABLE 15 Variables Affecting the Probability of Saying One Believes Hard Work and Perseverance Can Lead to Success, 2000

Independent Variable	Coefficient (standard error) [marginal effect]
Constant	2.96*** (0.77) [0.6]
Liberal[1]	-0.45** (0.19) [-0.09]
Conservative[1]	0.54*** (0.22) [0.11]
Household income ($1,000s)	0.002 (0.002) [0.0004]
Education (years)	-0.1** (0.04) [-0.02]
Age	-0.01* (0.01) [-0.002]
Married	-0.35 (0.26) [-0.07]
Children	0.53** (0.23) [0.11]
Black[2]	-0.25 (0.49) [-0.05]
White[2]	-0.004 (0.365) [-0.001]
Male	-0.24 (0.17) [-0.05]

N=398

NOTES:

1. Reference group: Political moderates.

2. Reference group: Nonblack minorities.

  * Coefficient is significant at the 0.10 level or higher.

 ** Coefficient is significant at the 0.05 level or higher.

*** Coefficient is significant at the 0.01 level or higher.

SOURCE: Campbell Public Affairs Institute, Maxwell Poll on Civic Engagement and Inequality [dataset] (Syracuse, N.Y.: Maxwell School of Citizenship and Public Affairs, 2006).

American National Election Study

The American National Election Study (ANES) survey is conducted biannually by the Center for Political Studies and the Survey Research Center at the University of Michigan. The surveys ask approximately 1,500 respondents questions about social trust, civic engagement, and political participation. Respondents also provide demographic information. One of the ways the ANES surveys gauge public opinion is through the use of "feeling thermometers," or 0–100 scales in which respondents are asked to give their opinions on other groups in society, where 0 denotes the most negative feelings possible for the group in question, and 100 is the most positive.

Table 16 summarizes the temperatures given by conservatives and liberals toward themselves and others.

TABLE 16 Thermometer Scores and Political Ideology, 2004

Temperatures Given by Those Who Say They Are...	Average Temperature Given to Liberals	Average Temperature Given to Conservatives	Percentage Giving Liberals a Temperature of 20 or Below	Percentage Giving Conservatives a Temperature of 20 or Below
Conservative or extremely conservative	39	81	23	0
Extremely conservative only	27	84	50	0
Liberal or extremely liberal	75	38	3	25
Extremely liberal only	75	23	5	65

N=1,212

SOURCES: American National Election Studies (ANES), National Election Studies [dataset] (Ann Arbor, Mich.: University of Michigan, Center for Political Studies [producer and distributor], 2004).

The Panel Study of Income Dynamics

A useful data resource for understanding *un*happiness is the Population Study of Income Dynamics (PSID), a national panel survey that has been conducted almost annually since 1968. The survey asks more than 7,000 families different combinations of questions on a broad range of issues, focusing in particular on income sources and uses. In 2001, the Center on Philanthropy at Indiana University sponsored a module of questions on charitable behavior.

The PSID asks respondents about happiness with the following question: "In the past 30 days, about how often did you feel: so sad nothing could cheer you up; nervous, restless or fidgety; hopeless; that everything was an effort; worthless?"

Table 17 presents the results of a probit regression of an affirmative response to the question about inconsolable sadness (where the respondent had experienced this at least once in the past month). Income is measured as "permanent income" to rule out transitory shocks. This is calculated as the inflation-adjusted average income for each respondent in the 1997, 1999, and 2001 PSID surveys.

TABLE 17 Variables Affecting the Probability of Saying One Has Felt "Inconsolably Sad" in the Past Month, 2001

Independent Variable	Coefficient (standard error) [marginal effect]
Constant	-0.21** (0.09) [-0.08]
Permanent income ($100,000s)	-0.09** (0.04) [-0.03]
Education (years)	0.005 (0.004) [0.002]
Age	0.0009 (0.0011) [0.0003]
Married	-0.34*** (0.03) [-0.12]
Children	0.03** (0.01) [0.01]
White[1]	-0.2*** (0.06) [-0.07]
Black[1]	-0.02 (0.06) [-0.01]
No religion[2]	0.16*** (0.06) [0.06]

N=6,552

NOTES:

1. Reference group: Nonblack minorities.

2. This is a dummy for those who said they had no religious affiliation. The Population Study of Income Dynamics (PSID) does not measure religion in terms of attendance.

  * Coefficient is significant at the 0.10 level or higher.

 ** Coefficient is significant at the 0.05 level or higher.

*** Coefficient is significant at the 0.01 level or higher.

SOURCE: Panel Study of Income Dynamics (PSID), Wave XXXII Computer File (Ann Arbor, Mich.: ICPSR, 2001), http://simba.isr.umich.edu.

The Social Capital Community Benchmark Survey

A major data source for charitable and civic activity is the Social Capital and Community Benchmark Survey (SCCBS). The SCCBS was undertaken from July 2000 to February 2001 by researchers at various American universities in collaboration with the Roper Center for Public Opinion Research and the Saguaro Seminar at Harvard University's Kennedy School of Government. The intent of the survey was to expose various hypotheses about civil society to empirical scrutiny. The SCCBS contained three types of questions. First, personal attitudes of individuals were probed, including self-assessments of happiness. Second, respondents were asked about their civic behavior, such as participation in voluntary community activities. Finally, the survey collected a full battery of sociodemographic measures for each respondent. The data consist of nearly 30,000 observations drawn from 41 communities across 29 states, as well as a nationwide sample.

The SCCBS asked respondents about their happiness with the following question: "All things considered, would you say you are very happy, happy, not very happy, or not happy at all?"

Table 18 compares the stated happiness for adherents of various religions. This table only looks at those who attend worship services at least once per week.

TABLE 18 **Religions and Stated Happiness, 2000**

Religious Group	Percentage Saying They Were "Very Happy"
Practicing Protestants	48
Practicing Catholics	42
Practicing Jews	50
People who practice other religions	40
Secularists	33

N=28,718

SOURCE: *Social Capital Community Benchmark Survey* (SCCBS) [machine-readable data file] (Cambridge, Mass.: Saguaro Seminar at the John F. Kennedy School of Government, Harvard University [producer]; Storrs, Conn.: The Roper Center for Public Opinion Research, University of Connecticut [distributor], 2000).

Chapter 8 focuses on the happiness effects of charitable giving and volunteering. Table 19 details the results of a probit regression of a dummy for saying one is "very happy" on measures of giving and volunteering, as well as a vector of demographics.

TABLE 19 Variables, Including Charitable Giving and Volunteering, Affecting the Probability of Saying One Is "Very Happy," 2000

Independent Variable	Coefficient (standard error) [marginal effect]
Constant	-1.11*** (0.06) [-0.42]
Gives	0.05** (0.03) [0.02]
Volunteers	0.24*** (0.02) [0.09]
Religious[1]	0.17*** (0.02) [0.06]
Secular[1]	0.01 (0.02) [0.002]
Household income ($1,000s)	0.005*** (0.0004) [0.002]
Age	0.002*** (0.001) [0.001]
Male	-0.12*** (0.02) [-0.04]
Married	0.32*** (0.02) [0.12]
Household size	-0.04*** (0.01) [-0.02]
Conservative[2]	0.1*** (0.02) [0.04]
Liberal[2]	-0.01 (0.02) [-0.003]
High school graduate[3]	0.17*** (0.04) [0.06]
College graduate[3]	0.22*** (0.04) [0.08]
Graduate education[3]	0.22*** (0.05) [0.08]

N=23,074

NOTES:

1. Reference group: Those who attend religious services, but irregularly.

2. Reference group: Political moderates.

3. Reference group: No high school diploma.

  * Coefficient is significant at the 0.10 level or higher.

 ** Coefficient is significant at the 0.05 level or higher.

*** Coefficient is significant at the 0.01 level or higher.

SOURCE: *Social Capital Community Benchmark Survey* (SCCBS) [machine-readable data file] (Cambridge, Mass.: Saguaro Seminar at the John F. Kennedy School of Government, Harvard University [producer]; Storrs, Conn.: The Roper Center for Public Opinion Research, University of Connecticut [distributor], 2000).

The Aging, Status, and Sense of Control Survey

The Aging, Status, and Sense of Control (ASOC) survey, conducted in 2001, examined the relationship between age and changes in the sense of control over one's life. Questions regarding mental health investigated difficulties in staying focused, feelings of sadness or anxiety, and enjoyment of life. Respondents were also asked about their health behaviors, including use of tobacco and alcohol, frequency of exercise, use of medical services including insurance coverage, and the number of prescription medications used. Demographic questions included age, sex, marital status, education, work status, marital and family relations, and socioeconomic status.

NOTES

Introduction: America's Pursuit of Happiness

1. Plato, *Euthydemus,* translated by Benjamin Jowett, Penn State University, www2.hn.psu.edu/faculty/ jmanis/plato/euthydem.pdf.

2. America's bold commitment to happiness reflected an optimism that made the new nation different from other countries. Thomas Jefferson, when asked years after drafting the Declaration what explained its contents, called it simply "an expression of the American mind." "Thomas Jefferson to Henry Lee, May 8, 1825," in *The Basic Writings of Thomas Jefferson,* edited by Philip S. Foner (New York: Halcyon House, 1950), p. 802.

3. Rajni Bakshi, "Gross National Happiness," 2005, Envirohealth Website, http://www.alternet.org/envirohealth/21083/.

4. In the early 1990s, nearly 100,000 Bhutanis were stripped of their citizenship (the government claiming they were Nepali migrants), and many still reside in UN-sponsored refugee camps outside Bhutan. The government, incidentally, simply announced that no harm to gross national happiness had occurred from this act. Sushil Sarma, "Bhutan Refugees on Hunger Strike," BBC News Online, February 18, 2003, http://news.bbc.co.uk/2/hi/south_asia/2774803.stm.

5. British psychologist Daniel Nettle, who wrote an elegant introduction to the study of happiness called *Happiness: The Science Behind Your Smile* (New York: Oxford University Press, 2005), identified the

three levels of happiness as "momentary feelings," "judgments about feelings," and "quality of life."

6. Catholic philosopher Deal Hudson's book calls this definition "psychological happiness." See Deal Hudson, *Happiness and the Limits of Satisfaction* (Lanham, Md.: Rowman and Littlefield, 1996).

7. Nettle, *Happiness,* p. 18; Aristotle is quoted in Darrin M. McMahon, *Happiness: A History* (New York: Atlantic Monthly Press, 2006), p. 45; Psalms 1:1–2.

8. Stefan Klein, *The Science of Happiness: How Our Brains Make Us Happy—and What We Can Do to Get Happier* (New York: Marlowe, 2002), ch. 3.

9. The PANAS questionnaire can be found at http://www.authentic happiness.sas.upenn.edu/.

10. My literary agent, Lisa Adams, also reminded me of the "evil eye" problem: Some people would never dare say they were "very happy" for superstitious fear that the cosmos would rip their happiness away out of sheer spite.

11. Will Wilkinson, "In Pursuit of Happiness Research: Is It Reliable? What Does It Imply for Policy?" *Policy Analysis* 590 (April 11, 2007), http://www.cato.org/pubs/ pas/pa590.pdf; Anna Wierzbicka, "'Happiness' in Cross-Linguistic and Cross-Cultural Perspective," *Daedalus: Journal of the American Academy of Arts and Sciences* 133, no. 2 (Spring 2006): 36.

12. D. Watson and L. A. Clark, "Self Versus Peer Ratings of Specific Emotional Traits: Evidence of Convergent and Discriminant Validity," *Journal of Personality and Social Psychology* 60 (1991): 927–940.

13. This study is described in Norbert Schwarz and Fritz Strack, "Reports of Subjective Well-Being: Judgmental Processes and Their Methodological Implications," in *Well-Being: The Foundations of Hedonic Psychology,* edited by Daniel Kahneman, Ed Diener, and Norbert Schwarz (New York: Russell Sage, 1999), pp. 61–84.

14. Stefan Klein discusses these famous studies on smiling in *The Science of Happiness.*

15. Finally, you now have evidence that your unhappiness is your parents' fault. See David Lykken and Auke Tellegen, "Happiness Is a Stochastic Phenomenon," *Psychological Science* 7, no. 3 (1996).

16. Martin E. P. Seligman, *Authentic Happiness: Using the New Positive Psychology to Realize Your Potential for Lasting Fulfillment* (New York: The Free Press, 2002).

17. BBC News, "Denmark 'Happiest Place on Earth'," July 28, 2006, http://news.bbc.co.uk/go/pr/fr/-/1/hi/health/5224306.stm; International Social Survey Program (ISSP), Zentralarchiv für Empirische Sozialforschung, *International Social Survey Programme*, 2002.

18. 2002 ISSP.

19. Shigehiro Oishi, Ed Diener, Dong-Won Choi, and Chu Kim-Prieto, "The Dynamics of Daily Events and Well-Being Across Cultures: When Less Is More," *Journal of Personality and Social Psychology* 93, no. 4 (2007): 685–698.

20. James A. Davis, Tom W. Smith, and Peter V. Marsden, principal investigators, *General Social Surveys, 1972–2004* [machine-readable data file] (Chicago: National Opinion Research Center [producer]; Storrs, Conn.: The Roper Center for Public Opinion Research, University of Connecticut [distributor], 2004).

21. Ibid.

22. Ruut Veenhoven, "Apparent Quality of Life: How Long and Happy People Live," *Social Indicators Research* 71 (2005): 61–86; Ruut Veenhoven, "The Four Qualities of Life: Ordering Concepts and Measures of the Good Life," *Journal of Happiness Studies* 1 (2000): 1–39.

23. If I am lucky, this book will stimulate more people to think about the importance of our nation's happiness—researchers, politicians, and everyday good citizens. In five years, perhaps those who take issue with my findings or disagree with my interpretation of the facts will produce more evidence on the subject. This would constitute success just as much as any research that found I was spot on in my conclusions, because it would mean we knew more and were better able to increase the happiness of our citizens.

Chapter 1: The Politics of Happiness

1. See Darrin M. McMahon, *Happiness: A History* (New York: Atlantic Monthly Press, 2006), p. 471.

2. Moore made these comments in a speech in Boston on July 28, 2004, in an event that coincided with the Democratic National Convention. For a transcript of the speech, see http://www.democracynow .org/article.pl?sid=04/07/28/1335239.

3. George Lakoff, *Don't Think of an Elephant: Know Your Values and Frame the Debate* (White River Junction, Vt.: Chelsea Green, 2004); Eric Salzman, "Meet George Lakoff," CBS News, January 15, 2004, http://www.cbsnews.com/stories/2004/01/15/politics/main593546 .shtml; Robert Altemeyer, *Enemies of Freedom: Understanding Right-Wing Authoritarianism* (San Francisco: Jossey-Bass, 1988); T. W. Adorno, E. Frenkel-Brunswick, D. J. Levinson, and R. N. Sanford, *The Authoritarian Personality* (New York: Harpers, 1950).

4. Jack Block and Jeanne H. Block, "Nursery School Personality and Political Orientation Two Decades Later," *Journal of Research in Personality* (2005).

5. Jonah Goldberg, "Right on the Couch," National Review Online, March 22, 2006, http://www.nationalreview.com/goldberg/goldberg 200603220735.asp.

6. Jon Gertner, "The Futile Pursuit of Happiness," *New York Times,* September 7, 2003.

7. James A. Davis, Tom W. Smith, and Peter V. Marsden, principal investigators, *General Social Surveys, 1972–2004* [machine-readable data file] (Chicago: National Opinion Research Center [producer]; Storrs, Conn.: The Roper Center for Public Opinion Research, University of Connecticut [distributor], 2004); Gallup, "Republicans Report Much Better Mental Health Than Others," November 30, 2007, http://www .gallup.com/poll/102943/Republicans-Report-Much-Better-Mental -Health-Than-Others.aspx.

8. 1974–2004 GSS.

9. Ibid.

10. 2004 GSS.

11. Ibid. Between married conservatives and single liberals in happiness are single conservatives and married liberals.

12. Ibid. The model here is a probit regression of a dummy for the answer "very happy" on political orientation and a vector of the demo-

graphics listed. The marginal effect is evaluated at the mean values of the covariates. The coefficient on "liberal" is insignificant, meaning that we cannot reject the hypothesis that liberals and moderates are equally unlikely to say they are very happy, compared with conservatives.

13. Jonah Goldberg, "Why 'Liberal' Doesn't Quite Fit." USA Today website, August 7, 2007, http://blogs.usatoday.com/oped/2007/08/why-liberal-doe.html.

14. 1996 GSS.

15. Stefan Klein, whose international bestseller *The Science of Happiness: How Our Brains Make Us Happy—and What We Can Do to Get Happier* (New York: Marlowe, 2002) looked systematically at the brain science behind life satisfaction, came to a startling conclusion about how to be happier: "We should want to change ourselves rather than our circumstances. The rest will come, because with a mind that is prepared for happiness, we will automatically seek out those situations that make us happy." In other words, the battle between collective action (changing circumstances) and private action (changing ourselves) is a battle in which one side has a clear edge in happiness. Again, according to Klein, modern neuroscience agrees with Eastern philosophy and the great thinkers of ancient Greece: For the sake of happiness, we should "anchor ourselves in good habits, because these form the mind" (p. 68).

16. George F. Will, "Happy Conservatives Irk Liberals," Seattle Post-Intelligencer website, March 1, 2006, http://seattlepi.nwsource.com/opinion/261161_will01.html; Pete Du Pont, "Pursue Happiness, Vote GOP," *Wall Street Journal*, November 29, 2004.

17. Albert Bandura, "Self-Efficacy," in *Encyclopedia of Human Behavior*, edited by V. S. Ramachaudran (New York: Academic Press, 1994), 4:71–81. Reprinted in H. Friedman, ed., *Encyclopedia of Mental Health* (San Diego: Academic Press, 1998). D. Kahneman, A. B. Krueger, D. A. Schkade, N. Schwarz, and A. A. Stone, "A Survey Method for Characterizing Daily Life Experience: The Day Reconstruction Method," *Science* 306 (2004): 1776–1780.

18. Elisabeth Lasch-Quinn, *Race Experts: How Racial Etiquette, Sensitivity Training, and New Age Therapy Hijacked the Civil Rights Revolution* (New York: Norton, 2001).

19. 2004 GSS.

20. 2004 American National Election Studies (ANES) (Ann Arbor: University of Michigan, Center for Political Studies [producer and distributor], 2004).

21. Quinnipiac University polling data (March 13, 2006); Arthur C. Brooks, "Taking America's Temperature," CBS News, June 6, 2006, http://www.cbsnews.com/stories/2006/06/05/opinion/main1682175.shtml.

22. 2002 and 2004 GSS.

23. 2004 GSS.

24. Ibid.

Chapter 2: Happiness Is a Gift from Above

1. David Van Biema, "Mother Teresa's Crisis of Faith," *Time*, August 23, 2007.

2. Ibid.

3. Karl Marx, *Critique of Hegel's Philosophy of Right* (Cambridge: Cambridge University Press, 1970); Christopher Hitchens, *God Is Not Great: How Religion Poisons Everything* (New York: Twelve Books, 2007).

4. As Ralph Waldo Emerson wrote in 1876, "All I have seen teaches me to trust the creator for all I have not seen." *The Complete Works of Ralph Waldo Emerson: Letters and Social Aims*, Centenary Edition (Boston: Houghton, Mifflin, 1903–1904), p. 302.

5. A joke that makes the point: A Catholic is marooned alone on a desert island. When he is finally discovered, the rescuers are amazed to find that the man has built a simple hut to live in, but next to it has also erected a magnificent church. They compliment him on his obvious deep and abiding faith, to which he replies, "Actually, I never go inside it—I like to sleep in on Sundays." A handy illustration of this point can be found in the attitudes of Catholics toward the difficult issue of abortion. Looking only at people who say they are "Catholics," we find that about a third favor the right of a woman to have an abortion for any reason— not far from the population average of 40 percent or so. The press regularly cites this fact as evidence that American Catholics are not

remarkably more pro-life than the rest of the public. But when we look only at Catholics who practice their faith regularly, support for abortion-on-demand drops to 10 percent. *Practicing* Catholics are, in point of fact, the most reliably pro-life group in America today. Similar findings on other attitudes and different religions all underscore the same point: Practice matters; affiliation does not. James A. Davis, Tom W. Smith, and Peter V. Marsden, principal investigators, *General Social Surveys, 1972–2004* [machine-readable data file] (Chicago: National Opinion Research Center [producer]; Storrs, Conn.: The Roper Center for Public Opinion Research, University of Connecticut [distributor], 2004).

6. 1972–2006 GSS. According to the 2004 GSS, 28 percent of Americans attend every week or more, whereas 39 percent attend once a year or less or have no religion. The 2000 Social Capital Community Benchmark Survey found that 33 percent attend every week, while 25 percent attend less than a few times per year or never. *Social Capital Community Benchmark Survey* (SCCBS) [machine-readable data file] (Cambridge, Mass.: Saguaro Seminar at the John F. Kennedy School of Government, Harvard University [producer]; Storrs, Conn.: The Roper Center for Public Opinion Research, University of Connecticut [distributor], 2000).

7. 2004 GSS.

8. 2000 SCCBS; 2004 GSS; Adam B. Cohen, "The Importance of Spirituality in Well-Being for Jews and Christians," *Journal of Happiness Studies* 3 (2002): 287–310. This study also contained data on fifty Jews, but there was too little variation in the data for the researchers to find statistically significant effects.

9. Katherine E. Wiegand and Howard M. Weiss, "Affective Reactions to the Thought of 'God': Moderating Effects of Image of God," *Journal of Happiness Studies* 7, no. 23 (2006): 23–40. In addition, regular churchgoers who feel "very close to God" are 27 percent more likely to be very happy than churchgoers who do not feel very close to God. This may have been the trouble for Mother Teresa. 2004 GSS.

10. Psychologists studying data on a sample of 200 Americans born in the 1920s found that by the time they were in their seventies, the two groups least afraid of dying were those who were "highly religious"

and those who were "not at all religious." P. Wink and M. Dillon, *Religion in Lives over Time: Tracking the Nature and Implications of Religion over Sixty Years of Life Course and Cultural Change*, unpublished manuscript (Durham: University of New Hampshire, 2007).

11. 1998 GSS. Thirty-six percent of those who were sure God existed were very happy, versus 28 percent who didn't believe in God, 12 percent who said there was no way to find out, 38 percent who said there was truth in one religion, and 20 percent who said there was little truth in any religion.

12. Thomas Bouchard, "The Genetics of Personality," in *Handbook of Psychiatric Genetics*, edited by K. Blum and E. P. Noble (Boca Raton, Fla.: CRC Press, 1997), pp. 273–296; H. H. Maes, M. C. Neale, N. G. Martin, A. C. Heath, and L. J. Eaves, "Religious Attendance and Frequency of Alcohol Use: Same Genes or Same Environments: A Bivariate Extended Twin Kinship Model," *Twin Research* 2 (1999): 169–179.

13. Robert D. Putnam, *Bowling Alone: The Collapse and Revival of American Community* (New York: Simon and Schuster, 2000), p. 333.

14. Jonathan Gruber, "Religious Market Structure, Religious Participation, and Outcomes: Is Religion Good for You?" National Bureau of Economic Research Working Paper 11377 (2005).

15. 2004 GSS. The quote from Saint Perpetua comes from Darrin M. McMahon, *Happiness: A History* (New York: Atlantic Monthly Press, 2006), p. 93.

16. George Bernard Shaw is widely quoted as saying, "The fact that a believer is happier than a skeptic is no more to the point than the fact that a drunken man is happier than a sober one. The happiness of credulity is a cheap and dangerous quality."

17. C. M. Cook and M. A. Persinger, "Experimental Induction of the 'Sensed Presence' in Normal Subjects and an Exceptional Subject," *Perceptual and Motor Skills* 85 (1997): 683–693; Steve Connor, "God Spot Is Found in Brain," *Los Angeles Times*, October 29, 1997.

18. Corry Azzi and Ronald Ehrenberg, "Household Allocation of Time and Church Attendance," *Journal of Political Economy* 83, no. 1 (1975): 27–56.

19. See Michael Betzold, "Appointment with Dr. Death" (Royal Oak, Mich.: Momentum Books, 1993); 2004 GSS.

20. 2004 GSS.

21. Arthur C. Brooks, "Philanthropy and the Nonprofit Sector," in *Understanding America,* edited by Peter Schuck and James Q. Wilson (New York: PublicAffairs, 2008): 539–562.

22. Pew Forum on Religion and Public Life, "Survey Shows Broad Public Support for the Displays," 2005, http://pewforum.org/publications/surveys/ten-commandments.pdf; 1998 GSS.

23. For this point about the Roman Catholic Church's monopoly in Spain and Italy, I am grateful to Larry Iannaccone.

24. 2006 GSS.

Chapter 3: Is Happiness a Family Value?

1. Carlos Brooks, the former Biter, will be eight years old in May 2008. He enjoys this anecdote and gave permission for me to use it.

2. James A. Davis, Tom W. Smith, and Peter V. Marsden, principal investigators, *General Social Surveys, 1972–2004* [machine-readable data file] (Chicago: National Opinion Research Center [producer]; Storrs, Conn.: The Roper Center for Public Opinion Research, University of Connecticut [distributor], 2004). Some economists have actually tried to put a monetary value on the happiness that people derive from marriage. The way they have done this is through the use of what economists call "shadow prices." These prices correspond to the amount of extra income an average person would have to earn to attain the same happiness boost that marriage brings. In 2002, two British economists estimated the annual value of marriage at $105,000. More importantly, they found that separation is equivalent to losing $255,000 per year. These high dollar amounts reflect not just the fact that marriage brings most people happiness, but also that it takes enormous amounts of money to change happiness levels much at all. The practical advice we can take home from these shadow prices is that if you have a choice of spending a few extra hours at work in search of higher pay or spending it cultivating your love life, you should nearly always take the latter option. Andrew E. Clark and Andrew J. Oswald, "A Simple Statistical Method for Measuring How Life Events Affect Happiness," *International Journal of Epidemiology* 31, no. 6 (2002): 1139–1144; Andrew E.

Clark and Andrew J. Oswald, "Satisfaction and Comparison Income," *Journal of Public Economics* 61 (1996): 359–381.

3. 2004 GSS. This regresses the "very happy" dummy on the full vector of demographics as well as a group of dummies for various marital statuses, using a probit model and assessing the marginal coefficient on "married." It is worth noting that in this model, "never married" does not differ significantly from divorced or widowed.

4. 2004 GSS.

5. R. E. Lucas, A. E. Clark, Y. Georgellis, and E. Diener, "Reexamining Adaptation and the Setpoint Model of Happiness: Reactions to Changes in Marital Status," *Journal of Personality and Social Psychology* 84 (2003): 527–539. This article finds that in some cases, after the happiness bounce from marriage wears off, people end up at a lower baseline happiness level than when they were single. No doubt this happens in cases of bad marriages, which we will discuss in a moment.

6. Daniel Nettle, *Happiness: The Science Behind Your Smile* (Oxford: Oxford University Press, 2005), p. 79; 2004 GSS.

7. D. T. Lichter, Z.-C. Qian, and L. Mellott, "Marriage or Dissolution? Transitions to Marriage Among Poor Cohabiting Women," Demography 43, no. 2 (2006): 223–240; Robert E. Rector, Patrick F. Fagan, and Kirk A. Johnson, "Marriage: Still the Safest Place for Women and Children," Heritage Foundation Backgrounder #1732 (2004).

8. 2004 GSS.

9. Tara Parker-Pope, "Quality of Marriage: Marital Stress May Be Harmful to Health," *Wall Street Journal,* May 20, 2004.

10. Daniel Gilbert nicely summarized these studies in *Stumbling on Happiness* (New York: Knopf, 2006), p. 225.

11. David Crary, "Key to a Good Marriage? Share Housework," Associated Press, July 1, 2007; 1990, 2004 GSS.

12. 2004 GSS. This model regresses a dummy for "very happy" on another for children and a vector of demographics.

13. 2004 GSS. This analysis regresses a measure of happiness on a scale from one to three, on a linear and quadratic term for children in the household as well as a full vector of demographic controls, using Ordinary Least Squares. The linear term is negative, while the quadratic term

is positive, suggesting that happiness is convexly negative in kids. I then differentiate the fitted equation, set the first-order condition to zero, and solve for the critical value of children, which is a global minimum.

14. *Social Capital Community Benchmark Survey* (SCCBS) [machine-readable data file] (Cambridge, Mass.: Saguaro Seminar at the John F. Kennedy School of Government, Harvard University [producer]; Storrs, Conn.: The Roper Center for Public Opinion Research, University of Connecticut [distributor], 2000). This considers families in which the parents are forty and under.

15. Daniel Kahneman, Alan B. Krueger, David A. Schkade, Norbert Schwarz, and Arthur A. Stone, "A Survey Method for Characterizing Daily Life Experience: The Day Reconstruction Method," *Science* 306, no. 5702 (2004): 1776–1780. The data did not distinguish between children of different ages, although the children were obviously living at home with their parents.

16. Martin Pinquart and Silvia Sorenson, "Influences of Socioeconomic Status, Social Network, and Competence on Subjective Well-Being Later in Life: A Meta-Analysis," *Psychology and Aging* 15, no. 2 (2000): 187–224.

17. 2004 GSS. Thirty-five percent of seniors with kids said they were very happy, versus 29 percent without kids. But regressing a dummy for "very happy" on a dummy variable for kids and a vector of demographic controls, using a probit estimation, yields an insignificant coefficient (p – 0.53) on the *children* dummy; Zhenmei Zhang and Mark D. Hayward, "Childlessness and the Psychological Well-Being of Older Persons," *Journals of Gerontology,* Series B: *Psychological Sciences and Social Sciences* 56 (2001): S311–S320; T. Koropeckyj-Cox, "Loneliness and Depression in Middle and Old Age: Are the Childless More Vulnerable?" *Journals of Gerontology,* Series B: *Psychological Sciences and Social Sciences* 53, no. 6 (1998): S303–S312.

18. 2004 GSS. The marginal effects of children and unconditional love work in the opposite direction from each other.

19. H. B. Gerard and G. C. Mathewson, "The Effects of Severity of Initiation on Liking for a Group: A Replication," *Journal of Experimental Social Psychology* 2 (1966): 278–287.

20. 2004 GSS.

21. See Deborah Blum, *Love at Goon Park: Harry Harlow and the Science of Affection* (Cambridge, Mass.: Perseus, 2002).

22. Robert Haveman and Barbara Wolfe, "The Determinants of Children's Attainments: A Review of Methods and Findings," *Journal of Economic Literature* 33, no. 4 (1995): 1829–1878.

23. Jocelyn Noveck and Trevor Tompson, "AP/MTV Poll: Happiness for America's Young People Often Means Family Ties, Faith, Belonging," Associated Press, August 20, 2007.

24. Kahneman et al., "Survey Method for Characterizing Daily Life Experience."

25. 2000 SCCBS.

26. Robert D. Putnam discussed many of the quality-of-life differences between socially connected communities and those where people are isolated in his book *Bowling Alone: The Collapse and Revival of American Community* (New York: Simon and Schuster, 2000).

27. L. L. Pearlin, M. A. Lieberman, E. G. Menaghan, and J. T. Mullan, "The Stress Process," *Journal of Health and Social Behavior* 22 (1981): 337–356; P. Cohen, E. Struening, G. Muhlin, L. Genevie, S. Kaplan, and H. Peck, "Community Stressors, Mediating Conditions and Well-Being in Urban Neighborhoods," *Journal of Community Psychology* 10 (1982): 377–391.

28. Similarly incorrectly, Arthur Schopenhauer said, "Loneliness is better than human company." Quoted in Wladyslaw Tatarkiewicz, *Analysis of Happiness* (The Hague: Martinus Nijhoff, 1976), p. 223.

29. Brendan Conway, "Europe Today," *Washington Times,* July 24, 2005; George Weigel, *The Cube and the Cathedral* (New York: Basic Books, 2005), p. 22; Patrick Festy, "Looking for European Demography, Desperately?" Population Division, Department of Economic and Social Affairs, United Nations, 2000 http://www.un.org/esa/population/publications/popdecline/festy.pdf.

30. Steven Ozment, "Diminishing Europe: The Good Life in Germany Does Not Include Children," *Weekly Standard* 13, no. 4 (October 8, 2007): 42; Pope Benedict XVI put it this way: "Europe is infected by a strange lack of desire for the future. Children, our future, are perceived as a threat to the present, as if they were taking something away

from our lives. Children are seen as a liability rather than as a source of hope." Joseph Ratzinger (now Pope Benedict XVI) and Marcello Pera, *Without Roots: The West, Relativism, Christianity, Islam,* translated by Michael F. Moore, with a Foreword by George Weigel (New York: Basic Books, 2006).

31. 2006 GSS.

32. 2004 GSS.

33. Tom Herman, "Marriage Penalty Expected to Ensnare More Couples," Associated Press, April 11, 2007.

34. See James Q. Wilson, *The Marriage Problem: How Our Culture Has Weakened Families* (New York: HarperCollins, 2002).

35. U.S. Bureau of the Census, "Poverty in the United States" (1999); U.S. Bureau of the Census, "Income, Poverty, and Health Insurance Coverage" (2003). The welfare reform legislation was called the Personal Responsibility and Work Opportunity Reconciliation Act (PRWORA) of 1996. The government no longer required recipients to be unmarried and unemployed. The main welfare program's name changed from Aid to Families with Dependent Children (AFDC) to Temporary Aid to Needy Families (TANF).

36. Ronald Lee and Tim Miller, "Population Policy and Externalities to Childbearing," *Annals of the American Academy of Political and Social Science* 510 (1990): 17–32.

Chapter 4: Staying Happy in the Age of Freedom and Insecurity

1. Armando Valladares, *Contra Toda Esperanza* (Madrid: Plaza and Janes, 1985).

2. This statistic on political prisoners renouncing their freedom comes from an introduction of Armando Valladares at an awards ceremony in 2003. See http://www.newsmax.com/archives/articles/2003/12/4/173407.shtml.

3. Johannes L. Jacobse, "The Patriarch and Fidel," Orthodoxy Today.org, February 5, 2004. In "'Pastors for Peace' Continue Support for Castro," *Presbyterian Layman,* April 14, 1999 (http://www.layman.org/layman/news/news-around-church/pastors-for-castro.htm), Mark Tooley of the Institute on Religion and Democracy reported on an

American delegation to Cuba led by a Baptist minister and former executive of the NCC that included several members of the U.S. Congress. In the minister's words, "I would be honored to have a person like Fidel as president of my own country." See also Digital Freedom Network, "Survivors of Tyranny" 2007, http://unix.dfn.org/printer _ArmandoValladares.shtml.

4. James A. Davis, Tom W. Smith, and Peter V. Marsden, principal investigators, *General Social Surveys, 1972–2004* [machine-readable data file] (Chicago: National Opinion Research Center [producer]; Storrs, Conn.: The Roper Center for Public Opinion Research, University of Connecticut [distributor], 2004). The GSS data used here are from the 2000 survey.

5. The English saying comes from J. Rufus Fears, "Freedom: The History of an Idea," Foreign Policy Research Institute's *Footnotes* 12, no. 19 (2007). As Thomas Jefferson put it, specifically in the context of the state, "a wise and frugal Government, which shall restrain men from injuring one another, shall leave them otherwise free to regulate their own pursuits of industry and improvement, and shall not take from the mouth of labor the bread it has earned." Thomas Jefferson, "The First Inaugural Address, 1801," in *The Complete Thomas Jefferson,* edited by Samuel K. Padover (New York: Tudor, 1943 [1801]).

6. In a 1934 fireside chat, Franklin Delano Roosevelt explicitly expanded "freedom" to encompass the welfare state: "I prefer and I am sure you prefer that broader definition of liberty under which we are moving forward to greater freedom, to greater security for the average man than he has ever known before in the history of America." Quoted in Peter D. McClelland, *The American Search for Economic Justice* (Cambridge, Mass.: Basil Blackwell, 1990), p. 110.

7. 2000 GSS. Traditionally, "freedom" and "liberty" are not equivalent, although occasionally they are used interchangeably. Freedom is an absence of constraints, while liberty is the absence of deliberative and coercive acts, usually by the government. In this discussion, I do not make much of this distinction for the sake of the exposition. President Lyndon B. Johnson, a clear philosophical follower of Roosevelt's concept of "freedom to" as opposed to "freedom from," clearly understood most Americans' definition when he told an audience in 1965

that "freedom is not enough"—we also must be given tangible things from others and the government. Lyndon B. Johnson, "To Fulfill These Rights," Commencement Address at Howard University, 1965.

8. 2000 GSS. This analysis regresses a dummy for "completely free" or "very free" on a full set of demographics, using a probit model.

9. Ibid. This regresses a dummy for saying "completely free" or "very free" on a vector of demographics, using a probit model. The coefficients are estimated at the average levels of the regressors.

10. Ibid. Unmarried women with kids feel less free than women without kids, but they still feel freer than secularist women.

11. 2000 GSS. This regresses a dummy for saying "very happy" on a dummy for feeling "completely free" or "very free" as well as all the listed demographics, using a probit model. The coefficients are estimated at the average levels of the regressors.

12. Ellen J. Langer and Judith Rodin, "The Effects of Choice and Enhanced Personal Responsibility for the Aged: A Field Experiment in an Institutional Setting," *Journal of Personality and Social Psychology* 34 (1976): 191–198.

13. 1996, 2004 GSS.

14. The index used here is the 2007 Index of Economic Freedom, created by the *Wall Street Journal* and the Heritage Foundation. The scores are based on laws governing economic freedom and their level of enforcement. See http://www.heritage.org/research/features/index/ about.cfm. The index measures economic freedom as a percentage; I have converted that to a 1–100 scale for ease of exposition. This analysis regresses the percentage of the population in thirty-three countries who said they were completely happy or very happy in the 2002 International Social Survey Programme data on the economic freedom scores from 2007. The regression is Ordinary Least Squares; the coefficient on economic freedom is 1.75 and highly statistically significant. International Social Survey Program (ISSP), Zentralarchiv für Empirische Sozialforschung, *International Social Survey Programme*, 2002.

15. See Serge A. Mikoyan, "Eroding the Soviet Culture of Secrecy: Studies in Intelligence," no. 11 (2001), Central Intelligence Agency, https://www.cia.gov/library/center-for-the-study-of-intelligence/csi -publications/csi-studies/studies/ fall_winter_2001/article05.html.

16. The "very happy" answer in the World Values Survey (WVS) is higher than that found in the General Social Survey, European and World Values Surveys Four-Wave Integrated Data File, 1981–2004, v. 20060423 (2006), European Values Study Foundation and World Values Survey Association, Aggregate File Producers: ASEP/JDS, Madrid, Spain; Tilburg University, Tilburg, the Netherlands (Aggregate File Distributors: ASEP/JDS and ZA, Cologne, Germany).

17. Bruno S. Frey and Alois Stutzer, "Happiness Prospers in Democracy," *Journal of Happiness Studies* 1 (2000): 79–102.

18. 2006 GSS.

19. 1998, 2000 GSS.

20. According to Durkheim, "At the very moment that . . . [the egoist] frees himself from the social environment, he still submits to its influence. However individualized a man may be, there is always something collective remaining—the very depression and melancholy resulting from this same exaggerated individualism. He effects communion through sadness when he no longer has anything else with which to achieve it." Émile Durkheim, *Suicide: A Study in Sociology* (New York: The Free Press, 1951 [1897]), p. 214.

21. 1998, 2004 GSS.

22. Ibid.

23. Barry Schwartz, *The Paradox of Choice: Why More Is Less* (New York: HarperCollins, 2004).

24. S. S. Iyengar, and M. R. Lepper, "When Choice Is Demotivating: Can One Desire Too Much of a Good Thing? *Journal of Personality and Social Psychology* 79 (2000): 995–1006.

25. Albert Einstein, Banesh Hoffman, and Helen Dukas, *Albert Einstein, the Human Side* (Trenton, N.J.: Princeton University Press, 1981).

26. Arthur C. Brooks, "Drink More, Earn More (& Give More)," *Wall Street Journal,* July 13, 2005, p. A14.

27. Thomas Jefferson made this point explicitly in the context of happiness when he said that "to close the circle of felicities" required the government to "restrain men from injuring one another." Thomas Jefferson, "The First Inaugural Address, 1801," in Padover, ed., *The Complete Thomas Jefferson.*

28. Abortion rights advocates frequently characterize the "pro-life movement" as one that seeks merely to impose private morality on other individuals, charging that it thus does not respect freedom. This argument is deeply mistaken. Of course, it is possible for reasonable people to disagree about when personhood deserving protected status begins, which is why people disagree about when abortion should be allowed: A minority would criminalize the practice at the moment of conception; others would prohibit it after the first trimester of pregnancy; and a large majority would criminalize it after the baby is viable. These are honest differences about when a fetus becomes a human.

29. "California Lawmaker Seeks to Ban the Spanking of Children Under 4 Years Old," Associated Press, January 20, 2007; Melissa Beecher, "Spanking a Sore Subject in Arlington," *Boston Globe,* Globe Northwest, March 26, 2006, p. 3.

30. Arthur C. Brooks, *Social Entrepreneurship: A Modern Approach to Social Value Creation* (Upper Saddle River, N.J.: Prentice-Hall, Forthcoming).

31. John D. Gartner, *The Hypomanic Edge: The Link Between (A Little) Craziness and (A Lot of) Success in America* (New York: Simon and Schuster, 2005).

32. For data on passengers, see http://www.transtats.bts.gov; Veronique de Rugy, "TSA Disaster," National Review Online, May 5, 2005, http://www.nationalreview.com/comment/de_rugy200505050751.asp.

33. William F. Buckley, "Security in the Air," *National Review* 53, no. 24 (December 17, 2001), p. 62; de Rugy, "TSA Disaster"; "TSA Relaxes Rules on Lighters, Breast Milk," Associated Press, August 19, 2007.

34. 2000 GSS. This conclusion comes from regressing a measure of happiness on measures of personal freedom, perceived societal freedom, and demographics. Personal freedom pushes happiness up while perceived societal freedom has no statistically significant impact on happiness.

Chapter 5: Does Money Buy Happiness?

1. Susan Vela, "Big Powerball Winners Check In, Punch Out," *Cincinnati Enquirer,* July 27, 2000; James Dao, "Instant Millions Can't

Halt Winners' Grim Slide," *New York Times*, December 5, 2005; "Powerball Winner Moving to Australia," *Kentucky Post*, July 27, 2000.

2. "For Lottery Winners, Trouble Followed Fortune," *USA Today*, November 28, 2005.

3. In the words of King Solomon, "I amassed silver and gold for myself, and the treasure of kings and provinces. . . . Yet when I surveyed all that my hands had done and what I had toiled to achieve, everything was meaningless, a chasing after the wind; nothing was gained under the sun." Ecclesiastes 2: 8–11. Or as Abd Er-Rahman III, the Moorish ruler of Spain in A.D. 960, poignantly put it, "I have now reigned about 50 years in victory or peace, beloved by my subjects, dreaded by my enemies, and respected by my allies. Riches and honors, power and pleasure, have waited on my call, nor does any earthly blessing appear to have been wanting to my felicity. In this situation, I have diligently numbered the days of pure and genuine happiness which have fallen to my lot. They amount to fourteen." Edward Gibbon used this quotation in *The Decline and Fall of the Roman Empire* (New York: Modern Library, 2003[1776–1788]), ch. 52.

4. James A. Davis, Tom W. Smith, and Peter V. Marsden, principal investigators, *General Social Surveys, 1972–2004* [machine-readable data file] (Chicago: National Opinion Research Center [producer]; Storrs, Conn.: The Roper Center for Public Opinion Research, University of Connecticut [distributor], 2004). All figures are inflation-adjusted to 2004 prices. The analysis involves regressing the percentage of respondents saying they are "very happy" on the real per capita gross domestic product (GDP) and a time trend intended to capture nonincome effects. The data are annual or semi-annual (twenty-five surveys conducted between 1972 and 2004), and the regressions are executed using Ordinary Least Squares. The coefficient on income is significant at the 5 percent level ($p = 0.05$).

5. Richard A. Easterlin, "The Worldwide Standard of Living Since 1800," *Journal of Economic Perspectives* 14, no. 1 (2000): 7–26.

6. Carol Graham and Stefano Pettinato, "Frustrated Achievers: Winners, Losers, and Subjective Well-Being in New Market Economies," *Journal of Development Studies* 38, no. 4 (2002): 100–140. Data

on Russian happiness: International Social Survey Program (ISSP), Zentralarchiv für Empirische Sozialforschung, *International Social Survey Programme,* 2002. In these data, 21 percent of Russians reported feeling very happy or completely happy.

7. BBC News, "Denmark 'Happiest Place on Earth,'" July 28, 2006, http://news.bbc.co.uk/go/pr/fr/-/1/hi/health/ 5224306.stm. According to economists Bruno S. Frey and Alois Stutzer in "What Can Economists Learn from Happiness Research?" *Journal of Economic Literature* 40, no. 2 (2002), "Income provides happiness at low levels of development but once a threshold . . . is reached, the average income level has little effect on average subjective well-being" (p. 416). One study by a prominent economist appears to refute this finding, showing that income increases raise happiness among rich nations as well as among poor ones. See Angus Deaton, "Income, Aging, Health and Well-Being Around the World: Evidence from the Gallup World Poll," National Bureau of Economic Research working paper 13317 (2007).

8. World Bank, 2005; World Development Indicators 2005 (Washington, D.C.: World Bank, 2005).

9. *Social Capital Community Benchmark Survey* (SCCBS) [machine-readable data file] (Cambridge, Mass.: Saguaro Seminar at the John F. Kennedy School of Government, Harvard University [producer]; Storrs, Conn.: The Roper Center for Public Opinion Research, University of Connecticut [distributor], 2000). The analysis regresses the percentage of the population that is "very happy" on the average household income in each community, using Ordinary Least Squares. Obviously, there are hungry people in America, a problem I do not intend to minimize. But the evidence suggests that sub-subsistence life in America and other developed countries has to do with problems other than underdevelopment and famine. The data on disposable income are from the Bureau of Economic Analysis, http://www.bea.gov/papers/pdf/DPI_MSA_Dunbar.pdf.

10. Philip Brickman, Dan Coates, and Ronnie Janoff-Bulman, "Lottery Winners and Accident Victims: Is Happiness Relative?" *Journal of Personality and Social Psychology* 36, no. 8 (1978): 917–927.

11. Panel Study of Income Dynamics (PSID), Wave XXXII Computer File (Ann Arbor, Mich.: ICPSR, 2001), http://simba.isr.umich.edu. This

analysis regresses (using a probit model) the likelihood of saying one was "inconsolably sad" over the past month on income, wealth, and a full vector of demographics. The income and wealth effects were estimated in separate models; when both are included, income is significant only at the 10 percent level ($p = 0.1$).

12. Adam Smith, *The Theory of Moral Sentiments* (Oxford: Oxford University Press, 1976[1759]), p. 149.

13. Richard Easterlin, "Explaining Happiness," *Proceedings of the National Academy of Sciences* 100, no. 19 (September 16, 2003): 11176–11183.

14. Bernard M. S. Van Praag and Paul Frijters, "The Measurement of Welfare and Well-Being," in *Well-Being: The Foundations of Hedonic Psychology*, edited by Daniel Kahneman, Ed Diener, and Norbert Schwarz (New York: Russell Sage, 1999), pp. 413–433.

15. Jon Gertner, "The Futile Pursuit of Happiness," *New York Times*, September 7, 2003.

16. Frey and Stutzer, "What Can Economists Learn from Happiness Research?"

17. Amos Tversky and Dale Griffin, "Endowment and Contrast in Judgments of Well-Being," in *Strategy and Choice*, edited by Richard Zeckhauser (Cambridge, Mass.: MIT Press, 1991), pp. 297–319.

18. S. Solnick and D. Hemenway, "Is More Always Better? A Survey on Positional Concerns," *Journal of Economic Behavior and Organization* 37 (1998): 373–383.

19. 1996 GSS. This analysis uses a probit estimation to model the likelihood of saying one is "very happy" on a dummy variable indicating one feels "very successful" or "completely successful," income, and the other demographics listed. The coefficients are evaluated at the margin using the mean value of the regressors.

20. But of course, it is unlikely that we will be equally successful if you make four times more than me: People who feel successful earn about a third more than others, on average.

21. Luisa Kroll and Allison Fass, "The World's Billionaires," *Forbes*, March 8, 2007, http://www.forbes.com/2007/03/07/billionaires-worlds-richest_07billionaires_cz_lk_af_0308billie_land.html; Austan Goolsbee, "For the Super-Rich, Too Much Is Never Enough," *New York Times*, March 1, 2007.

22. U.S. Securities and Exchange Commission Form 10-K (2006), http://www.oracle.com/corporate/ investor_relations/10k–2006.pdf.

23. In one study of New York City high schools, one researcher found that students whose first language was not English (who chronically score below average on tests) were frequently being taught test preparation instead of a standard English as a Second Language (ESL) curriculum. See Kate Menken, "Teaching to the Test: How No Child Left Behind Impacts Language Policy, Curriculum, and Instruction for English Language Learners," *Bilingual Research Journal* 30, no. 2 (2006): 521–546.

24. Charles Clotfelter and Philip Cook, *Selling Hope: State Lotteries in America* (Cambridge: Harvard University Press, 1989).

25. Robert H. Frank, *Luxury Fever: Money and Happiness in an Era of Excess* (Princeton, N.J.: Princeton University Press, 2000); Robert H. Frank, "Our Climb to Sublime; Hold On. We Don't Need to Go There," *Washington Post,* January 24, 1999, p. B01.

26. *Statistical Abstract of the United States* (Washington, D.C.: Government Printing Office, various years); 1972–2002 GSS. In this analysis, the percentage of the population saying it is "not too happy" is regressed on GDP per capita, government spending per capita, and a time trend, using Ordinary Least Squares.

27. Alexis de Tocqueville, *Democracy in America,* vol. 1 (New York: Vintage Books, 1945[1835]), p. 104.

28. The editors of *The Economist* put it nicely: "Capitalism can make you well off. And it also leaves you free to be as unhappy as you choose. To ask any more would be asking too much." "Happiness (and How to Measure it)," *The Economist,* December 23, 2006, p. 13.

Chapter 6: Inequality and (Un)happiness in America

1. The figures in this section come from the U.S. Census Historical Income tables. Inflation is neutralized with the chain-weighted price index from the *Statistical Abstract of the United States* (Washington, D.C.: Government Printing Office, various years). While looking at income quintiles is conventional, breaking up income groups using other cut points produces the same conclusions.

2. James A. Davis, Tom W. Smith, and Peter V. Marsden, principal investigators, *General Social Surveys, 1972–2004* [machine-readable data file] (Chicago: National Opinion Research Center [producer]; Storrs, Conn.: The Roper Center for Public Opinion Research, University of Connecticut [distributor], 2004); U.S. Census Bureau, http://www.census.gov/hhes/www/income/histinc/f04.html.

3. The quote by John Edwards comes from a speech he delivered on December 29, 2003, in Des Moines, Iowa. See http://www.gazette online.com/iowacaucus/candidate_news/edwards64.aspx.

4. Arthur C. Brooks, "The Left's 'Inequality' Obsession," *Wall Street Journal,* July 19, 2007, p. A16.

5. GSS 1972–2004; *Statistical Abstract of the United States* (various years).

6. *Social Capital Community Benchmark Survey* (SCCBS) [machine-readable data file] (Cambridge, Mass.: Saguaro Seminar at the John F. Kennedy School of Government, Harvard University [producer]; Storrs, Conn.: The Roper Center for Public Opinion Research, University of Connecticut [distributor], 2000). I regressed the percentage saying in each family that they were "very happy" on the income variance in each community as well as on the mean income level in each community. The coefficient on the variance was insignificant; the mean income level, in contrast, was significant, at the 10 percent level.

7. Campbell Public Affairs Institute, The Maxwell Poll on Civic Engagement and Inequality [dataset] (Syracuse, N.Y.: Maxwell School of Citizenship and Public Affairs, 2006).

8. According to the U.S. Basic Income Guarantee Network, a group of academics dedicated to achieving greater income equality in America, "equal citizenship is the overriding justification for moving along a path of decreasing income inequality among all persons." U.S. Basic Income Guarantee Network, "Unequal Income Is Unequal Citizenship: The Case Against Income Inequality," USBIG Discussion Paper No. 67, 2004.

9. This economist, Richard Layard, wrote: "If we make taxes commensurate to the damage that an individual does to others when he earns more, then he will only work harder if there is a true net benefit

to society as a whole. It is efficient to discourage work effort that makes society worse off." Richard Layard, *Happiness: Lessons from a New Science* (New York: Penguin Press, 2005), p. 228.

10. Vicente Navarro, *The Political Economy of Social Inequalities: Consequences for Health and Quality of Life* (Amityville, N.Y.: Baywood, 2000).

11. Maxwell Poll 2005.

12. Ibid. These results are based on probit models in which the beliefs about inequality are regressed on beliefs about the importance of work and perseverance, as well as a vector of the demographics listed. The marginal coefficients are estimated at the mean values of the regressors.

13. 2004 GSS.

14. John Mirowsky and Catherine E. Ross, "Aging, Status, and Sense of Control (ASOC), 1995, 1998, 2001," Computer file ICPSR03334-v2 (Columbus: Ohio State University [producer], 2001; Ann Arbor, Mich.: Inter-University Consortium for Political and Social Research [distributor], 2005–12–15). In this study, people were asked whether they agreed or disagreed with the statement that they were responsible for their own successes. Those who "agreed" or "agreed strongly" said they felt sad, on average, 0.96 days per week. Those who "disagreed" or "disagreed strongly" were sad an average of 1.2 days per week.

15. 2004 GSS. To measure the actual inequality people experience, we compare their income with that of others of their same sex, age, and education level—what economists call their "reference group." This analysis regresses a dummy variable indicating that someone says he or she is "very happy" on household income, the absolute distance of income to the reference income, the amount by which income exceeds (or falls short of) the reference, a dummy for a response that the person agrees that he or she has a good chance of improving living standards, and a vector of demographics. The marginal effects are estimated as the probit coefficients evaluated at the mean values of the regressors. Models in which each income measure is estimated separately (to ensure against collinearity problems in the full model) produce virtually identical results.

16. Andrew E. Clark, "Inequality-Aversion and Income Mobility: A Direct Test," Centre National de la Recherche Scientifique (CNRS) and Department and Laboratory of Applied and Theoretical Economics

(DELTA)–Fédération Jourdan Working Paper 2003–11 (2003); Claudia Senik, "What Can We Learn from Subjective Data? The Case of Income and Well-Being," CNRS and DELTA–Fédération Jourdan Working Paper 2003–06 (2003).

17. 2002 GSS.

18. As Irving Kristol put it, "The problem with our current welfare programs is not that they are costly—which they are—but that they have such perverse consequences for people they are supposed to benefit." Irving Kristol, "A Conservative Welfare State," *Wall Street Journal,* June 14, 1993.

19. George Orwell, *1984* (New York: New American Library, 1983), p. 40; Darrin M. McMahon, *Happiness: A History* (New York: Atlantic Monthly Press, 2006), p. 403.

20. *CIA Factbook,* 2007, https://www.cia.gov/library/publications/the-world-factbook/fields/2172.html. I calculate Gini coefficients by applying standard methods to the data on frequency of prayer, the response to questions about sacrificing for others, the degree of expressed optimism about life, and happiness, in the 2004 GSS. Of course, these indices can be rescaled in many ways that affect the Gini coefficients, but doing so in reasonable ways does not change the central point here in any material way.

21. Christopher Jencks, *Inequality: A Reassessment of the Effect of Family and Schooling in America* (New York: Basic Books, 1972). Jencks's work grew out of James S. Coleman's 1966 "Coleman Report" ("Equality of Educational Opportunity [Coleman] Study [EEOS]" [Washington, D.C.: U.S. Department of Health, Education, and Welfare, Office of Education/National Center for Education Statistics, 1966].)

22. Bruce Bartlett, "Income Mobility Belies Liberal Myth," National Center for Policy Analysis, August 23, 2000, http://www.ncpa.org/oped/bartlett/aug2300.html; "Movin' On Up" (editorial), *Wall Street Journal,* November 13, 2007, p. A24.

23. 2005 Maxwell Poll.

24. Ibid. These results are based on a probit model in which the beliefs about the importance of hard work are regressed on political views as well as a vector of demographics. The marginal coefficients are estimated at the mean values of the regressors.

25. Democratic National Committee, "Stop the Diversionary Tactics and Raise the Minimum Wage!" 2006, http://www.democrats.org/a/2006/08/stop_the_divers.php.

26. Stefan Klein describes this study in his book *The Science of Happiness: How Our Brains Make Us Happy—And What We Can Do to Get Happier* (New York: Marlowe, 2006), p. 185.

Chapter 7: Happiness Is a Full-Time Job

1. Marie Jahoda, Paul F. Lazarsfeld, Hans Zeisel, and Christian Fleck, *Marienthal: The Sociography of an Unemployed Community* (Chicago: Aldine, Atherton, 2002).

2. Ibid., pp. 37, 38, 71.

3. Ibid., p. 88.

4. These data are taken from the Organisation for Economic Co-operation and Development (OECD) Productivity Database, September 2006. They refer to the average number of hours worked annually per worker. See also Harry Mount, "Take a Holiday, Companies Tell Worried American Workaholics," *The Telegraph* (U.K.), August 21, 2006; Sarah Harper, "Late Life Work, Retirement, and Social Security for Women," in *Baby Boomer Women: Secure Futures or Not?* edited by Paul Hodge (Cambridge, Mass.: Global Generations Policy Initiative, 2006), pp. 93–98; and Sveinbjörn Blöndal and Stefano Scarpetta, "The Retirement Decision in OECD Countries," Economics Department Working Papers, No. 202 (Paris: Organisation for Economic Co-operation and Development, 1999).

5. Michael Elliott, "Europeans Just Want to Have Fun," *Time*, July 28, 2003.

6. Barbara Ehrenreich, *Nickel and Dimed* (New York: Metropolitan Books, 2001); James A. Davis, Tom W. Smith, and Peter V. Marsden, principal investigators, *General Social Surveys, 1972–2004* [machine-readable data file] (Chicago: National Opinion Research Center [producer]; Storrs, Conn.: The Roper Center for Public Opinion Research, University of Connecticut [distributor], 2004).

7. 2002 GSS. The "average income" used here corresponds to the adult population income mean.

8. Ibid. The "average income" used here corresponds to the adult population income mean. Daniel Kahneman, Alan B. Krueger, David A. Schkade, Norbert Schwarz, and Arthur A. Stone, "A Survey Method for Characterizing Daily Life Experience: The Day Reconstruction Method," *Science* 306, no. 5702 (2004): 1776–1780.

9. 2002 GSS.

10. 1998 GSS; Panel Study of Income Dynamics (PSID), Wave XXXII Computer File (Ann Arbor, Mich.: ICPSR, 2001), http:// simba.isr.umich.edu. Unlike money, leisure time does not seem to be related to social status—that is, people do not appear to gain any status from the amount of leisure time they enjoy. Recall the Harvard University study I described in Chapter 5 in which people were asked if they would prefer to earn $50,000 per year while everyone else earned $25,000, or $100,000 per year while others made $200,000. People tended to prefer the former. In the same study, the researchers also asked their subjects whether they would prefer two weeks of vacation when others had one week, or four weeks when others had eight. Only 18 percent picked the first option. S. Solnick and D. Hemenway, "Is More Always Better? A Survey on Positional Concerns," *Journal of Economic Behavior and Organization* 37 (1998): 373–383.

11. 2002 GSS. The probit model described regresses a dummy for a response of "very happy" on a dummy for reporting being very satisfied or somewhat satisfied with one's job, plus all the demographics listed. The coefficients are evaluated at the margin using the mean values of the covariates.

12. How do we know that job satisfaction pushes happiness up? The procedure to test this hypothesis uses a full-information maximum likelihood tobit model. I regress a 0–2 measure of happiness on a measure of job satisfaction and a vector of demographics; the instrument for job satisfaction is a measure of whether someone says his or her main source of satisfaction in life comes from work, which is strongly correlated with job satisfaction but largely uncorrelated with general happiness. The resulting coefficient on the predicted value of job satisfaction is large, positive, and significant. The appendix details this model.

13. Statistics bear out Frankl's beliefs. Indeed, when people were asked to rate on a scale of 1–7 the importance of getting a sense of meaning from a job, 84 percent of workers gave it a 6 or 7. 1982 GSS.

14. Victor Frankl, *Man's Search for Meaning* (New York: Pocket Books, 1984), p. 69.

15. For example, in 1928, the founder of the Roman Catholic movement Opus Dei, or "Work of God," taught that work can be a kind of prayer, advising his followers, "Put a supernatural meaning behind your ordinary work, and you will have sanctified your work." Josemaría Escrivá, *The Way (El Camino)* (London: Scepter, 2001), p. 135.

16. 2002 GSS.

17. Edward L. Deci and Richard M. Ryan, *Intrinsic Motivation and Self-Determination in Human Behavior* (New York: Plenum Press, 1985).

18. Mihaly Csikszentmihalyi, *Flow: The Psychology of Optimal Experience* (New York: HarperPerennial, 1990).

19. See Charles Murray's excellent discussion of the balance between challenge and ability in predicting flow in Charles Murray, *In Pursuit of Happiness and Good Government* (New York: Simon and Schuster, 1988). For the Aristotelian Principle, see Edward Banfield, Allan Bloom, and Charles Murray, "The Pursuit of Happiness: Then and Now," *Public Opinion* (May/June 1988), p. 42.

20. According to some of the most authoritative psychological research on the subject, people have an "intrinsic need to be self-determining." Deci and Ryan, *Intrinsic Motivation*, p. 107.

21. 2002 GSS; 2001 PSID. This analysis regresses measures of happiness on a dummy for at least a month of unemployment in the past decade and a full vector of demographics.

22. 2002 GSS. While 41 percent who say it is not at all true that their job security is good say they are not too satisfied or not at all satisfied with their jobs, only 6 percent of workers who say it is very true that they enjoy good job security give this response. Rafael Di Tella, Robert J. MacCulloch, and Andrew J. Oswald, "Preferences over Inflation and Unemployment: Evidence from Surveys of Happiness," *American Economic Review* 91, no. 1 (2001): 335–341; David G. Blanchflower, "Is

Unemployment More Costly Than Inflation?" National Bureau of Economic Research Working Paper No. 13505 (2007).

23. 2002 GSS. In a regression of a measure of happiness on a dummy for retired status and a full vector of demographics, the coefficient on retirement actually becomes positive, although not significant at a high level.

24. 2001 PSID.

25. Ibid. The conclusion here is reached via a probit model of a dummy variable for saying one has been inconsolable over the past month on a vector of demographics and dummies for welfare receipt and unemployment.

26. See D. S. Hiroto, "Locus of Control and Learned Helplessness," *Journal of Experimental Psychology* 102 (1974): 187–193.

27. 2002 GSS.

28. Ibid.

29. Ibid.

30. Corporate Leadership Council, *Employee Retention: New Tools for Managing Workforce Stability and Engagement* (Washington, D.C.: Corporate Executive Board, 1998).

31. Mount, "Take a Holiday."

32. Arthur C. Brooks, "Right-Wing Heart, Left-Wing Heart," April 11, 2006, CBSNEWS.com.

33. 2002 ISSP.

34. Richard Layard, *Happiness: Lessons from a New Science* (New York: Penguin Press, 2005), p. 174.

Chapter 8: The Secret to Buying Happiness

1. Lynn Franey, "KC's Secret Santa revealed," *Kansas City Star*, February 23, 2007.

2. Associated Press, "Illness Unmasks Generous 'Secret Santa,'" November 16, 2006.

3. Lynn Franey, "Secret Santa Larry Stewart Dies at 58," *Kansas City Star*, January 12, 2007.

4. *Social Capital Community Benchmark Survey* (SCCBS) [machine-readable data file] (Cambridge, Mass.: Saguaro Seminar at the John F.

Kennedy School of Government, Harvard University [producer]; Storrs, Conn.: The Roper Center for Public Opinion Research, University of Connecticut [distributor], 2000).

5. Panel Study of Income Dynamics (PSID), Wave XXXII Computer File (Ann Arbor, Mich.: ICPSR, 2001), http://simba.isr.umich.edu.

6. 2000 SCCBS. This analysis regresses the population percentage giving to charity on the percentage saying they are very happy.

7. James A. Davis, Tom W. Smith, and Peter V. Marsden, principal investigators, *General Social Surveys, 1972–2004* [machine-readable data file] (Chicago: National Opinion Research Center [producer]; Storrs, Conn.: The Roper Center for Public Opinion Research, University of Connecticut [distributor], 2004).

8. P. L. Dulin and R. D. Hill, "Relationships Between Altruistic Activity and Positive and Negative Affect Among Low-Income Older Adult Service Providers," *Aging and Mental Health* 7, no. 4 (2003): 294–299.

9. David Sloan Wilson and Mihaly Csikszentmihalyi, "Health and the Ecology of Altruism," in *The Science of Altruism and Health*, edited by S. G. Post (Oxford: Oxford University Press, 2006), p. 6.

10. 1998 International Social Survey Program (ISSP), Zentralarchiv für Empirische Sozialforschung, *International Social Survey Programme*, 1998. This analysis regresses the population percentage volunteering for charitable, political, or religious causes on the percentage saying they are very happy. See http://www.essex.ac.uk/news/2004/nr2004 0924b.htm.

11. Much of this research has been sponsored by the famous Institute for Research on Unlimited Love (IRUL), which is housed within Case Western University's prestigious medical school. Much of the research sponsored by IRUL has been devoted to collecting and analyzing data establishing a causal link between giving and life satisfaction. IRUL's director, Professor Stephen Post, has documented IRUL's remarkable findings in his book *Why Good Things Happen to Good People: The Exciting New Research That Proves the Link Between Doing Good and Living a Longer, Healthier, Happier Life*, which he coauthored with Jill Niemark (New York: Broadway, 2007).

12. Elizabeth Midlarsky and Eva Kahana, *Altruism in Later Life* (Newbury Park, Calif.: Sage, 1994), ch. 6.

13. Alan Luks, *The Healing Power of Doing Good: The Health and Spiritual Benefits of Helping Others* (New York: Fawcett, 1992); Alan Luks, "Helper's High: Volunteering Makes People Feel Good, Physically and Emotionally. And Like 'Runner's Calm,' It's Probably Good for Your Health," *Psychology Today* 22, no. 10 (1988): 34–42.

14. T. Field, M. Hernandez-Reif, O. Quintino, S. Schanberg, and C. Kuhn, "Elder Retired Volunteers Benefit from Giving Massage Therapy to Infants," *Journal of Applied Gerontology* 17 (1998): 229–239.

15. D. McClelland, D. C. McClelland, and C. Kirchnit, "The Effect of Motivational Arousal Through Films on Salivary Immunoglobulin A," *Psychology and Health* 2 (1988): 31–52.

16. Jorge Moll, Frank Krueger, Roland Zahn, Matteo Pardini, Ricardo de Oliveira-Souza, and Jordan Grafman, "Human Fronto-Mesolimbic Networks Guide Decisions About Charitable Donation," *Proceedings of the National Academy of Sciences* 103, no. 42 (2006): 15,623–15,628; Shankar Vedantam, "If It Feels Good to Be Good, It Might Be Only Natural," *Washington Post*, May 28, 2007, p. A1.

17. Dharol Tankersley, Jill Stowe, and Scott A. Huettel, "Altruism Is Associated with an Increased Neural Response to Agency," *Nature Neuroscience* 10 (2007): 150–151.

18. See Arthur C. Brooks, *Who Really Cares* (New York: Basic Books, 2006), ch. 3.

19. S. C. Baker, C. D. Frith, and R. J. Dolan, "The Interaction Between Mood and Cognitive Function Studied with PET," *Psychological Medicine* 27, no. 3 (1997): 565–578.

20. Stefan Klein, *The Science of Happiness: How Our Brains Make Us Happy—and What We Can Do to Get Happier* (New York: Marlowe, 2006), p. 42.

21. C. Hardy and M. Van Vugt, "Nice Guys Finish First: The Competitive Altruism Hypothesis," *Personality and Social Psychology Bulletin* 32 (2006): 1402–1413.

22. Internal Revenue Service, "Selected Itemized Deductions, Schedule A, 1990–2000," http://www.irs.gov/pub/irs-soi/01inded.pdf; Patrick M.

Rooney, Kathryn S. Steinberg, and Paul G. Schervish, "A Methodological Comparison of Giving Surveys: Indiana as a Test Case," *Nonprofit and Voluntary Sector Quarterly* 30, no. 3 (2001): 551–568.

23. Rodney Balko, "The Road to Hell . . . ," Reason Online, http://www.reason.com/blog/show/116966.html.

24. Arthur C. Brooks, "Is There a Dark Side to Government Support for Nonprofits?" *Public Administration Review* 60, no. 3 (2000): 211–218.

25. See Brooks, *Who Really Cares,* ch. 3.

26. Arthur C. Brooks, "Philanthropy and the Nonprofit Sector," in *Understanding America,* edited by Peter Schuck and James Q. Wilson (New York: PublicAffairs, 2008), pp. 539–562.

27. Arthur C. Brooks, "The Effects of Income Redistribution on Giving Behavior," manuscript (2007).

28. Michael Rushton and Arthur C. Brooks, "Government Funding of Nonprofit Organizations," in *An Integrated Theory of Nonprofit Finance,* edited by Dennis R. Young (Lanham, Md.: Lexington Books).

29. Giving USA Foundation, *Giving USA* (Glenview, Ill.: Giving USA Foundation, 2007). The data in this section are contained and described in Brooks, *Who Really Cares.*

30. 2003 PSID, 2000 SCCBS.

31. When we regress charitable giving on political beliefs, religious behavior, family structure, and other demographics, the difference between liberals and conservatives becomes statistically insignificant.

32. 2000 SCCBS.

Conclusion: Happiness Lessons for Our Leaders

1. This is very similar to a thought experiment proposed by Charles Murray in his famous book *Losing Ground: American Social Policy, 1950–1980* (New York: Basic Books, 1984).

2. These statistics come from the National Election Pool. See http://www.beliefnet.com/story/155/ story_15546_1.html.

3. George Washington, Fifth Annual Message to Congress, Philadelphia, December 3, 1793. See Yale Law School, http://www.yale.edu/lawweb/avalon/presiden/sou/washs05.htm.

4. The axiom is a paraphrase of the Apostle Paul in his first letter to Timothy: "For the love of money is a root of all kinds of evil: which some reaching after have been led astray from the faith, and have pierced themselves through with many sorrows." 1 Timothy 6:10.

5. These income figures are according to the U.S. Census, 2007, http://www.census.gov/prod/2007pubs/p60–233.pdf. "Average" here is the statistical mean.

6. Christian Bjørnskov, Axel Dreher, and Justina A. V. Fischer, "The Bigger the Better? Evidence of the Effect of Government Size on Life Satisfaction Around the World," *Public Choice* 130 (2007): 267–292.

7. A. Afonso, L. Schuknecht, and V. Tanzi, "Public Sector Efficiency: An International Comparison," *Public Choice* 123 (2005): 321–347.

Appendix: The Data on Happiness

1. My last book, *Who Really Cares* (New York: Basic Books, 2006), uses similar empirical procedures to this one, but on charitable giving. It contains an appendix that looks at many of the same issues as this one—indeed, I am basing my discussion here on that book's appendix.

2. See http://www.heritage.org/research/features/index/about.cfm.

3. The Maxwell School at Syracuse University is my home institution. However, I am not personally involved in the administration of this poll.

ACKNOWLEDGMENTS

The great (well, mostly great) thing about writing a book about happiness is that literally everyone is an expert, eager to tell you what they think about the subject. If this were a book entitled *Onions: A Brief History*, I'm sure I would not have benefited so much from the abundant suggestions of friends, neighbors, and strangers. I am grateful to hundreds of folks who have talked to me about happiness and unhappiness over the past year. But there are a few people in particular whom I wish to thank formally.

This is the second book I have had the privilege to write in collaboration with my editor at Basic Books, Lara Heimert. Lara's brilliance, insightfulness, energy, and optimism make even the third round of editing a manuscript something to look forward to. Others at Basic provided invaluable help and support as well, including David Steinberger, John Sherer, Michele Jacob, Greg Houle, Robert Kimzey, Kathy Streckfus, and Brandon Proia. I am also grateful to my literary agent Lisa Adams, who helped me develop the core ideas in this book, and who made it possible for me to publish these ideas outside the walls of academia.

The American Enterprise Institute's National Research Initiative gave me extraordinary financial and intellectual support for this project. I am deeply indebted to Henry Olsen, who suggested the collaboration with AEI that I have enjoyed since the spring of 2007. I am also grateful to AEI's leaders, Chris DeMuth and David Gerson, and to numerous AEI scholars who gave me exceptionally helpful suggestions and ideas, including Karlyn Bowman, David Frum, Christina Hoff Sommers, Leon Kass, Allan Meltzer, Charles Murray, Michael Novak, Alex Pollock, and Sally Satel. In addition, I would like to thank AEI interns Daniel Chew and Jon Flugstad for their research assistance, and AEI staff members Chris Pope and Diana Steinmeyer for administrative support. Funding for this project through AEI was generously provided by the Searle Freedom Trust, for which I wish to thank the Trust and its president, Kim Dennis.

I continue to be amazed at the support my work receives from The Maxwell School of Citizenship and Public Affairs and Whitman School of Management at Syracuse University. I am grateful to the Bantle family for their generous endowment of my Chair, and to the leaders of the school and university—in particular, Chancellor Nancy Cantor, Provost Eric Spina, and my dean, Mitchel Wallerstein—make it possible for me and my colleagues to work in areas (like happiness research) that are important, but not always within traditional academic boundaries. The staff of the Campbell Public Affairs Institute, Bethany Walawender and Kelley Coleman, provided administrative assistance for this project. I also had excellent research support from Matt Lenkowsky, Jessica Haynie, and Nick Bailey.

Many friends and colleagues read various chapter drafts along the way and indulged me by brainstorming about key ideas. Many of their suggestions led to changes in the book. These people include Scott Allard, Colin Beavan, Jeff Brooks, Rev. Sam Candler, Steve Gardner, Deal Hudson, Larry Iannaccone, Byron Johnson, Amy Kass, Leslie Lenkowsky, Steve Lux, John J. Miller,

Mike Morris, David Mustard, Fr. Richard John Neuhaus, Grover Norquist, Chuck North, David Van Slyke, Rod Stark, Scott Walter, Doug Wolf, and Karl Zinsmeister.

A number of the ideas presented here were shaped and formed in work I did with my friends at SmithBucklin and the William E. Smith Institute for Association Research in Chicago. I am particularly grateful to my friend Henry Givray, SmithBucklin's CEO, for his intellectual and creative support.

I had the opportunity to develop many of the themes of this book in the pages of the *Wall Street Journal,* for which I thank my editors Howard Dickman and Tunku Varadarajan. Other journals and magazines that published work related to my happiness research are the *New York Sun, Condé Nast Portfolio, The American, City Journal,* and *National Review Online.* I also discussed several of the key themes of this book on Michael Medved's radio show.

Virtually all of data for this book are publicly available from the National Opinion Research Center, the Inter-University Consortium for Political and Social Research, the Roper Center for Public Opinion Research, and the University of Michigan. I wish to thank these organizations for making high-quality survey data freely available to scholars. The original empirical research used for this book simply would not exist without the work of these organizations.

I am particularly indebted to my intellectual partner (and wife), Ester Munt-Brooks, who—as an American by choice instead of by birth—has constantly reminded me why our great nation is fundamentally a happy one and deserves to be so, and who challenged me on every weak point in this book. The book is dedicated to our three children—Quimet, Carlos, and Marina—who endured being told many times over the past year not to interrupt while Mom and Dad were discussing America's gross national happiness.

INDEX

Sartre, Jean-Paul, 74
Saudi Arabia, 199
SCCBS (Social Capital and
    Community Benchmark
    Survey), 227–228, 237n6,
    249n9, 252n6
Seat belt laws, 103
Secularism, 42–44, 48–49, 52–56,
    194, 197–198
  family values and, 75, 76–77
  restrictions on freedom and, 88
Self
  -esteem, 179, 180
  -reports, 6–8
Seligman, Martin, 11–12
Senior citizens, 180–181, 190. *See
    also* Retirement
September 11th terrorist attacks, 200
Sexuality, 22, 27, 142
  family values and, 60, 65, 68, 71
  feminism and, 60
  marriage and, 65
  monkey love experiments and, 71
  restrictions on freedom and, 89,
    94, 95, 98
Shaw, George Bernard, 238n16
Silence of the Lambs, The (film), 57
Smith, Adam, 118
Smoking, 85, 98–99, 118
Social
  engineering, 81
  welfare net, 107–108
Social Democratic Party, 76
Socialism, 92
Sociology, 94
Socrates, 1–3
Solitary confinement, 84
Something Beautiful for God
    (documentary), 41
Soviet Union, 91–92, 95–96, 114, 146
Spain, 53, 54, 75, 156
Speech, freedom of, 86–87
Spirituality, 45, 49
Stalin, Josef, 52, 146

Standard of living, 90, 142
Stanford University, 96
State of the Union Address, 86–87
Steinem, Gloria, 60
Stereotypes, 22, 25
Stewardship, 81
Stewart, Larry, 175
Stewart, Potter, 4
Stress, 25, 59–60, 63, 64, 181
"Strict father" model, 24
Student groups, 33
Substance abuse, 11. *See also*
    Alcoholism; Drug use
Success, 140, 142, 163
  addiction to, 124
  downside to, 123
  materialism and, 126, 132
  perceptions about, 123–125
  search for meaning and, 163
Suicide, 94
Suicide (Durkheim), 94
Supreme Court (United States), 4, 23
Survey Research Institute, 225
Switzerland, 92, 171
Syracuse University, 223, 262n3

Taliban, 97
Taxation, 89, 99
  Alternative Minimum Tax, 78
  charity and, 185–186, 189
  coercive nature of, 205
  Earned Income Tax Credit, 173
  estate, 145
  family values and, 59, 77–80
  government spending and, 129–130
  inequality and, 138, 145, 148
  punitive, 145, 202
  "two Americas" theme and, 134
Telecommuting, 169
Television, 34, 67
Ten Commandments, 53
Tennessee, 116
Terrorism, 35, 103–106, 108, 200
Texas, 177–178